THE KINGDOM
OF GOD

THE KINGDOM OF GOD

A guide for Old Testament study

Francis Breisch, Jr.

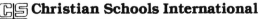 **Christian Schools International**
3350 East Paris Ave. SE, Box 8709
Grand Rapids, Michigan 49518-8709

CHRISTIAN SCHOOLS INTERNATIONAL
3350 East Paris Ave., SE
P.O. Box 8709
Grand Rapids, Michigan 49518-8709

©1958 by NATIONAL UNION OF CHRISTIAN SCHOOLS
(now CHRISTIAN SCHOOLS INTERNATIONAL)
Printed in the United States of America
All rights reserved

20 19 18 17 16

ISBN 0-87463-207-2

The development of *The Kingdom of God* was made possible with
grants from Christian Schools International Foundation and
Canadian Christian Education Foundation, Inc.

PREFACE

The youth of today are the leaders of tomorrow. And the destiny of the Church in the next generation hinges, humanly speaking, upon the training that the young people receive today. If the young people are neglected, the Church will lose its vitality; if they are ill-informed, the Church will lose its effectiveness; if they are divorced from the Word of God, the Church will lose its life. The Church of tomorrow will be characterized by a living, vibrant faith only to the degree that the young people are taught the Scriptures today.

The importance of teaching God's Word to young people is widely accepted in theory, but frequently ignored in practice. In recent years we have witnessed a renewed interest in biblical studies. Many books and pamphlets dealing with the Bible have been published. Yet there has been virtually nothing produced which meets the needs of those who teach Bible to high school students. As a step toward filling this gap, the National Union of Christian Schools has sponsored the writing and publication of this guide for Old Testament study.

From the outset it seemed desirable to center this guide around a theme. That the theme should be *The Kingdom of God* seemed necessary. No other theme so well summarizes the message of the Old Testament. It exhibits the unity which exists in the Old Testament. It shows the historical development of God's work of redemption. It emphasizes the fact that the entire Old Testament prepares for the coming of Christ, the eternal King. To trace the growth of the Kingdom of God is to keep one's finger on the pulse of God's redemptive program. Throughout the guide I have attempted to point out the various ways in which the Kingdom of God comes to expression in the Old Testament.

Tracing the Kingdom of God through the Old Testament requires an understanding of the historical development of God's plan. For this reason I have included introductory material for each book and have arranged the books in chronological order. Rather than follow the order of the English Old Testament, the guide takes up the books in the order in which it is estimated they were written. The historical books form the backbone of this guide. The poetical and prophetical books are inserted after the history of the time in which they were written. It is hoped that these features will make it easier to see the way in which God's kingdom developed over the centuries.

The fact that this volume is designed primarily for high school students is reflected in both form and content. The vocabulary has been geared to the high school student. Technical terms have been defined as simply as possible. Some interesting problems have been ignored. Others have been greatly simplified. The handling of higher criticism is a case in point. The subject cannot be ignored, but neither can it be presented in any great detail. So it has been introduced at only a few points. In those cases the position of higher criticism has been presented very briefly. And the refutation has been limited to an uncovering of the basic unbelief on which higher criticism rests.

A few comments about the use of the various parts of the guide may be in order. The outlines are designed for memorization. For that reason they are short. And the biblical references of the outlines have been restricted in most cases to chapters, even when accuracy might demand that division come in the middle of a chapter. The exercises are designed to provide a challenge for all students. The factual questions should not be too difficult for most high school students. The thought questions are more difficult. It is recognized that in many cases more exercises are provided than a teacher may wish to assign. This provides opportunity for selection by the teachers. It is recommended that along with the work given in the exercises the teacher require the reading of some portions of each book in the Old Testament, so that the students will continually be confronted with the living Word of God. Finally, it should be noted that where use is made of direct quotations, only the name of the author is given. The books from which the quotations are taken are listed in the references at the end of the book. The biblical quotations in this guide are from the American Standard Version.

I wish to express my deep appreciation for the assistance given me by the Rev. Edward Bossenbroek, Mr. John Bos, Mr. Sidney Dykstra, Mr. Nelvin Vos, and Mr. Edwin Walhout, whose suggestions and criticisms have been extremely valuable. I am also indebted to Baker Book House, Wm. B. Eerdmans Publishing Company, Henry H. Halley, and Zondervan Publishing House for permission to quote from the books listed in the references. A special debt of gratitude is due to Dr. Edward J. Young and the Wm. B. Eerdmans Publishing Company for permission to use the chart on page 131, which has been adapted from a similar chart in Dr. Young's *An Introduction to the Old Testament.* Lastly, I would like to acknowledge the indirect contributions to this work made by my former teachers at Westminster Theological Seminary, who by precept and example instilled a love for the inspired Word of God.

May the Lord our God grant that this book may serve to increase in the hearts of our young people a love for the Kingdom of God and for the Christ who is our eternal King.

FRANCIS BREISCH, JR.

CONTENTS

Part IV The Period of Theocratic Decline

Part V The Period of Theocratic Transition

INTRODUCTION

Chapter 1

Introduction

This book is intended to be your guide as you study the Old Testament. The study which we are beginning must cover a great deal of material. And that material will not all be the same. There is in the Old Testament a great variety of subject matter. This variety helps to make our study interesting. But before we turn to this variety, it is necessary to notice some facts which will provide unity for our study. In order to do justice to our study of the parts of the Old Testament, we must first survey the Old Testament as a whole.

The Old Testament Is God's Word

It is impossible to study the Old Testament fairly and honestly without first recognizing and acknowledging one basic fact. The Old Testament is God's revelation to men. It is not the entire revelation of God, but all of the Old Testament is God's Word. Unless we start with this fact, our study of the Old Testament is doomed to failure. Some people claim that this is a human idea, imposed upon the Old Testament by men. It is not. It is found in the Old Testament. It is also found in the New Testament. The Bible testifies clearly to its divine authorship.

It is impossible to present all the evidence to support this statement. Nor is it necessary for us to do that. Let us simply notice that over four hundred times the Old Testament says about its message: "Thus saith Jehovah." And notice what the New Testament says about the Old Testament. "For no prophecy ever came by the will of man: but men spake from God, being moved by the Holy Spirit" (II Peter 1:21). In other words, God's Word declares that it is God's Word, and for Christians that is enough. The Westminster Confession of Faith presents this thought beautifully. After listing some of the "incomparable excellencies" of the Scripture which move us to esteem it highly, it adds, "our full persuasion and assurance of the infallible truth, and divine authority thereof, is from the inward work of the Holy Spirit, bearing witness by, and with the Word in our hearts." God the Holy Spirit, who dwells in the hearts of His people, teaches us that the Bible is His revelation to us. Beyond this we need no proof.

The Old Testament Is Inspired

While we affirm that the Bible is God's Word, we do not maintain that God wrote it directly. No hand from Heaven wrote the Old Testament as it traced the message of doom on Belshazzar's wall. The books of the Old Testament were written by men. This fact poses a question: How can books written by men be God's Word? The Bible gives its own answer: By means of inspiration (II Tim. 3:16). By inspiration we mean that God guided the authors of the Old Testament books in such a way that they wrote what He wanted them to write. God did this in a wonderful way. He did not ignore the personalities of the authors. He did not force them all to use the same style. He used them as they were, or perhaps we should say, He prepared for their work. They received His word and wrote it, each in his own style, each with his own vocabulary, each according to his own education. But what they wrote was not their own; it was God's. The words they used were the words chosen by God, and the thoughts they expressed were God's revelation to men.

We cannot understand precisely how this took place. That is not strange. There are many things in life that we accept without understanding them. Why should we be surprised that we cannot understand everything about such a wonderful and mysterious subject as God's inspiration of His Word? As Christians we must humbly confess that we cannot fathom the ways of God. We do not understand in order that we may believe; we believe in order to understand. And when we believe that God inspired the writers of the Old Testament, the door is opened for us to understand what He has written.

The Old Testament Is Infallible

By our recognition that the Old Testament is God's inspired Word, several facts about that Word are brought to our attention. We then recognize that the Old Testament is infallible. This simply means that there are no errors in it. It does not mean that the writers of the Old Testament knew everything. There were many things they did not know. But when they wrote, under the inspiration of the Holy Spirit, they were kept from any error. After all, they wrote God's words. And it is impossible for God to make an error. Man may not always know what is truth. God always does. He is omniscient; He knows everything. Whether it be history or science or a basic truth of redemption, God knows it. Moreover, it is impossible for God to lie. He Himself tells us that (Titus 1:2). He is altogether holy, of purer eyes than to look upon iniquity. Thus it is impossible that there should be any errors in the Old Testament. Let us never forget what Jesus said about it, "thy word is truth" (John 17:17).

We should realize that not all people believe that the Old Testament is infallible. Unbelievers often take great pleasure in pointing out

places where they think the Bible is wrong. Even some people in Christian churches are influenced by such men, and give up their belief in
the infallibility of Scripture. In this scientific age of ours, we are told,
belief in infallibility is impossible. This is not true. Science has never
proven the Bible to be wrong. On the contrary, it has often shown
that the Bible is right and its critics are wrong.

Archaeology Supports the Old Testament

The science of archaeology, which deals with the remains of past
civilizations, studies the Bible more directly than any other science.
And archaeology supports the Bible. A few examples, chosen from
many, will show that this is so. For many years scoffers laughed at
the story told in Exodus 5 about the Israelites making bricks without
straw. Impossible, they said. The ancient peoples always needed a
binding material for their bricks. But excavations made at the Egyptian
city of Pithom, which was built by the Israelites (Ex. 1:11), proved
otherwise. In these buildings the lower courses of brick were made
with good chopped straw. The middle courses were made with less
straw, and much of that was stubble. The upper courses were made
without any straw. This agrees perfectly with the biblical story. A
second example comes from Jericho. Although sceptics had denied that
the walls of Jericho fell miraculously as pictured in Joshua 6, excavations at the site of ancient Jericho showed that this is precisely what
happened. There is no evidence of the walls being battered in. "The
bricks that composed the east wall lie as a streak down the eastern
slope gradually getting thinner, with conspicuous traces of a general
fire. Thus the outer wall fell outwards, and down the hillside, quite
flat, making it possible for the invaders to enter 'every man straight
before him'" (Halley). Time after time the critics of the Bible have
been silenced by the findings of archaeology.

Thus we see that science attests the infallibility of the Bible. But
notice this. Science does not prove that the Bible is infallible. The
infallibility of the Bible is proved by its divine authorship. It needs
no human proof. Science can show that particular statements of the
Bible are true, but it can never provide an adequate foundation for our
belief in an infallible Bible. Only God can do that.

The Old Testament Is Important

When we see that the Bible is God's Word, we also recognize that
the Old Testament is authoritative. It speaks with all the authority
of God Himself. We who are God's creatures, and especially we who
are His children, must obey His Word. What He says we must believe;
what He commands we must do. Neither doubt nor disobedience can
be tolerated. And this is so simply because it is God who speaks to us
in the Old Testament. If the Old Testament contained the ideas of

men about God, we would be free to accept or reject their thoughts. But since it is God who speaks, we have no choice but to believe and to obey.

Since the Old Testament is part of God's Word, it is applicable to our lives. If it were merely a human account of the religious experiences of the ancient Jews, this would not be true. We might find it interesting, but insist that it was of no value to us. Changing times and differing cultures might make their example nearly worthless to us. But the Old Testament is God's Word, and God's Word does not change. His holiness and righteousness, His lovingkindness and mercy, His wisdom and grace are the same today as they were thousands of years ago. Therefore we can discover in the pages of the Old Testament directions as to how we may please God. In fact, Paul tells us that the things which happened to the Israelites were recorded for our benefit. Since this is true, our study of the Old Testament must be practical. We must continually ask ourselves how these things apply to us. Therefore, we must approach our study of the Old Testament in a spirit of prayer, asking God to reveal to us His will as it is contained in His inspired Word.

The Authors of the Old Testament

We have seen that it is impossible properly to understand the Old Testament without taking into account its divine origin and its infallible character. We must also recognize that it is impossible properly to understand the Old Testament unless we have some knowledge of its historical background. The Old Testament is a collection of thirty-nine books. Two of these books, Psalms and Proverbs, are themselves collections, containing the writings of various authors. So we can see that God used many men to write the Old Testament. In addition, He used men who lived at various times in the history of Israel. The earliest books of the Old Testament were probably written about 1500 B.C., and the last book was not written until about 400 B.C. So the writing of the Old Testament covers a period of a thousand years or more. What is more, they were written in various parts of the Middle East. Most of them originated in Palestine, but some came from Mesopotamia (modern Iraq), and some from Egypt or the Sinai Peninsula.

All of these factors point to the great diversity which is present in the books of the Old Testament. Yet, in spite of all these differences, there is one factor which links all the books and their authors together. All these authors were members of God's chosen people. All these books originated within the framework of the covenant nation. And the covenant nation was a divinely constituted organization. It was the Church of God in the Old Testament. The common religious framework which unites all the writers of the Old Testament provides a unified approach to spiritual matters. By their various backgrounds God prepared these men to provide a well-rounded picture of His redemptive work. By their common faith in Him He prepared them to give a true and unified picture of that work.

The Collection of the Old Testament

The writers of the Old Testament recorded God's revelation as He had given it to them. As these books appeared, the Jews recognized that they were God's Word and gradually gathered them into a collection. This collection is known as the Jewish canon. (A canon is simply a list, in this case a list of inspired books.) The Jewish canon was exactly the same as our Old Testament. The collection was completed by the early part of the fourth century B.C. It has remained the same ever since. One point needs to be made clear. The collectors of the Hebrew canon, whoever they may have been, did not give these books authority by including them in the canon. The Old Testament Church, when it made this collection, acknowledged by including these thirty-nine books that they were recognized as having divine authority because they were inspired by God. These books showed their inspiration clearly; they were included in the canon. Other religious books did not possess the marks of inspiration; they were rejected.

The Divisions of the Old Testament

As the books of the Old Testament were collected, they fell into three groups — the Law, the Prophets, and the Writings. This grouping is a natural one. The Law, consisting of the five books of Moses, was the first written revelation that Israel had. It also contained the basic revelations of God, such as those at Mount Sinai, which were the foundation of Israel's religious and civil life. It is natural that these books should have a unique place in the thinking of the pious Jew. The second group, the Prophets, derives its name from the office held by the authors of the books. A prophet was a man who was called of God to receive His revelation and to communicate it to the people. The Prophets is divided into two groups, Former and Latter. The Former Prophets are all anonymous. The authors of Joshua, Judges, Samuel, and Kings remain unknown, but their works testify to their prophetic office. As they present in their books the history of Israel, they portray it as a revelation of God's redemptive work. The Latter Prophets include Isaiah, Jeremiah, Ezekiel, and the Twelve, whom we call the Minor Prophets. These books were written by the men whose names are attached to them. They include some history, but chiefly they contain the words of prophecy spoken by these prophets. The third group is called the Writings. In this group there are several types of books. Included are poetical books, historical books, and five books used by the Jews in their sacred festivals. These books have one thing in common. They were written by men who were not prophets. That is the distinguishing feature of the Writings.

The Purpose of the Old Testament

In our study of the Old Testament, we must never think of it as a complete unit. It is like a house that is finished on three sides. The one end is left open, because there is another room to be added. And that room is the most important room of the house. It is the New Testament. The entire Old Testament exists to provide an introduction to the New Testament. This is true because Christ is the center of the biblical story. The Old Testament points forward to Him. The New Testament centers around Him. So in our study of the Old Testament, we must always have our eyes to the future, looking ahead for the rising of the Sun of Righteousness.

The Typology of the Old Testament

One of the means by which the Old Testament points to Christ is its system of types. A type may be defined as something (a person, object, or event) in the Old Testament which is designed by God to resemble and foreshadow something in the New Testament. In the Old Testament God taught the same truths as in the New Testament. But they were not taught as clearly. In the Old Testament God prepared certain things so that they would point forward to the New Testament expression of His truth.

Perhaps we can better understand typology (the study of types) if we see its connection to symbolism. Certain historical events symbolize divine truths. They teach lessons. And this is no accident. God designed it that way. Take, for example, the brass serpent which Moses prepared. The historical purpose for which that serpent was made was to save the Israelites from death by snake bite. It did that. Anyone who looked at it was healed. Now if any Israelite thought about that brass serpent for awhile, he would see that it taught a lesson. It taught him that faith in God was really the means by which he was saved from death. He believed God, he looked, he was healed. He learned the lesson that faith in the God-provided remedy was absolutely necessary. That was the symbolism of the brass serpent.

The typology of the serpent is like its symbolism. But as a type the serpent points forward to that which is a higher revelation of the same truth. The serpent is a type of Christ, who is the God-appointed remedy for sin. And here too it is necessary to have faith in the God-provided remedy. "And as Moses lifted up the serpent in the wilderness, even so must the Son of man be lifted up; that whosoever believeth may in him have eternal life" (John 3:14, 15). This is the typical lesson of this incident.

So we see that God taught Israel certain lessons through symbols. The same lessons, spelled out in New Testament language, are called types. Israel's symbols are the Church's types.

We will find some types presented as such in the New Testament. In Hebrews, for instance, the tabernacle and its worship are presented as types of the way that we now approach God through Christ. But there are other types which are not mentioned in the New Testament. We must seek for these types too. If a person, event, or object was a symbol for Israel of old, then we may examine it to see if it is a type for us. By means of these types we shall have our attention drawn constantly to the New Testament. Types are one method by which "The New is in the Old concealed; the Old is in the New revealed."

The Theme of the Old Testament

In choosing a theme for our study it is important that we look ahead to Christ and to the New Testament. We need a theme as a highway to direct our travel through the Old Testament. There are so many side roads we could travel, so many interesting lanes into which we could take excursions. But there we would lose sight of the whole picture which the Old Testament presents. We want to follow one road, and we want to be sure that our road is the main highway that will lead us directly to Christ and the New Testament. We find this highway in the theme "The Kingdom of God." We will see in our study how this constitutes the main line of thought in the Old Testament. We will see how every book contributes to this basic theme.

The Theme of the New Testament

But before we do this we should jump forward to the New Testament and assure ourselves the same highway is to be found there. And here too we find it to be a main thoroughfare. We are told that Jesus came "preaching the gospel of God and saying, The time is fulfilled and the kingdom of God is at hand" (Mark 1:14, 15). Many of Jesus' parables were about the Kingdom. When He announced the founding of His church He said, "I will give unto thee the keys of the kingdom . . ." (Matt. 16:19). After the Resurrection He taught His disciples about the "things concerning the kingdom of God" (Acts 1:3). And when He returns in glory He will come as "KING OF KINGS, AND LORD OF LORDS" (Rev. 19:16). The road marked "The Kingdom of God" is the highway that leads from one end of the Bible to the other. It is the road we shall walk together.

Before we begin our journey it would be well to survey the road ahead. Our journey will take us through various stages of the Kingdom of God. The Kingdom does not suddenly appear in perfect final form. Instead it develops, much as a plant does. It does not grow by additions, as earthly empires grow by adding new areas of land. It grows as does a plant, by the development of something that is already present. We might compare it to a tulip bulb. If you hold a bulb in your hand, you hold a tulip. The tulip is hidden in the bulb.

But you cannot find it by cutting the bulb apart. You must plant it and allow it to grow. In a similar way God planted the seed of His kingdom in the earth of human history. He watered it abundantly with His grace. And it grew — first a shoot, then a plant, a bud, and finally the perfect flower. In the Old Testament we will not find the flowering. That is reserved for the New Testament. But we will be privileged to see the early stages of development. And that is a wonderful story.

The Outline of the Old Testament

We are now ready to trace the development of God's kingdom in the Old Testament. We should have an outline for our study before us. In order that we may see the development clearly, we will divide the time covered by the Old Testament into periods. Each period will tell us something about the Kingdom of God. The outline also includes the historical events which mark the boundaries of each period.

The Period of:	From:	To:
I. Theocratic Beginnings	Creation	Exodus
II. Theocratic Establishment	Exodus	Reign of Saul
III. Theocratic Development	Reign of Saul	Reign of Solomon
IV. Theocratic Decline	Reign of Solomon	Exile
V. Theocratic Transition	Exile	Coming of Christ

This is not the only possible outline of the Old Testament. But if you will examine the Table of Contents, you will see that this outline is a guide to our study.

In this outline the word *theocratic* is used repeatedly as a synonym for Kingdom of God. For example, "The Period of Theocratic Beginnings" could also be called "The Period of the Beginning of the Kingdom of God." But that is clumsy. The term *theocratic* is easier to use. Since the word may be unfamiliar, let us examine it. The word *theocratic* resembles the word *democratic*. *Democratic* comes from two Greek words — *demos* (people) and *kratos* (power). It means that the power resides in the people. So a democratic government is a government "of the people, by the people, and for the people." *Theocratic* likewise comes from two Greek words — *theos* (God) and *kratos* (power). It means that the power resides in God. God is the ruler. And since God is an absolute monarch, *theocratic* refers to the Kingdom of God.

The Dates of the Old Testament

In addition to an outline, it is essential to our study that we have in mind a few very important dates. Since the Old Testament may use much space dealing with a short period of time, and may pass over a longer period of time in silence, we can become confused as to when various people lived and various events occurred. The only solution to that problem is the memorization of a few dates. The dates

given below are not exact. They are close approximations which should
be easy to memorize.

Call of Abraham	2100 B.C.	Fall of Israel	720 B.C.
Exodus	1450 B.C.	Fall of Judah	600 B.C.
Saul becomes king	1050 B.C.	End of Old Testament	400 B.C.
Division of kingdom	930 BC.		

EXERCISES

Factual questions

1. What is the most basic fact about the Old Testament?
2. How can we show from the Bible that it is God's Word?
3. How are we convinced that the Bible is God's Word?
4. What is inspiration? How did God inspire the biblical writers?
5. What is infallibility? Is the Old Testament infallible?
6. Why is the Old Testament authoritative?
7. How should we study the Old Testament?
8. How are the Old Testament writers different from each other? How are they the same?
9. When was the canon of the Old Testament completed?
10. Into what three parts is the Old Testament divided?
11. What does each part contain?
12. How did the Jews decide into which section a book should go?
13. Why is the Old Testament not complete in itself?
14. What is the difference between a type and a symbol?
15. In what fashion does God's kingdom grow?

Thought questions

1. Why is faith important in the study of the Bible?
2. Considering what has been said about the Old Testament, try to decide how you should study it.
3. Is it possible for science to prove the Old Testament wrong about history, geography, etc.?
4. If the Bible were proven to be wrong about historical matters, could we still trust it as a guide to spiritual truth?
5. Is it true that the Old Testament is really a man-made book, since men decided which books should be included?
6. What is the difference between growth by organic development and growth by addition?
7. Make a list of some things from the Old Testament that you think are types.

Memory

1. Outline of Old Testament.
2. Dates of Old Testament events.

PART ONE

THE PERIOD OF
THEOCRATIC BEGINNINGS

Chapter 2

The Five Books of Moses

NAMES

Pentateuch is not a biblical name. It is derived from the Greek and means simply "five books." It has been applied for a long time to the first five books of the Bible. The Jews themselves referred to these books as the Torah, that is, the Law. Either of these titles can be used to designate the five books written by Moses.

The Bible refers to the Pentateuch by a variety of terms. Some of these are: the law of Moses; the book of the law; the law of God; the law of Moses, the man of God. These terms are composed of various combinations of four words — law, book, Moses, and God. These words express well the major points to remember about the Pentateuch. "Law" expresses the legal character of the Pentateuch, which contains many of God's laws to men. "Book" shows that the Pentateuch is intended to be permanent. "Moses" identifies the human author of the books, and "God" points to the divine author, by whose inspiration Moses wrote. If we keep these terms in mind, we will always have a proper approach to our study of the Pentateuch.

PURPOSE

In the Pentateuch God gives us a picture of the earliest historical development of the theocracy. The five books, taken together, enable us to understand how God laid the foundations of His kingdom. Everything in the Pentateuch is designed to accomplish this end. The Pentateuch is not simply history. It does not attempt to present or explain everything which happened. There are places where it passes over large periods of time in silence. For example, the four hundred and thirty years in Egypt are scarcely mentioned. The thirty-eight years of wilderness wandering are summarized briefly. These omissions are explained by the fact that during these periods nothing happened which advanced the development of God's kingdom. Moses wrote with a purpose in mind — to trace the beginnings of the Kingdom of God. Therefore he chose his material carefully, so that this story would stand out clearly, and not be lost amidst the clutter of unnecessary information.

AUTHOR

What the Bible Says

For centuries Christians and Jews have agreed unanimously that Moses was the human author of these books. This belief has a solid

20

basis in the testimony of God's Word. There is not a part of the Bible that questions the Mosaic authorship of the Pentateuch. On the contrary, every part of the Bible affirms that Moses wrote these books. The Pentateuch contains at least six places where Moses is said to write certain events or revelations from God (Ex. 17:14; 24:4-8; 34:27; Num. 33:1, 2; Deut. 31:9, 22). One of them, Deuteronomy 31:9, is especially significant. It tells that Moses not only wrote the law of God, but delivered it to the Levites for safekeeping. The rest of the Old Testament also assumes that the Pentateuch is the work of Moses. Already in Joshua we have a reference to "the book of the law of Moses" (Josh. 8:31). From the time of Joshua to the time of Ezra, the repeated, unanimous testimony of the Old Testament presents Moses as the author of the Pentateuch. In the New Testament Christ names Moses as the author of certain statements which are found only in the Pentateuch (Matt. 19:8; Mark 10:5). And He speaks of the "law of Moses" (Luke 24:44). In fact, throughout the Bible, every reference to the law means the Pentateuch, and wherever the author of the Pentateuch is named, it is Moses. This does not mean that Moses wrote every word of the Pentateuch. For instance, Deuteronomy 34 deals with his death and the mourning that followed it. This was surely added by another inspired writer. But, in the main, the Pentateuch comes from God through Moses.

What Men Say

With such a weight of evidence in favor of the Mosaic authorship of the Pentateuch, one would expect to find unanimous agreement on this matter. But as a matter of fact, such agreement is sadly lacking. There are many men who deny that Moses wrote the Pentateuch. And these are men who are scholars, and who have applied their scholarship to the study of the Bible. Why do they deny what the Bible so clearly teaches? First of all, they do not believe that the Bible is the Word of God. While some may state this more openly than others, basically it is true of all the Higher Critics, as they are called. They think that the Old Testament must be studied as a piece of human literature. They do not hesitate to declare that it can be, and is wrong at many places. They are sure that it is wrong when it presents Moses as the author of the Pentateuch. They believe that it was written much later, and that the author used Moses' name to gain recognition for his work.

You see, by taking this view the Critics can explain away some features about the Pentateuch which they do not like. For instance, the Pentateuch contains some prophecies which were fulfilled. These the Higher Critics explain by claiming that the book was written after the fulfillment, and the prophecy was included in the book to impress the readers. In a similar manner, the miracles of the Pentateuch are explained as mere legends of an early age, which did not actually happen. You may wonder why these men work so hard to explain away these things. The answer is really quite simple. If these men admit that Moses wrote these books, if these prophecies are real prophecies and these miracles are true miracles, then the God presented in the Pentateuch must also be real. If He is real, they should love Him and obey Him. But they do not do so, and they do not want to do so. This makes them sinners. But they do not want to admit that they are sinners before God. They do not want to face the demands of a sovereign God. So they simply deny that the Pentateuch presents an accurate picture of God. And to deny the God of the Pentateuch, they must deny that Moses wrote the Pentateuch.

The Problem of the Critics

If Moses did not write the Pentateuch, who did? And when? These are fair questions to put to the Higher Critics. And if we did so, each one would give a different answer. And each one would be sure that the others were wrong and that he was right. They can only agree on one point — that Moses did not write the Pentateuch. They cannot agree at all about how it did come into existence. This disagreement is an indication that they do not speak the truth.

We cannot afford to ignore such men as we study the Old Testament. We must never forget that they exist, for some day we may meet them. Many people teach the views of higher criticism as the truth. We must know about this false position. But we must always remember that these men speak as they do because they deny that the Bible is God's Word. They do not have the light of the Holy Spirit. And we do not want to be led by those who themselves walk in darkness.

EXERCISES

Factual questions

1. What does Pentateuch mean? Torah? To what books do they refer?
2. What words does the Bible use to describe the Pentateuch? What does each word emphasize?
3. What is the main story of the Pentateuch?
4. Who is the human author of the Pentateuch? What biblical proof can be found for this?
5. Why do men deny the Mosaic authorship of the Pentateuch?
6. On what important question do Higher Critics differ?

Thought question

1. What do the Higher Critics lack that is necessary for understanding the Bible?

Chapter 3

The Destruction of the First Theocracy

Genesis

PURPOSE

The Old Testament deals with the nation of Israel. Israel's history is presented, her poetry is preserved, and the words of her prophets are recorded. Why is the Word of God so interested in this one nation? The Old Testament itself answers that question. Israel is God's covenant nation. It is in Israel that God established His theocracy in Old Testament times. But this answer raises other questions. Why did God have a covenant nation? And how did Israel become that nation? These questions are answered in Genesis. The first book of the Bible thus provides a foundation for the rest of the Old Testament. It shows why God separated a people for Himself. It also shows how Israel became the people whom He separated for Himself. Genesis provides an introduction to the story of the theocracy which God founded in Israel. In the first eleven chapters of Genesis we learn why God limited the theocracy to a single nation.

OUTLINE

ANALYSIS

The Creation

The first chapter of Genesis, which presents the creation of the heavens and the earth, emphasizes the sovereignty of God. It shows clearly that God, and God alone, is the creator of the universe. Thirty-four times we are told that God acts — God created, God saw, God said,

God divided, God made, etc. This work of God reveals His infinite power. This is shown especially by the fact that all this is done simply by commanding. It is not by laboring, but by speaking the word of His power that God creates the universe.

We note also that the world as it was created was just what God wanted it to be. The repeated statement "and it was so" shows that God's purpose was fully realized. And when each act of creation is finished, we read that "it was good." The final picture of creation displays God's pleasure in that which He has made — "and, behold, it was very good" (Gen. 1:31). Genesis 1 pictures the sovereign God bringing to pass by His almighty word that which is good in His sight.

Why is the doctrine of creation important? Because it teaches that everything belongs to God because He created it. Therefore He has the sovereign right to dispose of all His creatures as He wills. He who is the source of all things is therefore also the ruler of all things. This is set forth beautifully in Psalm 24:1:

> *The earth is Jehovah's, and the fulness thereof;*
> *The world, and they that dwell therein.*
> *For He hath founded it upon the seas,*
> *And established it upon the floods.*

Man's Place in Creation

Man is the highest of God's creatures. He is the crowning work of creation. This is presented in four ways:

1. Man was made last. In Genesis 1 we notice that the simpler creatures were made first. Each step in creation prepares for the following steps. Man comes last, and this points to his high position.

2. Before man was created we read these words, "And God said, Let us make man . . . ." This might be called a conference between the persons of the Godhead. Nowhere else in the creation narrative do we find such a conference. Man must be the crown of creation to receive this special concern by God.

3. Man is the only creature that is made in the image of God. Surely this likeness to the Creator indicates that man is the highest creature.

4. Man was given dominion over the other creatures. In Genesis 2 this is expressed by the fact that man is given the task of naming the animals.

The First Theocracy

This picture of man, the highest creature, standing between God and the rest of creation, presents the first theocracy. God is the sovereign ruler, by virtue of creation. He has made man in the image of God, placed him in the world, and has given him the task of ruling as God's vice-ruler. In this we have all the elements of a divine kingdom. Man rules the world. Yet he does not rule for himself. He rules in behalf of God, and willingly acknowledges God as his own ruler.

This first theocracy was perfect. There was no flaw in it. But it was not necessarily permanent. God set before man a choice. He gave to man the command to abstain from eating the fruit of the Tree of the Knowledge of Good and Evil. He warned man that if he ate of it he would die. This warning does not only refer to physical death. It also includes spiritual death, which is separation from God. Spiritual death leads to physical death, which is the separation of body and soul.

When God said that disobedience would mean death, He implied that obedience would bring eternal life. This was a covenant between God and man. God told man precisely what to do. He told him what would happen if he obeyed or disobeyed. Man's actions would decide his future. We call this the covenant of works, because under this arrangement man was to earn eternal life by obeying God.

Sin and Redemption

Man's testing in the covenant of works ended in failure. He sinned, and ate the forbidden fruit. The sentence of death was immediately imposed. Adam and Eve died spiritually. God also put His curse upon the man and the woman. Until the time when spiritual death brought physical death upon them, life would be made more difficult by this divine curse. Sin brings misery as well as death.

But God did not curse only man. He also cursed the serpent. And His curse upon the serpent contained a promise of redemption (salvation from sin and the effects of sin) for man. God said, "I will put enmity between thee and the woman, and between thy seed and her seed: he shall bruise thy head, and thou shalt bruise his heel" (Gen. 3:15). Notice what is included in this promise.

1. God promises salvation by declaring that He will put enmity between the seed of the woman and that of the serpent. "I will put enmity" shows that God will undo the results of the Fall. By sinning, man had become Satan's friend and God's enemy. God is going to save man by restoring man to fellowship with Him. This will make man the enemy of Satan, as he was before he sinned.

2. This salvation will be certain, because it is based on God's action. He says that He will put enmity. It is to be a sovereign salvation, because only God's sovereign work could guarantee man's salvation.

3. God promises a saviour, the seed of the woman, who will destroy Satan. This is a promise of Christ. There can be no salvation apart from Him. The first promise of redemption includes a promise of Christ, and the entire Old Testament prepares for His coming.

4. This saviour will suffer at the hands of Satan. This suffering will be part of His redemptive work.

In this promise we have the seed of the new Kingdom of God. The first theocracy was destroyed, and immediately God set into operation the forces which would produce the second theocracy which will continue forever. From this seed the plant of God's redemptive kingdom will grow. The rest of the Bible is dedicated to tracing the growth of that plant.

The Growing Effects of Sin

But before continuing that story, Moses presents to us just how awful sin really is. The sin of Adam did not affect only him. By his first sin he infected all his descendants as well. Since that time man is born in sin, and has a sinful nature. The effects of this sinful nature are now set forth. It has been suggested by some writers that the period between the Fall and the Flood was one in which God withheld His grace to a large degree, so that men might see how awful sin really is, and what misery it brings. Sin erupted in the first murder, when Cain killed Abel. But Cain at least tried to hide his sin. The second murderer mentioned shows a greater hardness of heart. Lamech admits his act, and composes a song about it. Thus the picture of the growing effects of sin is painted.

Not all Adam's children are of Cain's evil line. There is another line, descending from Seth. This line retains at least some knowledge of Jehovah. But sin also affects the Sethites. Genesis 5 shows that death, the result of sin, did not bypass them. The fact that Enoch escaped death only spotlights the fact that everyone else experiences death. His experience was unique. Sin was everywhere, and everywhere it brought forth death.

Just before the Flood sin reached its peak. Notice the cause. "And it came to pass, when men began to multiply on the face of the ground, and daughters were born unto them that the sons of God [the children of Seth] saw the daughters of men [the children of Cain] that they were fair; and they took them wives of all that they chose. And Jehovah said, My Spirit will not strive with man for ever . . ." (Gen. 6:1-3). Here is a lesson that every Christian young person should take to heart. Marriage with unbelievers is disastrous for the Christian, for the Church, and for the world. Christian homes are one of the main barriers against the spread of sin. Intermarriage breaks down this barrier. It was in this way that open sinfulness spread throughout the entire world just before the Flood.

Notice what is said of man in Genesis 6:5. "And Jehovah saw that the wickedness of man was great in the earth, and that every imagination of the thoughts of his heart was only evil continually." This exposes the sinfulness of man's heart. But in this case that sinfulness was turned loose in the world. Notice how great man's sin is.

1. It begins at the very center of his personality — the imaginations of the thoughts of his heart. It is not simply on the surface, limited to a few evil deeds.

2. It includes everything which comes from his heart. His thoughts are "only evil continually." His sin is so great that it excludes all good.

3. It extends to everything that he does — "the wickedness of man was great in the earth."

By putting these statements together, it becomes clear that there is no good in man. Swelling from the very core of his being, his sins extend wherever the influence of man is felt. And the corruption that fills the earth as a result of this sin calls for divine punishment. That punishment was soon inflicted.

The Flood

The purpose of the Flood was to destroy sinful man and the results of his sin from the earth. "And God said unto Noah, The end of all flesh is come before me; for the earth is filled with violence through them; and, behold, I will destroy them with the earth" (Gen. 6:13). This end was achieved. The Flood destroyed man and beast from the face of the earth. Of course, not all life was destroyed. God called Noah to build the ark to save himself, his family, and a pair of each type of animal. This was a representative group through whom God would again populate the earth. By thus saving a remnant from the physical punishment of sin, God pictures the fact that He will save His church from the eternal punishment of sin.

The Flood fulfilled its purpose, and when that was done God brought the remnant forth from the ark. Then God made a covenant with Noah, which we call the covenant of nature. In this covenant God promised that never again would the course of nature be interrupted by a flood, nor would mankind again be destroyed, until God's plan of history is completed. This covenant is important for the development of the theocracy. It guarantees stability in the world. It assures us that there will be a stage on which the drama of redemption can be played without interruption until the last act is completed.

Noah himself became living proof that redemption was still needed. The Flood could not erase the sin from the human heart and Noah soon became the one through whom sin first manifested its ugly presence in the regenerated world. And Noah's descendants quickly turned away from God. They planned the Tower of Babel, by which they intended to avoid being scattered. To prevent them from fulfilling their purpose, God changed their languages so they could not understand each other, and scattered them abroad. This prepared the way for the next step in God's plan. Mankind as a whole had failed. Now God was ready to separate a people, that through them He might redeem the world. This separation begins with Abraham.

EXERCISES

Factual questions

1. What is the purpose of Genesis?
2. What is emphasized in the first chapter of Genesis?
3. List the various actions performed by God in Genesis 1 and give references.
4. Why is the doctrine of creation important?
5. How do we know that man was the highest of God's creatures?
6. What was man's position in the first theocracy?
7. Write out the words of God in Genesis 2 which show what was required of man in the covenant of works.
8. What are the parts of the first promise of redemption?
9. List the evidences of the growth of sin in Genesis 4-6, giving references.
10. What was the cause of the Flood?
11. Show from Genesis 6:5 how great man's sinfulness is.
12. What was the purpose of the Flood?
13. Why did God save Noah and his family?
14. Why is the covenant God made with Noah important?
15. Write out the verse from Genesis 11 which shows the purpose of the Tower of Babel.

Thought questions

1. What do we mean when we say that man was created in God's image?
2. What does the Bible mean when it says that God rested?
3. Compare the way in which Cain's conscience affects him with the working of Lamech's conscience. What can we learn from this?
4. What lesson can we learn from Genesis 6:1-5?
5. What does it mean that man is totally depraved? Prove man's total depravity from Scripture.
6. What was wrong with the building of the Tower of Babel?
7. Read again the definition of the first theocracy. Now show from Scripture that sin really destroyed this relationship.

Memory

1. Outline of Genesis.
2. Psalm 24:1, 2.
3. Genesis 6:5.

Chapter 4

The Promise of the New Theocracy

Genesis

PURPOSE

In many ways the second part of Genesis is different from the first. Here we see God narrowing the limits of His work. Instead of dealing with the whole human race, God now works with one man and his descendants. But there is a close connection between the two sections. The first part served to show us why God limited His Old Testament kingdom to a single nation. The human race as a whole had failed. So now God begins to purify mankind by separating a single nation from the rest of mankind. This nation will be His instrument in purifying all men. The second part of Genesis tells us how God began to separate His chosen nation from other men.

ANALYSIS

God's Kingdom and the Covenant of Grace

The new stage in God's redemptive work begins with Abraham. Abraham receives the promise that God will establish a new theocracy with him and with his family. This promise comes in the form of a covenant. A covenant is an arrangement or an agreement in which two parties understand completely what is expected of each. God is a covenant God. He does not leave His people ignorant of what He expects of them. Nor does He leave them in ignorance of what He will do for them. We have already seen that God makes covenants with men. First He entered into the covenant of works with Adam. Next He made His covenant of nature with Noah. Now He establishes His covenant of grace with Abraham. This covenant is given in three stages. The first comes at the time of Abraham's call, found in Genesis 12. The second occurs in a vision related in Genesis 15. In Genesis 17 God formally establishes His covenant with Abraham. It is important that these chapters be carefully studied so that it will be understood what God promised Abraham and what He required of Abraham in each of these stages.

It is by means of this covenant of grace with Abraham that the way is paved for the establishment of the new theocracy. But Genesis does not record the actual establishment of this theocracy. Abraham did

29

not see the fulfillment of the promises God gave to him. Nor did his immediate descendants see the promises fulfilled. That fulfillment was reserved for a later time. They received the promises, and they lived in complete faith in those promises of God. God was their God and they were His people. This was enough to satisfy them. And so they lived with God, waiting for Him to do what He had promised. As they waited, God guided their lives, and pictured in them some of the important truths about His kingdom.

God's Blessings and Abraham's Life

The life of Abraham teaches us two important lessons. The first is that God gives real blessings to His people. Some men think that the only benefit of religion is the ability it gives us to have proper attitudes toward life. In other words, the value is all in our heads. But that is simply not true. God's kingdom contains many blessings for His people. And these are real blessings. Some of them we receive in this life and others we will receive in the life to come. God displayed this fact in Abraham's life. He gave Abraham many blessings. As you read about his life, look for these blessings. They show us that God's kingdom is the source of much good for God's people.

The life of Abraham also teaches us what our response to the theocracy must be. Abraham is called the father of believers. His whole life was a life of faith. A careful reading of the story of his life will reveal instance after instance in which his faith is displayed. In Hebrews 11 we also have a few of these manifestations of faith listed. Remember, as you look for evidences of faith, that faith in God is revealed by obedience to God. This is the second lesson of Abraham's life. God's blessings are to be received by faith.

God's Choices and Abraham's Seed

The life of Isaac is much different from that of his father Abraham. Here our attention is directed to the supernatural way in which God works in His kingdom. The birth of Isaac illustrates this fact. Abraham and Sarah thought that they had the only answer to a great problem. Abraham needed a son so that the promise could be fulfilled. So they used a device which was an accepted custom in those times. Abraham had a son who was born of Hagar, Sarah's maid. This was the natural answer, since Sarah was too old to have any children. But God would not accept the natural answer. He provided a supernatural answer. Isaac was born of Sarah in her old age. This and other incidents in the life of Isaac illustrate the fact that the theocracy is brought about by supernatural action.

Jacob teaches us that membership in God's kingdom is based upon election. It is not because of what we are, but because of God's choosing us that we become members of the theocracy. In the birth of Isaac, God displayed His supernatural method of working. But in the birth of Jacob, His election is displayed. In the case of Isaac we could find a reason why God might choose Isaac and not Ishmael. But in the case of Jacob there is no such reason. In fact, everything points in the other direction. But Jacob is chosen, and this is the result of God's electing love. That it was not due to Jacob's character is clear from the story of his early life. At first he was a despicable character. But later in his life he becomes a true saint of God. This shows us a second truth about God's election. God does not choose us because we are good but in order that He might make us good.

God's Guidance and Israel's Early History

The early history of Israel is the story of the lives of the patriarchs, Abraham, Isaac, and Jacob. After this the family begins to enlarge. Jacob has twelve sons, who are to become the fathers of the tribes of Israel. Of these the most prominent is Joseph. This is natural, since he prepares the way for the next step in the biblical narrative — the Exodus. But we should also notice that Joseph is one of the Old Testament characters who may be called a type of Christ. By that we mean that the events which occur in his life have a striking resemblance to the events in the life of our Lord. As an example, compare the treatment Joseph received from his brothers with the words of John 1:11, "He came unto his own, and they that were his own received him not."

The book of Genesis ends with the blessings which Israel bestows upon his sons. These blessings are prophetic, and foretell the fortunes of the various tribes of Israel. Of special importance is part of the blessing upon Judah.

> *The sceptre shall not depart from Judah,*
> *Nor the ruler's staff from between his feet,*
> *Until Shiloh come;*
> *And unto him shall the obedience of the peoples be.*
> —GEN. 49:10.

This asserts that Judah will be the ruler of Israel, and out of Judah shall come a special ruler. This is a prophecy of Christ.

CONCLUSION

So the book of Genesis brings us to the end of the period of promise. In it we see the first theocracy established by creation and destroyed by sin. We see the wrath of God upon a sinful world expressed in the Flood. And then we see the beginning of a new theocracy, given in the form of a promise to Abraham and his children. This new theocracy is the subject of the rest of the Bible. God is still perfecting His kingdom. It will come to its perfection only when Christ returns from Heaven to judge the living and the dead. So Genesis is truly the foundation of the Bible. It provides the basis on which the entire redemptive plan of God rests. One could not write *Finis* at the end of Genesis. It is like an introductory chapter. There is much more to follow.

EXERCISES

Factual questions

1. What is the purpose of the second part of Genesis?
2. What do the three patriarchs teach us about the theocracy?
3. What blessings did God promise Abraham in Genesis 12, 15, and 17?
4. What requirements did God set before Abraham in those chapters?
5. In what ways did Abraham express his faith in God? Gen. 12; 13:7ff.; 18:22ff.; 22.
6. How is God's supernatural action displayed in Isaac's life? Gen. 22 , 24.
7. What events in Jacob's early life show that God did not choose him because he was good? Gen. 25:27ff.; 27; 30:31ff.
8. What events in Joseph's life remind you of the life of Christ? Gen. 37:18ff.; 39:7ff.; 45.

Thought questions

1. Would God ever tell a Christian today to sacrifice his son? Explain your answer.
2. Is there an element of "poetic justice" in the way Laban treated Jacob?
3. Why did God wrestle with Jacob? What does the change of name mean? Gen. 32:22ff.
4. Was it right for Joseph to trick his brothers?

Map Work

1. On a map of the Middle East locate:

Ur of the Chaldees	Gerar
Haran	Beersheba
Bethel	Mount Moriah
Memphis	Hebron
The Negeb, also	Dan
called the South	Damascus

2. Trace the journeys of Abraham in Genesis 12-14 and 20-22.
3. Compare your map with a modern map, and list the modern countries through which Abraham passed.

Memory

1. Genesis 12:3.
2. Genesis 17:7.

PART TWO

THE PERIOD OF
THEOCRATIC ESTABLISHMENT

Chapter 5

The Covenant People Are Delivered

Exodus

PURPOSE

The book of Exodus continues the narrative of Genesis. It is intended to show how God brought about the organization of the covenant nation. That which was prepared for in Genesis now takes place in Exodus. In the first part of Exodus we see the people of Israel redeemed from their bondage in Egypt. This is a necessary step toward their organization as a nation. It is also typical of the redemption from sin.

OUTLINE

   I. Israel is delivered from Egyptian bondage Exodus 1-18
  II. Israel receives the covenant at Sinai   Exodus 19-24
 III. Israel receives its sanctuary for worship   Exodus 25-40

ANALYSIS

God's Promises Are Fulfilled

Exodus cannot be understood without Genesis. The events which take place here are based on promises given there. You will recall that Abraham received certain promises, but never saw the fulfillment of those promises. The central promise of the covenant of grace required no waiting — God was the God of Abraham. But the threefold promise of a land to be received, a nation to be formed, and a blessing to be bestowed upon all men through Abraham was not fulfilled in the time of the patriarchs. It is in Exodus that the fulfillment begins. Here we see the seed of Abraham formed into a great nation. Here we see set into motion the forces which gave unto Israel the promised land of Canaan as her own land. But not yet is the third part of the promise fulfilled. That must await the coming of Him who is the great Seed of Abraham. It is in Christ that Abraham becomes a blessing to all the world.

In Exodus we also see the fulfillment of another word of God to Abraham. "Know of a surety that thy seed shall be sojourners in a land that is not theirs, and shall serve them; and they shall afflict them four hundred years; and also that nation, whom they shall

34

serve, will I judge: and afterward shall they come out with great substance" (Gen. 15:13, 14). The first part of Exodus is concerned with precisely this.

When Did the Exodus Occur?

When Jacob descended into Egypt to sojourn there he had a family numbering seventy souls. He was received by Pharaoh with great honor, and given the good land of Goshen for a residence. But the favored status of Israel gave way to slavery and bondage when "there arose a new king over Egypt, who knew not Joseph" (Ex. 1:8). Who was this king? Why did he not know Joseph? When did these events occur?

The history of Egypt is reckoned according to dynasties, or ruling families. The first thirteen dynasties are Egyptian. But then Egypt was conquered by a Semitic people known as the Hyksos, or the Shepherd kings. These people composed dynasties fourteen through seventeen. Then the native Egyptians arose, threw off the yoke of foreign rule, and established the native eighteenth dynasty. From this time on Egypt was ruled by Egyptians.

Scholars do not agree exactly where Israel fits into this picture, but the following account seems most in accord with the biblical facts. Joseph came to Egypt during the latter part of the twelfth dynasty or early in the thirteenth dynasty, when the Egyptians ruled their own land. The descendants of Jacob were already settled in Egypt when the Hyksos invasion took place. The Hyksos treated the Israelites kindly, for they were of the same racial background and of the same occupation. But when the Egyptian revolt ended the Hyksos rule, the new Pharaoh forgot about Joseph and remembered only that the Israelites were much like the hated Hyksos. As a result, he determined to reduce them to a state where they could never aid any invader. To this end he placed them in bondage.

Israel's Bondage Pictures Our Sin

This bondage was not simply political dependence. The Bible clearly pictures it as slavery of the worst kind. It was intended to make them perpetual slaves, forever unable to free themselves. This bondage had religious implications. God taught Israel to look back on her redemption from the bondage of Egypt as the basis of her religion. Israel was God's people because He had redeemed her. So we see that the release from bondage symbolized the redemption from sin, and that bondage itself symbolized that cruel captivity in which man is kept by sin.

To release Israel from Egyptian bondage God prepared a redeemer. Moses occupies a place of unique importance in the Old Testament. He was God's servant who had charge of the Old Testament Church of God. In this he is compared to Christ, who is the head of the New Testament Church. We might find many ways in which Moses' life was like Christ's. But the important point is the work each did. Moses was God's instrument in redeeming His people from Egyptian bondage; Christ was God's instrument in redeeming His people from the bondage of sin. Moses was the typical redeemer; Christ was the actual redeemer.

When God's time had come for Israel to be redeemed, God appeared to Moses in the burning bush. There He revealed Himself as I AM THAT I AM. This name is closely connected to the name Jehovah. Both have the same meaning. They refer to the unchangeableness of God, especially as it is concerned with His covenant. Thus they indicate that He is the one who is faithful to keep all His covenant promises. The revelation of this name was appropriate for this time when the promises made to Abraham were about to be fulfilled.

The Exodus Pictures Our Redemption

The release of Israel from bondage typifies the release of God's people from sin. When we remember this fact, we can learn much from the events which took place.

1. We see God's power displayed in the plagues which He brought upon Egypt. These were miracles, showing the supernatural power of the God of Moses. God could have brought Israel out of Egypt without this display of power. He could have caused Pharaoh to submit without a battle. But He says to him, "For this cause have I made thee to stand, to show thee my power, and that my name may be declared throughout all the earth" (Ex. 9:16). By means of these plagues God also magnified His power by comparing it to the weakness of the gods of Egypt, since the Egyptians worshiped some of the things which were stricken.

2. We see the grace of God to Israel displayed by the division that He makes between Israel and Egypt. The first plagues strike all alike; but beginning with the fourth Israel was exempted from them. This was a manifestation of God's love. Having chosen Israel to be His people, He now shelters her from the plagues.

3. The last plague brought death to the first-born. From this plague Israel was not automatically excluded. The Passover is given as the means whereby Israel shall escape this plague. The sacrifice of a lamb and the sprinkling of the blood on the doorposts and lintel provide salvation from death. Here we see pictured the grand truth that sin must be removed by sacrifice if the punishment of sin is to be avoided. How clearly this points to Christ, our Passover Lamb who was sacrificed to take away the sin of the world.

4. The Passover meal shows that expiation (taking away of sin) is followed by fellowship with God. That is the meaning of this meal.

It is like the peace offerings, of which we shall learn in Leviticus. It symbolizes that the eater is actually eating in God's presence. It showed the Israelites how precious they were to God.

5. In the release from Egypt we also see that the salvation of God's people includes the destruction of their enemies. This idea is present in the dreadful plagues. It comes to its climax at the Red Sea, where the Israelites are safely delivered and Pharaoh and his army are drowned.

6. In the story of their journey to Sinai we learn that God does not redeem His people and then forget them. We see how He continually protects His people from their enemies and provides for all their needs.

All of these points are also true of the redemption from sin which God provides for His people. The study of the Exodus should make us understand our salvation better and appreciate it more.

(Note: The name of the body of water that Israel crossed is really the "Reed Sea" or "Sea of Reeds." Israel probably did not cross the Red Sea as we know it, but a smaller, shallower body of water located somewhere along the present Suez Canal.)

EXERCISES

Factual questions

1. What is the purpose of the book of Exodus?
2. What promises to Abraham are fulfilled in Exodus?
3. How did Pharaoh oppress Israel? Ex. 1.
4. What does this bondage symbolize?
5. What does I AM THAT I AM mean?
6. What signs did God give Moses? Ex. 4.
7. What was the result of the first appearance of Moses and Aaron before Pharaoh? Ex. 5.
8. What six lessons may we learn from the redemption from Egypt that are also true of our redemption from sin?
9. List the ten plagues. Ex. 7-11.
10. From which plagues was Israel excluded?
11. Describe the Passover lamb. Ex. 12.
12. What was to be done with it? Ex. 12:6ff.
13. What natural means did God use to part the Red Sea? Ex. 14:21ff.
14. What was manna? When did it appear? Ex. 16:4ff.

Thought questions

1. How did God prepare Moses for his task?
2. Why does God begin the Ten Commandments by saying, "I am Jehovah thy God, who brought thee out of the land of Egypt, out of the house of bondage"?

3. How is the Passover lamb like Christ?
4. Why did God do so many miracles at this time?

Map Work

1. On a map of Egypt and the Sinai Peninsula locate the following cities or areas:

Rameses	Elim
Succoth	Rephidim
Pi-hahiroth	Wilderness of Sin
Marah	

2. Trace the journey of Israel as far as Sinai.
3. Draw symbols to picture the events which occurred at:

Red Sea	Wilderness of Sin
Marah	Rephidim

Memory

1. Outline of Exodus.
2. Exodus 15:11.

Chapter 6

The Covenant Nation Is Organized

Exodus

PURPOSE

The purpose of Exodus, as we have seen, is to present the story of the organization of Israel as the covenant nation. We have taken note of the first step in that process. Now, in the second part of the book, we come to the formal procedure by which Israel becomes the theocratic nation.

ANALYSIS

God's Covenant with Israel

God has brought Israel out of Egypt and down the Sinai Peninsula to Mount Sinai. Here it was that He had called Moses. Here He had promised Moses, "When thou hast brought forth the people out of Egypt, ye shall serve God upon this mountain" (Ex. 3:12). Here the covenant was to be made.

The purpose of the covenant is made plain in Exodus 19:5, 6a: "Now therefore, if ye will obey my voice indeed, and keep my covenant, then ye shall be mine own possession from among all peoples: for all the earth is mine: and ye shall be unto me a kingdom of priests, and a holy nation." It is by means of this covenant that Israel is organized into a nation. But she was not an ordinary nation. Israel was to be a God-centered nation. She would be a theocracy, a nation ruled by God.

The covenant is here presented as being voluntary. That is, Israel can choose to enter the covenant or not to enter it. And the means of entering is obedience. Is this a covenant of works? Not at all. Remember that this covenant is made after the exodus from Egypt. And that exodus is the symbol and type of redemption. It is as a redeemed people that Israel becomes the covenant nation. The obedience required from Israel is that obedience to the redeeming God which always follows His redeeming work.

There is a purpose behind this demand for obedience. It stresses the fact that the nation about to be organized is distinct from other nations. It is a theocracy. It is not man, but God, who makes the laws of Israel. Therefore, it is not man but God who rules. In Israel there can be no distinction between church and state. They are identical. They have the same head. The God whom they worship is the ruler. The God who rules them is the object of their worship.

The Law of God

This close union of religion and government is found even in the Ten Commandments. The commandments are broad principles. They are applicable far beyond the borders of Israel. They are the sum of God's requirements for all of mankind. But notice how they begin, "I am Jehovah thy God who brought thee out of the land of Egypt, out of the house of bondage" (Ex. 20:1). The call to obey these commandments is based upon what God has done for Israel.

The Ten Commandments are for all men in every age. They are ethical standards which flow from the very nature of God Himself. When properly understood — as Jesus understood and explained them— they cover all of life and demand nothing less than perfect love and perfect obedience to God. They tell us how we are to worship God and how we are to treat our fellow men. They are broad principles which apply to all the situations of our lives.

Just because the commandments are broad and general, and just because the problems of life are so practical and specific the commandments must be applied to the various situations of life. As Christians, we are responsible for doing that for ourselves, using all of God's Word as our guide, and with the Holy Spirit as our teacher. But in the young theocratic nation, it was necessary for God to spell out in detail just how the commandments were to be applied to Israel's life. So God did not give Israel just the unchangeable moral law; that is, the commandments, the standard of right and wrong; He also gave the civil law and the ceremonial law. The civil law contains God's rules for Israel's life. The ceremonial law contains God's rules for Israel's worship. But in Israel life and worship were closely united. Therefore we often find the ceremonial and the civil laws presented together. We make the distinction to aid our understanding. The Bible simply presents the ordinances of God.

The Tabernacle

In the theocratic nation, it was necessary that the worship of God should be central in all of life. In fact, if God had made the people into a nation, and had not given them their form of worship, they would not have become a truly theocratic nation. The giving of the instruction for building the tabernacle is closely connected with the giving of the law. In the giving of the law the God who redeemed His people from bondage asserts His right to rule them. In the giving of the tabernacle the God who is their ruler asserts His right to declare how He shall be worshiped.

The tabernacle lies at the center of all Old Testament worship. The temple was simply a permanent sanctuary, built on the pattern of the tabernacle. We can get some idea of the purpose of the tabernacle by the names that are given to it. It is called:

1. The dwelling place, to signify that here God dwells among His people and is truly their God.

2. The tent of meeting, to show that here God meets with His people and has fellowship with them.

3. The tent of testimony, because it testifies constantly to the covenant which God had made with His people.

4. The holy place, because it is set apart from everything else by virtue of God's presence there. It is to be viewed with reverent awe, and God's ordinances concerning it are to be scrupulously obeyed.

The form of the tabernacle, and the placing of the various articles of furniture, is indicated in the sketch below.

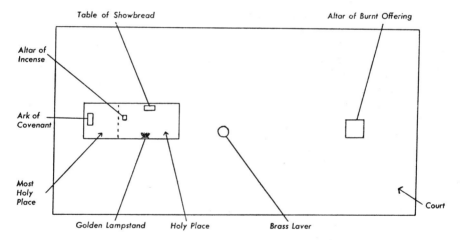

The Priests

The worship ritual in the tabernacle was performed by the priests. God had promised to make Israel a kingdom of priests, but she had not yet attained to that position. The entire nation of Israel was not yet sufficiently advanced spiritually to be allowed to enter the house of God. So a group of Israelites, taken from the tribe of Levi, were to represent their brethren and serve as priests. They were given the responsibility of carrying out the ritual of worship on behalf of their fellow Israelites. They were mediators between God and man. This was not their own idea. They were chosen for this task by God. In this they were types of Christ, "the one mediator between God and man."

The Typical Meaning of the Tabernacle

The tabernacle was the divinely appointed place of worship for Israel. It was the place where God dwelt with His people, and they could fellowship with Him. The tabernacle has a typical meaning as well. It finds its New Testament reference in Christ. John 1:14 reads literally, "And the Word became flesh and tabernacled among us." In Christ we see God dwelling among men in the form of man. Christ did not stop dwelling among men when He ascended into Heaven. He still dwells in His church by His Spirit. And when, in Revelation, John pictures the perfect consummation of God's redemption, it is introduced by the angel cry, "Behold, the tabernacle of God is with men" (Rev. 21:3). This is what the tabernacle typifies—the perfect fellowship of God and His people. In New Testament times that is the fellowship of Christ and His church.

The Furniture in the Court

The altar of burnt offering was the focal point of Israel's worship. Here the sacrifices and offerings were brought. This altar can represent only one thing. It is the Old Testament symbol of the sacrifice of Christ for the sins of His people. "For if the blood of goats and bulls, and the ashes of a heifer sprinkling them that have been defiled, sanctify unto the cleanness of the flesh: how much more shall the blood of Christ, who through the eternal Spirit offered himself without blemish unto God, cleanse your conscience from dead works to serve the living God?" (Heb. 9:13, 14)

Also in the court was the brass laver, where the priests washed their hands and feet before entering the tabernacle or serving at the altar. This washing signified that they were purified, and therefore able to deal with holy objects. So too there must be a purification of God's people if they are to worship Him properly. No longer is there a distinct order of priests. Through Christ all Christians have been made priests. But we still need to be purified. This is done by "the washing of regeneration and renewing of the Holy Spirit" (Titus 3:5). The brass laver symbolizes and typifies the cleansing work of the Holy Spirit, beginning with regeneration and including our sanctification. By this work the sacrifice of Christ is applied to us individually, and we are prepared to fellowship with God.

The Furniture in the Holy Place

In the holy place we find the golden lampstand, the table of showbread, and the altar of incense. Of these three the altar stood closest to the veil behind which lay the most holy place. Here, at the very entrance to the holy of holies, incense was burned morning and evening using live coals plucked from the fire of the brass altar. The symbolical meaning of this was evident even to the Old Testament saints. "Let my prayer be set

forth as incense before thee," prays David (Ps. 141:2). And in
Revelation the incense is connected with the prayers of the saints. This
is also its significance for us. Prayer is "the chief part of the thankfulness which God requires of us" (Heidelberg Catechism). It is part of
our worship of God. In fact it is that part of our worship in which
we draw nearest to God.

The table of showbread stood along the north wall of the sanctuary.
On it in two piles were twelve loaves of "presentation bread." On
each pile was a jar of frankincense. Most likely there were also two
jars of wine. These were all placed on the table on the morning of the
Sabbath and remained there until the next Sabbath. What did they
mean? They represented the fruits of the land. To the Israelite they
symbolized the fruits of righteousness which he was to produce. And
this is also what they typify for us. This is what we bring as an
offering to God. The symbolism does not exclude the material gifts we
bring to God as part of our worship. But the emphasis is on that which
makes the gifts worthwhile, a life which is lived to God's glory.

The golden candlestick, or better, the golden lampstand, was made
of pure gold. It held seven golden lamps, in which olive oil was burned.
These were lit every night, so that there would always be illumination in
the house of God. The symbolism of the lampstand is most difficult.
Probably it typifies the light of truth which shines forth from us, and
brings glory to God. Then it would picture our worship of God
through witnessing, both with life and with lips.

The Furniture in the Most Holy Place

The only article of furniture in the most holy place was the ark of
the covenant. This was a box of wood covered with gold. Its top was
a slab of solid gold, from which rose the figures of two cherubim. This
was called the mercy seat. The pillar of fire which symbolized the
presence of God descended upon this mercy seat. This was the fact to
which all the tabernacle pointed — that God dwelt among His people.
It symbolized that they could enter into the very presence of God. But not
all Israel could enter. Not even all the priests could enter, but only the
high priest, once a year. And he came with blood, in order to obtain
forgiveness. This pointed forward, as the author of Hebrews indicates,
to Christ, the great High Priest, who entered into the very presence of
God in Heaven with His own blood shed for us. And when His work
is fully completed, and we are glorified with Him, we ourselves shall
stand in the presence of God Almighty. So the ark of the covenant is the
type of our present entrance into God's presence "in Christ." And it is
the type of the coming glory, when we shall be with Him for all
eternity.

The Covenant Nation Has a Tragic Beginning

The giving of the law and the giving of the tabernacle were events of the utmost importance. Coupled with the redemption from Egypt, they form the foundation for all the national life of Israel. Henceforth Israel was the covenant nation, chosen from among all the nations of earth to serve the living God. But she was still far from the theocratic ideal, in which every Israelite would gladly serve Jehovah and Him alone. No sooner had she been constituted as the covenant nation than the people fell into sin. The tragic story of Exodus 32-34 proves again that this covenant was not made with the people of Israel because they were worthy, but because God had chosen them in sovereign love.

When the golden calf had been destroyed, when Israel had been punished, when Moses had obtained forgiveness for the people, then the tabernacle was built. And the book closes on a glorious note, "the glory of Jehovah filled the tabernacle" (Ex. 40:34). The covenant God takes up His residence with the covenant nation.

EXERCISES

Factual questions

1. What is the purpose of this second part of Exodus?
2. What was the purpose of the covenant God made with Israel?
3. What was the place of obedience in the covenant?
4. What three types of laws are found in Exodus? Explain each.
5. What is the connection between the giving of the law and the giving of the tabernacle?
6. What names are given to the tabernacle and what does each mean?
7. Considering 1 cubit as 18 inches or 1½ feet, give the dimensions for the court, the tabernacle proper, and each article of furniture. Ex. 25-30.
8. Why were priests ordained in Israel?
9. What does the tabernacle typify?
10. What is the typical meaning of the altar of burnt offering?
11. What is the typical meaning of the brass laver?
12. What is the typical meaning of the altar of incense?
13. What is the typical meaning of the table of showbread?
14. What is the typical meaning of the golden lampstand?
15. What is the typical meaning of the ark of the covenant?
16. What did the people do while Moses was on Mount Sinai? Ex. 32.
17. How were they punished? Ex. 32:15ff.
18. What favor did Moses ask of God? Ex. 33:17ff.
19. What happened to Moses as a result of his talking with God? Ex. 34:29ff.

Thought questions

1. Exodus 21 and 22 contain some of the civil laws which apply the principles of the Ten Commandments. Frame some modern problems where these laws could apply. Example: A man had a dog which was known to bite, but he refused to tie it. One day it bit a boy. The boy's father demanded that the dog be killed and that the owner pay $5,000 damages. Should the judge grant this? See Ex. 21:28-32.

2. Do any of the decisions of the problems in question 1 differ from our laws? If so, which are better?

3. What were the people expected to learn from the thunder and lightning on Mount Sinai?

4. What made the sin of the golden calf so terrible?

5. How were the children of Levi blessed as a result of their action in this sin?

6. Did Moses really see God?

Chapter 7

The Covenant Nation Receives Its Laws

Leviticus

PURPOSE

The book of Leviticus contains the laws which God gave to His covenant nation. Having been formally organized as the theocracy, Israel now needed to receive her laws from her divine ruler. These laws were intended to make her like her ruler. God's holiness is both the reason and the example for Israel's holiness.

OUTLINE

I.	Laws for holy worship	Leviticus 1-16
II.	Laws for holy living	Leviticus 17-27

ANALYSIS

In Exodus we saw that Israel received the tabernacle as the place where she should worship Jehovah. We saw how every part of the tabernacle was designed to teach Israel—and us too—how sinful man is to have fellowship with God. In Leviticus we find directions given regarding the sacrifices which were the primary means of worship in the tabernacle.

God commanded that Israel worship Him through five classes of offerings—the burnt offering, the meal offering, the peace offering, the sin offering, and the trespass offering. Each of these was to be offered under certain conditions. Each had a special meaning. Each can teach us something about our fellowship with God.

The Burnt Offering

The burnt offering is mentioned first because it was the most common. It was offered twice daily for all Israel, as part of the regular tabernacle worship. Any Israelite might also voluntarily bring a burnt offering. Since the other offerings share many of the elements of the burnt offering, we shall examine it more fully than the others.

The worshiper who came to present a burnt offering had to bring with him an animal. A bullock, a sheep, or a goat was permitted. In case of poverty, he might bring a turtledove or young pigeon. The sacrifice had to be the very best, a male without blemish. Bringing this into the

46

court, the worshiper first laid his hands on it, then slew it on the north side of the altar. The priests then sprinkled the blood of the sacrifice upon the altar. After this the animal was cut into pieces and all the pieces placed on the altar and burned.

Several of the actions required in this offering make its meaning plain. The laying of the worshiper's hands on the animal signifies that something is transferred from one to the other. This is the uniform meaning of this action in the Bible. In this case there is only one thing that can be transferred—the sin of the man. By the laying on of hands the animal becomes the bearer of the worshiper's sins.

This shows us why the sacrifice was killed. The animal which bears the worshiper's sins must now pay the penalty of sin. That is the idea in all Old Testament sacrifice. It is said that the burnt offering is "accepted for him to make atonement for him" (Lev. 1:4). To atone means to cover. Atonement is the covering over of sins, blotting them out. The animal's blood was shed as a sacrifice to take away sin. The worshiper's sin had been laid upon the animal. Now the death of the animal represented the payment of the penalty due to the worshiper. And, the penalty having been paid, the sins could no more be counted against him.

The sprinkling of the blood on the altar signified that this was so. The animal was polluted by sin. But the death of the animal paid for that sin. Consequently the blood of the animal, which represents its life, is no longer considered as sinful. It can now be sprinkled on the holy altar. It is now acceptable to God. By this act the worshiper was assured that his sin and guilt was removed.

Finally, the sacrifice was burned on the altar "for a burnt-offering, an offering made by fire, of a sweet savor unto Jehovah" (Lev. 1:9). This brings us to the climax of the burnt offering. Since sin was removed and the worshiper was forgiven, his sacrifice was burned on the holy altar. And since the sacrifice represented him, this burning pictured the worshiper himself rising as a "sweet savor unto Jehovah." The burnt offering thus symbolized the consecration of the worshiper to his God. In the burnt offering he was presenting himself, first to be cleansed from sin and then to be pleasing to God.

This offering was presented twice daily for all Israel. By this the goal and purpose of the covenant nation was expressed. The sin of Israel was symbolically acknowledged and atoned for. And the smoke of the sacrifice ascending to God declared that God's covenant people were offering themselves to Him, so that He might delight in them.

The Meal Offering

Closely connected to the burnt offering, and often presented with it, was the meal offering. (This is called the meat offering in the

Authorized Version. But "meat" used to refer to all sorts of food. Now it is used only for flesh. So the word used gives a mistaken impression. It was grain, not meat, that was offered.) The meal offering had nothing about it to signify the removal of sin. That is the reason why it was not offered alone. The grain, along with oil, frankincense, and wine, was partly burned and partly given to the priests for their food. This offering, composed of the fruits of the ground, pictured the fruits of righteousness. Like the burnt offering, it symbolized consecration. But where the burnt offering symbolized the consecration of the whole man, the meal offering especially had in view the expression of consecration in holy living.

The Peace Offering

The procedure for the peace offering was the same as that for the burnt offering until the blood had been sprinkled. But then the whole animal was not burned. The fat, or tender parts, was burned. This symbolized the presentation of the animal to God. Part of the animal, the breast and the right shoulder, was given to the priest. The remainder was returned to the offerer to be eaten. This eating was part of the offering. It symbolized eating with Jehovah. And eating together, in Oriental countries, signifies fellowship, communion, oneness. So the peace offering symbolized most beautifully that for which the whole sacrificial system existed—fellowship between God and His people.

The Sin Offering

The sin offering was provided for the Israelite who had committed a sin "in error." If anyone committed a sin in deliberate defiance of God's law there was no offering for his sin. He was to be executed. But for the sinner who sinned through lack of knowledge, or lack of will power to resist temptation, or in the heat of passion, God provided this offering. It consisted of an animal to be slain, except in the case of the poorest people. They could bring grain unmixed with oil or incense. The animal was slain and the blood was brought into God's presence by being sprinkled on the altar (in most cases), applied to the horns of the altar (for a ruler of the people), or applied to the altar of incense (when the high priest or the whole congregation sinned). Then part of the animal was burned before Jehovah, and the rest was disposed of in a way that signified that it was holy. This offering signified that the guilt of the offerer was taken away.

The Trespass Offering

The trespass offering is closely connected to the sin offering. It appears that it was intended only for those sins which were an invasion of the rights of God or of a fellow man. The trespass offering differs from the sin offering only slightly. The sacrifice was always a ram.

The blood was always put on the brass altar. And the worshiper had to return what he had gained by violating the right of another, with an additional twenty per cent for damages. This offering showed that it was necessary, not only that sin be covered, but that God's justice be satisfied.

The Meaning of the Sacrifices

We should have no difficulty in recognizing that all these sacrifices point to Christ. The sacrifices themselves are not enough. The intelligent and pious Old Testament worshiper must have recognized that fact. The animal could never be a satisfactory substitute for the man. If God accepted animal sacrifices, it must have been because there was a perfect sacrifice yet to come. The pages of the New Testament leave us without doubt on this score. Again and again the work of Christ is explained in terms of the levitical sacrifices. And it is the slaying of the animal that pictures Christ's work most directly. His death, the perfect sacrifice made by the great High Priest, truly makes atonement for sin. It is the reality of which the Old Testament sacrifices were simply shadows.

So from Leviticus we learn again one of the most simple and yet most profound truths of the Bible. We cannot have fellowship with God unless and until our sins have been covered through the shed blood of Jesus Christ. Then and only then can we present our bodies "a living sacrifice, holy, acceptable unto God" (Rom. 12:1). Then and only then can we enter into that fellowship which "is with the Father, and with his Son Jesus Christ" (I John 1:4).

The Meaning of the Day of Atonement

Finally, in connection with the sacrifices, we must briefly refer to the Day of Atonement. On the tenth day of the seventh month all Israel gathered together. On that day sin offerings were presented for the high priest and for the people. Only on this day was the blood of these sacrifices carried into the holy of holies and sprinkled on the mercy seat. This ceremony was the most important single event of the Jewish year. By this annual sacrifice all Israel's sins were atoned for, and the covenant nation was able again to offer the burnt offerings of consecration daily. We should not be surprised to find that the writer of Hebrews uses this as a picture of Christ's work. "For Christ entered not into a holy place made with hands [as the high priest entered the most holy place on the day of atonement], like in pattern to the true; but into heaven itself, now to appear before the face of God for us: nor yet that he should offer himself often, as the high priest entereth into the holy place year by year with blood not his own; else must he often have suffered since the foundation of the world: but now once at the end of the ages hath he been manifested to put away sin by the sacrifice of himself" (Heb. 9:24-26).

The Meaning of Holiness

In Leviticus we learn also of that which makes men clean and unclean (Lev. 11-15). The terms "clean" and "unclean" have a special meaning. That which is "unclean" pollutes or defiles the one who touches it, so that he is not able to enter the tabernacle and worship God. This distinction between clean and unclean was intended to remind Israel constantly of the sin that is in man. Man's sin has affected the world. As a result of sin, not everything in the world is fit for the worship of a holy God. The restrictions involved in the avoidance of the unclean things taught Israel that she must be holy, as God is holy.

Holiness is the central thought of Leviticus. The sacrifices and ritual were means whereby the defilement of sin could be removed. Hand in hand with this went God's instructions for Israel's conduct. Leviticus contains both civil and ceremonial laws. And the point of these laws is set forth in Leviticus 19:2, "Speak unto all the congregation of the children of Israel, and say unto them, Ye shall be holy; for I Jehovah your God am holy."

Holiness involves living according to God's standard set forth in His law. And this law is primarily religious. Nowhere in Leviticus is there any suggestion that Israel can live right without worshiping right. Worship is the warp and woof of the fabric of Israel's life. In the instructions given for a holy life, much attention is paid to the religious. The conduct of the priests is emphasized, since they represent the people before a holy God. And the life of Israel is built around her religious feasts. The weekly Sabbath (every seventh day), the annual feasts (half of them in the seventh month), the sabbatical year (every seventh year) and the year of jubilee following the seventh sabbatical year made up the framework of Israel's life. All these feasts reminded Israel of her relationship to God. And the constant repetition of seven (a number often used to symbolize God or perfection) suggested that God required of them nothing more than a faithful keeping of His laws and statutes. All this was a perpetual reminder that Israel was a holy people unto Jehovah.

CONCLUSION

The Meaning of Leviticus

The book of Leviticus is often neglected. To some extent that is understandable, for it hardly seems to have any bearing on our present-day problems. But when we read Leviticus in the light of the New Testament, especially in connection with the epistle to the Hebrews, we will discover how up-to-date Leviticus is. The Old Testament presents the same Christ as does the New Testament. To see Him in the types and shadows of the ancient Church as well as in the clearer revelation of this dispensation is to increase in understanding. And to increase in understanding of Christ is to increase in love and worship and service. And is that not the goal of every Christian?

EXERCISES

Factual questions

1. What is the purpose of Leviticus?
2. What various types of offerings are mentioned in Leviticus?
3. What could the worshiper bring as a sacrifice?
4. What is represented by the laying on of hands?
5. Why was the animal killed?
6. What is signified by the sprinkling of the blood?
7. What does each type of offering symbolize?
8. Decribe the animals, the fish, and the birds that are unclean. Lev. 11:1-19.
9. What did the distinction between clean and unclean signify?
10. What feasts did Israel have to keep? Lev. 23.
11. What happened during the sabbatical years? Lev. 25.
12. What happened during the year of jubilee? Lev. 25:8ff.
13. How were the laws in Leviticus connected to Israel's future? Lev. 26:3ff.

Fill in the blanks from Leviticus 16.

On the Day of Atonement, Aaron put on _____ garments. He took a _____ for a _____ and a _____ for a _____ for himself. From the people he took two _____ for a _____ and a _____ for a _____. Having killed the _____, he took its _____ in a basin, and a _____ containing _____ from the _____, and a handful of _____. In the tabernacle he _____ the incense and sprinkled the _____ on the ark _____ times. This made atonement for the sins of _____ and his _____.

He did the same with the blood of one _____ (chosen by lot) to make the atonement for the sins of _____. Then Aaron laid his _____ on the head of the remaining _____ and confessed upon it the _____ of Israel. The _____ was then taken into the wilderness. Then Aaron took off the _____ garments, bathed himself, put on his regular priestly garments, and offered _____ for _____ and for _____. The man who took the _____ away and those who burned the _____ and _____ outside the camp had to _____ themselves and their clothes before returning into the camp.

Thought questions

1. Why did sacrificial animals have to be without blemish?
2. Why were Nadab and Abihu killed for offering "strange fire"? Lev. 10.
3. Why were the priests required to meet higher standards than the people? Lev. 21, 22.

Memory

1. Outline of Leviticus.
2. Leviticus 19:2.

Chapter 8

The Covenant Nation Is Disciplined

Numbers

PURPOSE

The book of Numbers continues the history of Israel where it ended in Exodus. (Leviticus, of course, contains law, not history.) In Numbers we see the children of Israel brought to the border of the land of promise. The story of their travels to that point is intended to show us how God trained or disciplined His covenant nation so that they would be ready to receive the land which He had promised them.

OUTLINE

     I. Israel's discipline for travel   Numbers 1- 9
    II. Israel's discipline for obedience Numbers 10-21
  III. Israel's discipline for conquest Numbers 22-36

ANALYSIS

Preparing to Leave Sinai

After the tabernacle had been built and consecrated and God had taken up residence in the most holy place, it was time to begin preparations for moving. Sinai was made holy by the events which had occurred there. But it was not the promised land. Israel had to travel to the land of Canaan, for it was in that land that God had promised to establish His theocratic nation. Therefore He gives instructions which would prepare Israel for travel.

A census of the available fighting men was taken. They numbered 603,550. On the basis of this number, it has been estimated that the entire group would be approximately two and one-half million. This is certainly not impossible. It shows how greatly God had blessed Israel in Egypt, even when they were in bondage. But a group this large could not wander through the wilderness in undisciplined fashion. To travel and to camp with a people like this would demand careful planning.

God Himself did the planning. The tribes were each given a specific side of the tabernacle on which they were to camp. As a result, the camp of Israel was always in the form of a square with the taber-

53

nacle in the center. Three tribes were on each side of the tabernacle. Of these three, one tribe was marked out by God as the leader. When it was time to move, the nation marched by tribes. The order of march was also prescribed by God. In this way the large multitude could do all things in an orderly fashion.

At the time of the first Passover, God had declared that the first-born of Israel were His, to be consecrated for His service. But now God chose the tribe of Levi to take the place of the first-born. They were to aid the priests and to carry the tabernacle when the camp moved. At God's command, they were consecrated for these tasks.

As Israel left Sinai, she was not to forget that she was a holy nation, separated unto God. Therefore, for twelve days the heads of the tribes brought sacrifices and offerings to God. And in order that they might never forget that they were a redeemed people, God again told them that they were to keep the Passover annually. They celebrated this feast before they left Mount Sinai.

The Trip to Canaan

Israel was now prepared to travel. And so they began the trip to the land of Canaan going up the east side of the Sinai Peninsula. But as they traveled they showed that they needed to learn to be obedient to God. They sinned with awful frequency. The great test of their willingness to obey God came at Kadesh-barnea. Here they were on the borders of the promised land. Here they sent spies into the land and learned that it was indeed a good land. But when they were informed that it was inhabited by giants who dwelt in walled cities, they refused to believe that Jehovah would give them the land. And for this unbelief they were punished. Part of the punishment involved forty years of wandering in the wilderness. During this time all the Israelites who were twenty years or older at the time of testing would perish. Since they refused to believe that God would give them the land, they would never enter it.

Little is said about those forty years. A few incidents, generally connected with sin, are related. But we get the impression that the discipline of those forty years was not in vain. The people did not become sinless, but they trusted God more. When the forty years were almost gone, God directed their feet eastward. He brought them to the area east of Jordan. Here they met and conquered Sihon and Og, two great and powerful kings. God showed them that when they trusted Him He would give His covenant nation victory over the strongest of foes.

The kings of Moab and Midian saw that God gave Israel the victory over these powerful foes. They began to fear what Israel would do to them. So they sought aid from Balaam, a heathen prophet who knew about Jehovah, but did not worship Him. He tried to force God to curse Israel. Balaam's altars and sacrifices resembled the pulling of strings of a marionette by a puppeteer. They were supposed to make Jehovah do what Balaam wanted done. But Jehovah is not manipulated by men. He caused Balaam to bless Israel instead of cursing her. One of these blessings is a beautiful prophecy of Christ:

> *I see him, but not now;*
> *I behold him, but not nigh:*
> *There shall come forth a star out of Jacob,*
> *And a sceptre shall rise out of Israel,*
> *And shall smite through the corners of Moab,*
> *And break down all the sons of tumult.*
> —NUM. 24:17.

When Israel learned of this (and they must have learned about it, since Moses recorded it in detail) they were assured again that God was able to give them the victory over all opponents. Neither mighty armies nor heathen gods could stand against Jehovah, the God of Israel.

Preparations for Entering Canaan

As they stood on the borders of Canaan, a census of this new generation was taken. Israel now numbered 601,730 fighting men. This was a slight decrease.

At this time God also prescribed new offerings. The burnt offering was already being offered morning and evening. Now, in addition, special offerings were to be brought on every Sabbath, on the first day of every month, and at the scheduled feasts. These would involve a sizable number of animals. Here we see God's tender care for His people. When they were in the wilderness, which could not pasture large flocks, these special offerings were not required. Now that they are entering a land flowing with milk and honey, the new sacrifices are added. God always supplies what He requires His people to give Him.

Before the entrance final preparations needed to be made. Moses could not enter Canaan. Joshua was appointed to replace him. Reuben, Gad, and half the tribe of Manasseh desired the lands of Sihon and Og for their inheritance. This was granted, with the understanding that they send fighting men across Jordan to help conquer the land of Canaan. In full faith that they would conquer the land, the principles for dividing it were set forth before they had ever set foot in the land.

CONCLUSION

Obedience is the first requirement of the theocracy. Any people is expected to obey its ruler. In the theocracy, the ruler is God. Therefore obedience is also a religious duty. Israel had to be disciplined so that she would learn to obey. This discipline did not consist simply of punishment for sin. The strict rules for camping and traveling, the

victories which followed obedience and the defeats which followed
disobedience, and the added prescriptions for worship were also means
of discipline. This discipline worked. It was this disciplined generation
that wrested the land of Canaan from the heathen nations. It was this
generation that was obedient to God's law.

Factual questions   EXERCISES

1. How does Numbers get its name? Num. 1, 26.
2. What is the purpose of Numbers?
3. In what order did Israel march? Num. 2; 10:13ff.
4. What was the position of the tribe of Levi in Israel? Num. 3:5ff.
5. Draw a sketch of the camp of Israel placing the tabernacle in the
   center, the Levites around it by families, and the rest of the
   tribes around the Levites. Specify directions. Num. 2.
6. Did the Levites touch the tabernacle furniture when they carried
   it? Why? Num. 4.
7. There are seven sins of Israel listed in Numbers 11:3-35; 11:35-
   12:15; 13:1-14:45; 15:32-36; 16:1-35; 20:1-13; 21:4-9. Fill
   in the following information for each.
   Place   Sinner(s)   Sin   Punishment
8. By what sign did God show that Aaron was His chosen priest?
   Num. 17.
9. What does the brass serpent typify? Num. 21:4ff.; John 3.
10. What does the New Testament say about Balaam? II Peter 2:
    12ff.; Jude; Rev. 2:12ff.
11. What did the addition of new offerings at this time teach Israel?
12. What two laws concerning heiresses were occasioned by the
    daughters of Zelophehad? Num. 27, 36.
13. Why did Reuben, Gad, and the half-tribe of Manasseh want land
    on the east side of Jordan? Num. 32.

Thought questions
1. Compare the census of Numbers 1 with that of Numbers 26 and
   tell which tribes increased and which decreased. Then read again
   the prophecies of Jacob in Genesis 49. Can you see the prophecies
   being fulfilled in Reuben, Simeon, Manasseh (Joseph's son)?
2. Why was the decision of Israel at Kadesh-barnea so important?
   Num. 13, 14.
3. Why was Israel to refrain from fighting with Edom? Num. 20.
4. How would conquering Sihon and Og help conquer Canaan?

Memory
1. Outline of Numbers.
2. Numbers 24:17.
3. Numbers 6:24-26.

Chapter 9

The Covenant Nation Is Consecrated

Deuteronomy

PURPOSE

The name Deuteronomy means "second law." This title is not strictly accurate. (The names of the books are not inspired, but were given later by men.) Deuteronomy does not simply repeat the laws given earlier. It contains a "summary of the whole law and wisdom of the people of Israel, in which those things which related to the priests and Levites are omitted, and only such things included as the people in general needed to know" (Luther, quoted in Keil and Delitzsch). The book is composed chiefly of three addresses given by Moses to the people. In them he speaks to Israel as a father to his children. He has only one goal in mind—that Israel, when she enters her land, shall be true to Jehovah. Everything in Deuteronomy points to the renewal of the covenant between God and His covenant nation.

OUTLINE

    I. Moses' first address — a review of God's guidance
            Deuteronomy 1- 4
   II. Moses' second address — a review of God's covenant
            Deuteronomy 5-26
  III. Moses' third address — a call to covenant obedience
            Deuteronomy 27-30
  IV. Moses' farewell and death   Deuteronomy 31-34

ANALYSIS

The First Address

Deuteronomy begins with the record of a speech in which Moses reminds Israel of her past history. This is good preparation for the following speech, which will deal with the covenant. The burden of the first speech is God's care for Israel in spite of Israel's disobedience. Moses reminds the people how God provided elders to judge them, how they rebelled against God at Kadesh-barnea, and how God had just recently given them victories over Sihon and Og. He also recalls how he had entreated God for permission to enter Canaan, but had been refused because of his sin.

The Second Address

This speech begins with a repetition of the Ten Commandments. You should remember that the commandments are found in Deuteronomy 5 as well as in Exodus 20. This restatement of the moral law of God is followed by a strong warning against apostasy (falling away from God). Then Moses sets forth a series of laws. These laws are given to guide Israel when she enters Canaan. There are laws which deal with worship, laws which deal with the proper organization of government for a theocratic nation, and laws which explain what it means in practice to love your neighbor as yourself.

The Third Address

The first two speeches lead to this third address. Moses calls Israel to renew her covenant with God. He directs how this is to be done when they have entered Canaan. They are to make an altar as a permanent record of the covenant, and are to perform a ceremony in which the blessings and the cursings of the covenant are solemnly proclaimed by the Levites and acknowledged by the people. To these instructions the people give assent. (And when they entered Canaan they faithfully followed these instructions. Read about it in Deuteronomy 27 and Joshua 8:30-35.) Then Moses, like a loving father, implores his children to keep this covenant which God has made with them.

The End of Moses' Work

Now Moses has come to the end of his mission. It is time to enter Canaan. But he may not enter because of his sin at Meribah. Joshua has been chosen to replace Moses. Now he is consecrated for that task. Then, like a true patriarch, Moses blesses the people. Alone, he ascends into Mount Nebo, to the high peak called Pisgah. From that vantage point God shows him the promised land. But Moses enters instead into a better land. There, alone with God, he leaves this life and begins his heavenly rest.

CONCLUSION

We have come to the end of the Pentateuch. These books by Moses are designed to trace the history of the theocracy until the time when Israel was about to occupy her own land. Each book has contributed to that goal:

1. Genesis has shown the need for a separate people and has described the calling of that people in Abraham.

2. Exodus has pictured the formal organization of Abraham's children into the covenant nation.

3. Leviticus has set forth the laws by which the theocratic nation is to be a holy nation.

4. Numbers has traced the ways in which the covenant nation was disciplined to serve God faithfully.

5. Deuteronomy tells how Israel was consecrated for the task of conquering Canaan.

It is obvious that we cannot stop at the end of the Pentateuch. The story of God's kingdom does not end here. But Moses' work in recording the development of the theocracy is finished.

EXERCISES

Factual questions

1. What is the purpose of Deuteronomy?
2. Why were the Israelites defeated by the Amorites? Deut. 1:26ff.
3. Why was Israel able to defeat Sihon and Og? Deut. 2:26-3:11.
4. Does Moses expect Israel to avoid apostasy? Deut. 4:15ff.
5. What past experiences should convince Israel that she has not received the land because of her righteousness? Deut. 9: 6ff.
6. Who could use the cities of refuge? Deut. 19.
7. How were the Israelites to treat a captured city in other lands? In the land of Canaan? Deut. 20:10ff.
8. What will be some results of disobedience to the covenant? Deut. 28:15ff.
9. How often was the covenant to be read before the people? Deut. 31:9ff.
10. Where was Moses buried? Deut. 34.
11. What is the purpose of the Pentateuch?
12. How does each book in the Pentateuch help to achieve the purpose of the Pentateuch?

Thought questions

1. Why did God give the Ten Commandments twice?
2. Is the covenant recorded in Deuteronomy the same as that recorded in Exodus? If so, why was it renewed?
3. Israel did disobey the covenant. Can you recall from Israel's history the fulfillment of the curses found in Deuteronomy 28: 20-35, 58-68?
4. When Moses died, who remained of those who had been at Kadesh-barnea?

Memory

1. Outline of Deuteronomy.
2. Deuteronomy 6:4, 5.
3. Deuteronomy 18:18.
4. Deuteronomy 29:29.

Chapter 10

The Covenant Nation Receives Its Land

Joshua

INTRODUCTION

Former Prophets

When we come to Joshua, we leave behind us the first major section of the Old Testament—the Law or the Pentateuch. No longer are we studying books that were written by Moses. We are now in the Former Prophets. The group of books entitled "Prophets" includes all the Old Testament books written by prophets. This group is divided into two parts — the Former and the Latter Prophets. Our study of the Latter Prophets will come later. (See Chapter 29.) The Former Prophets include the books of Joshua, Judges, Samuel, and Kings.

We do not know who wrote any of the Former Prophets. Tradition tells us that they were written by prophets. The contents of the books agree with that tradition. These are books of history. But they do not simply record the facts of history. They choose, from all the events which occurred in Israel, those facts which most clearly trace the development of God's kingdom and emphasize God's work in the midst of His people. They present history from a religious point of view. They are interested in displaying the hand of God in history. In this way the Former Prophets provide a background for the Latter Prophets. Without the history contained in these books, the prophecies found in the Latter Prophets would be almost meaningless.

Joshua

Joshua, like the rest of the books in the Former Prophets, is anonymous. But, although we cannot identify the author we can determine approximately when the book was written. We know that it could not have been written by Joshua himself, because it contains several items which occurred after Joshua's death. (However, some short sections may have been written by Joshua and included in the book by a later author.) On the other hand, it could not have been written very long after Joshua's death. For one thing, the harlot Rahab was still living. "She dwelt in the midst of Israel unto this day, because she hid the messengers" (Josh. 6:25). Most likely the book was written within ten or fifteen years

60

after the death of Joshua by someone who knew Joshua well and had been an eyewitness of the things recorded in the book.

PURPOSE

The book of Joshua shows how Israel was brought into the land of Canaan. This was a fulfillment of God's promise to Abraham. This was the final step in the establishment of the theocratic nation. Israel was formally organized, had received her laws, and was now given possession of the land in which the theocracy was to develop.

OUTLINE

    I. Israel conquers the promised land   Joshua 1-12
   II. Israel divides the promised land   Joshua 13-24

ANALYSIS

Preparation for Conquering Canaan

Moses was dead, and the people had mourned for him thirty days. Now God appeared to Joshua, the chosen successor, and encouraged him. Joshua began by sending spies to Jericho. When they returned with the report that the heathen trembled for fear of Israel, the time for action had come. God added to that fear by bringing Israel across the Jordan by a miracle. When the ark of the covenant, the symbol of God's presence, was carried into the Jordan (which was at flood stage at this time of year), the waters were stopped above them, and they crossed on dry ground. If the Israelites had needed any assurance that Jehovah was with them, this miracle surely would have provided it. In order that this lesson might not be lost on future generations, Joshua erected two memorials of twelve stones, as a reminder of God's mighty deeds.

Israel now camped at Gilgal on the west side of Jordan. Here Israel displayed by her actions that she realized her need of obeying God's covenant. During the time of wilderness wandering, the covenant sign of circumcision had been neglected. Now it was administered to all who were uncircumcised. This was a reminder to them of God's covenant with Abraham. It was also, on their part, a promise to be faithful to that covenant.

At Gilgal the people of Israel also celebrated the Passover. It was forty years to the month since they had left Egypt. Some scholars believe that the Passover was not celebrated from the time Israel left Sinai until this day in Gilgal. If so, this was the first time in thirty-eight years that Israel had received this reminder of God's redeeming grace by which she had been brought out of Egypt. How important this lesson was at the beginning of a time of warfare! Reminded both of God's faithful covenant and of His redeeming grace, Israel was prepared for her task.

As a final encouragement to Joshua, the Angel of Jehovah (who is really the Son of God) appeared to Joshua and announced that He would lead Israel in battle.

Conquest of Southern Canaan

The stories of the capture of the important Canaanite cities of Jericho and Ai are very familiar. But we must not allow familiarity to blind us to the lessons set forth therein for Israel and for us.

Israel's strategy must have seemed strange to the inhabitants of Jericho. Perhaps it seemed strange to the Israelites as well. But there was a reason for it. All were to learn that the victory was not of Israel, but of God. In a miraculous manner Jericho was opened wide to the swords of Israel's warriors that it might be clear to all that Jehovah led the children of Israel to victory.

The story of Ai emphasizes clearly the truth that God's covenant nation must be holy in order to receive God's blessing. As long as the sin of Achan goes unpunished, Israel cannot win a victory. But when the sinner has been stoned, the city is quickly taken.

The incident of the deceitful Gibeonites who pretended that they had come from a far country, was a lesson to Israel that it was not enough to trust in one's own wisdom. For lack of asking Jehovah what to do, Israel was tricked into disobeying God's express command to spare none of the Canaanites. Nevertheless God turned even this evil to good. The other Canaanites united to attack Gibeon for making this alliance with Israel, and Joshua was able at one sweep to break the back of Canaanite power in the southern part of Canaan.

A Problem in Ethics

The conquest of Canaan poses a problem for some people. When the people of Israel captured the Canaanite cities they killed everyone. Neither man, woman, nor child was spared. This was not their own idea. They did it by express command of God. "But of the cities of these peoples, that Jehovah thy God giveth thee for an inheritance, thou shalt save alive nothing that breatheth" (Deut. 20:16). In the eyes of some people, this is not in accord with the nature of God. The very idea that God would require such cruelty is unthinkable to them.

Actually the problem is not as great as it is made to appear. We must simply remember that God punishes sinners. He punished sinners among the people whom He had chosen as His own. Remember Nadab and Abihu, Korah, Dathan, and Abiram, Achan! He also punishes the sins of other men. And the Canaanites were terrible sinners. God had said to Abraham that his seed would not yet inherit Canaan because "the iniquity of the Amorite is not yet full" (Gen. 15:16). By now their iniquity was filled up. That the harlot Rahab was apparently a respectable citizen of Jericho is one piece of evidence. And much more is available to us through archaeology. We have learned that the Canaanite religion was composed of immoral sexual practices. It also involved sacrificing first-born children to the gods. The Canaanites were ripe for punishment. "Archaeologists who dig in the ruins of the Canaanite cities wonder why God did not destroy them sooner than he did" (Halley).

We must also remember that Israel was commanded to be holy. We have seen from her past history how prone the people were to murmur against Jehovah and even to follow other gods. The utter destruction of the Canaanites was commanded as a means of preserving Israel from following the sinful religions of the heathen.

Conquest of Northern Canaan

The destruction of the Amorite confederation which attacked Gibeon had opened the way to the capture of all the south. A similar confederation, led by the king of Hazor and including all the city-states of north Canaan, now formed to fight against Israel. But Joshua attacked swiftly, apparently catching the enemy in a confused and unprepared state, and scattered them. This one victory gave Israel control of the northern part of Canaan.

Distribution of the Land

Although not all the land was conquered, the time had come to begin dividing it. Reuben, Gad, and the half-tribe of Manasseh had received their inheritance east of Jordan. At a meeting in Gilgal the inheritances were decided by lot. In this way it would be God, not man, who determined the land each tribe should receive. The first lots fell to Judah and to the sons of Joseph—Ephraim and Manasseh. They received the best and most important sections. As a result they became the most important tribes in Israel. This was in accord with the prophecy of Jacob, made centuries before.

The remaining tribes were told to search out the land and describe it to Joshua. After this was done, they met again in Shiloh and the other seven tribes received their inheritance. The map on page 64 shows the approximate location of each tribe. The tribe of Levi received no inheritance. Instead, the Levites were given forty-eight cities in which to dwell. Of these, six had already been designated as cities of refuge. They are also placed on the map.

Conclusion

We will miss the point of Joshua if we simply regard the book as history which tells how Israel conquered and divided her land. It is that, but it is more than that. We must never forget the promise to Abraham.

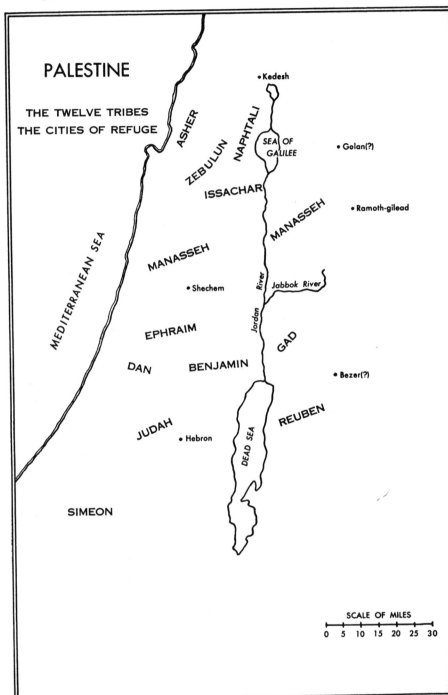

PALESTINE

THE TWELVE TRIBES
THE CITIES OF REFUGE

• Kedesh

ASHER

ZEBULUN

NAPHTALI

SEA OF GALILEE

• Golan(?)

ISSACHAR

MANASSEH

• Ramoth-gilead

MEDITERRANEAN SEA

MANASSEH

• Shechem

Jabbok River

Jordan River

EPHRAIM

GAD

DAN   BENJAMIN

• Bezer(?)

JUDAH   • Hebron

DEAD SEA

REUBEN

SIMEON

SCALE OF MILES

0   5   10   15   20   25   30

That promise made the receiving of the land a religious matter. It connects this story with the covenant faithfulness of God.

The story of Joshua also points forward. Time and again the book of Joshua speaks of rest. The goal of all this struggle and conflict was that Israel might *rest* in her land. This is typical. Canaan always had a symbolical meaning. It spoke to Israel of the rest that they should have in God — a higher, spiritual rest. So too it speaks to us of the Sabbath rest that remains for the children of God. Canaan is a type of the heavenly rest. It pictures the eternal glory that awaits God's children. And Joshua, who was God's servant to give Israel her rest, must be considered a type of that later Joshua (Hebrew form of Jesus) in whom God's people are given their perfect rest.

EXERCISES

Factual questions

1. What books are included in the Former Prophets?
2. Why are these books classified as prophetical?
3. When was Joshua written?
4. What is the purpose of the book of Joshua?
5. What agreement was made between Rahab and the two spies? Josh. 2:8ff.
6. What was the purpose of the twelve stones? Josh. 4.
7. What four events took place at Gilgal? Josh. 5:2ff.
8. What was Achan's sin? Josh. 7.
9. How did the Gibeonites deceive Israel? Josh. 9:3ff.
10. What miracles marked the battle at Gibeon? Josh. 10:10ff.
11. What lessons could Israel learn from the battles of the southern campaign?
12. How can we justify the extermination of the Canaanites?
13. Which tribes received the choicest portions?
14. What inheritance did Caleb receive? Josh. 14:6ff. What did Joshua receive? Josh. 19:49ff.
15. What was the procedure for using the cities of refuge? Josh. 20.
16. What did the eastern tribes do as they returned home? Josh. 22:10ff.
17. How did they explain this action? Josh. 22:13ff.
18. What choice did Joshua put before Israel? Josh. 24:14ff.
19. How long did Israel serve Jehovah? Josh. 24:29ff.

Thought questions

1. What can we learn about Jericho and her inhabitants from the story of Rahab in Joshua 2?
2. In the light of what happened at Kadesh-barnea, did Joshua act wisely when he sent out spies? Why?

3. Look up Canaanites in a Bible dictionary or Bible encyclopedia and make a report on them.

4. How many lessons can you derive from the conquest and division of Canaan that can be applied to our Christian life and to the inheritance of glory that awaits us?

Map Work

1. Draw a map of Palestine and locate the following places on it:

Gilgal	Gibeon
Jericho	Hebron
Ai	Waters of Merom
Bethel	Hazor

Memory

1. Outline of Joshua.
2. Joshua 1:8, 9.

PART THREE

THE PERIOD OF
THEOCRATIC DEVELOPMENT

Chapter 11

The Covenant Nation Forsakes Jehovah

Judges

With the book of Judges we enter into a new period in the history of the Old Testament. The reception of the land under Joshua was the final step in the period of theocratic establishment. Now we turn to the development of that which has been established.

It would be wonderful to be able to record that Israel continued to progress onward and upward without any failure or backslidings. But such is not the case. On the contrary, the history of Israel is marked by continual sin and rebellion. Often the Israelites are spoken of as a stiff-necked and disobedient people. Think back over the history already studied, and it will be evident that this is so. Now, at the beginning of this period of theocratic development, we find Israel falling from the high estate to which God has brought her. The book of Judges presents a terrible picture. Yet, in it all, God is working and is developing His kingdom. Even though the surface movement of history seems to be flowing against the fulfillment of God's plan, beneath the surface the irresistible current of the divine purpose moves on to the appointed end.

The next step in God's purpose is the development of a theocratic kingdom, that is, a nation ruled by a king who in turn acknowledges that he is simply a minister of the God of Israel. The development of that kingdom begins with the period of the judges and continues until David, the theocratic king, rules over Israel.

PURPOSE

The purpose of Judges is to show that Israel needs a king. Ideally, a king might not be necessary. But actually, Israel is a nation of spiritual children. Her immaturity is reflected in her worship. God gave her visible expressions of spiritual truths in the tabernacle and the offerings. So it is not strange that the great truth of the theocracy, that God is her ruler, should be displayed by means of an earthly king who was subject to God's law.

The history of Israel given in Judges shows that Israel needed a strong leader if she was to be true to God. The judges provided temporary leadership. But the whole period is characterized by the statement with which Judges ends, "In those days there was no king in Israel: every man did that which was right in his own eyes" (Judges 21:25). This presents the problem of the times, and also shows where the answer lies. Israel needs a theocratic king. In the period of the judges Israel was made conscious of that need.

INTRODUCTION

Date of Writing

Judges, like the rest of the Former Prophets, is anonymous. But the time of its writing can be fixed rather closely. The statement, "In those days there was no king in Israel" seems to imply the contrasting statement, "as there is now." If that is so, then Judges was written no earlier than the beginning of Saul's reign.

Another statement in the book helps us decide on the latest possible date of composition. In Judges 1:21 we are told that "the Jebusites dwell with the children of Benjamin in Jerusalem unto this day." But when David had reigned in Hebron for seven years he did what none before him had been able to do. He routed the Jebusites from their stronghold in Jerusalem and made it his capital. From that time on the statement in Judges would be inaccurate. So Judges must have been written during the reign of Saul or the early reign of David. Tradition says that it was written by Samuel, but that cannot be proved right or wrong.

Nature of Contents

Judges is not simply a book of history. It does not attempt to tell us everything that happened during this period of 350 years. Everything that is included in the book is related to three great facts which the book sets forth.

1. Faithfulness to Jehovah results in national unity; unfaithfulness results in disintegration into tribes which are sometimes at odds with each other.

2. Faithfulness to Jehovah results in the complete possession of Canaan; unfaithfulness results in oppression by other nations.

3. Throughout Israel's checkered history God is faithful to His covenant and shows His mercy to His people.

This selection of material shows that Judges was written from the viewpoint of a prophet. History is a revelation of the purposes and works of God. The prophet who wrote this book took pains to make that clear.

OUTLINE

I. The rapid growth of Israel's apostasy   Judges 1, 2
II. The historical results of Israel's apostasy   Judges 3-16
III. The moral consequences of Israel's apostasy   Judges 17-21

Although the book of Judges treats the stories in the third part of this outline separately from the history in the second part, this does not mean that the episodes occur at a later date. As a matter of fact, most scholars think that they occurred early in the period of the judges. The stories are added after the history to give us a clear picture of what life in Israel was like at this time.

ANALYSIS

Israel's Downward Path

While Joshua lived, Israel obeyed God and carried out the responsibilities of the covenant. But when Joshua died, and when the generation that had conquered Canaan under his leadership passed away, the new generation turned away from God. No strong leader arose to replace Joshua, and the Israelites could not walk by faith alone. Gradually their attempts to rid the land of the Canaanites became less and less vigorous. Eventually they did not try to remove them, but simply made them bond servants. Finally God sent an angel to tell Israel that the Canaanites would remain in the land and be a plague to Israel.

The Cycle of Israel's History

From this time on until the end of the period of the judges the history of Israel followed a pattern:

1. The children of Israel turned away from Jehovah and served the gods of the heathen. This is called apostasy.

2. As a punishment, God sent other nations to oppress Israel.

3. When the oppression became too great, Israel cried to God for deliverance.

4. God raised up judges to deliver Israel from her oppressors.

5. The people obeyed and worshiped Jehovah for a time (usually until the judge died) and "the land had rest."

These five points can be remembered with the aid of five words beginning with R:

Relapse (apostasy)	Release
Retribution (punishment)	Rest
Repentance	

As you read the history of the judges you will see this pattern again and again.

The Judges of Israel

There are twelve judges mentioned in the book of Judges. We should know the six most important ones, and the oppressing nations from whom they delivered Israel.

Judge	Defeated nation
Othniel	Mesopotamia
Ehud	Moabites
Barak and Deborah	Canaanites
Gideon	Midianites
Jephthah	Ammonites
Samson	Philistines

None of these judges delivered or judged all of Israel. At this time there was little national spirit. An oppressor could attack and occupy one part of Israel without being attacked by the other tribes. This is especially obvious in the case of the last two judges mentioned. Many scholars believe that the oppression by Ammon (which was primarily over the eastern tribes) and the oppression by the Philistines (which was primarily in the southwestern part of the country) took place at the same time.

Who Were the Judges?

When we read the word "judges," we are likely to put into the term the idea of judges as we know them. These judges of Israel were not men who presided over courts of law. At least, that was not their primary task. First of all, they were military leaders. God raised them up to deliver the people from those who were oppressing them. In order to do this they had to win military victories over the enemies of Israel. Only after these victories did they begin to rule. In their ruling they were much like kings, but on a smaller scale.

The judges were men of faith. Of the six judges listed above, Barak, Gideon, Jephthah, and Sampson are included in the eleventh chapter of Hebrews—the catalogue of Old Testament heroes of faith. (Othniel is probably missing because so little is said of him in Judges. Read the story of Ehud carefully and you will see why he is not included.) These men did not think of themselves as military heroes. They were servants of Jehovah. The battles they fought were religious battles and the victories they won were given them by God. The song of Deborah and Barak (Judges 5) clearly shows that fact. These judges were beacon lights of faith in an age that was dark with sin.

The judges were also men of their time. They may have been the best specimens of Israel's piety and valor, but they shared many of the faults of the people. Gideon is an example of this. After his marvelous victory over Midian he made a golden image which led him astray and the people of Israel with him.

Samson as a Typical Judge

In Samson we can see both the best and the worst in Israel. His life is typical of the children of Israel. In one sense Samson was the ideal Israelite, the picture of what Israel should have been. He was a Nazirite from birth. (A Nazirite was one who was especially separated to God. He was placed under certain restrictions. One restriction was that he could not cut his hair. Most Nazirites followed the restrictions for just a short period. Samson was a Nazirite for life.) As a Nazirite Samson pictured the fact that Israel was separated to God. As God was with him and strengthened him, so God was also with Israel to provide for all her needs.

But Samson was far from being a Nazirite at heart. His heart was far from God, at least during part of his life. He fell into sin, especially the sin of adultery. As a result he lost the strength and blessing which God had given him. In this he symbolized Israel's actual experience. By committing spiritual adultery and going after other gods, Israel sacrificed God's blessing and was oppressed by the surrounding nations.

The Spirit of the Age

The two stories which make up the final part of Judges give us insight into the age in which these things took place. The idolatry of Micah, the willingness of a Levite to be a private priest of a false god, the audacious theft of Micah's gods and priest by the tribe of Dan, and the worship of those false gods by the Danites make us realize that this people had fallen far from that time of faith when they had conquered mighty foes. The wicked conduct of the men of Gibeah and the terrible method the Levite used to broadcast their crime show us that the time of Judges was one when conscience was stifled and evil was running wild. We are reminded of the conduct of the people of Sodom and Gomorrah just before their destruction. The war of the other tribes against Benjamin indicates clearly that there was no national spirit in Israel.

There is a good reason why this section comes last. We have read about the judges and their exploits. Now we are shown that the judges were insufficient. And these stories are interlaced with the comment, "in those days there was no king in Israel." The spirit of the age testifies clearly that Israel desperately needed a king.

CONCLUSION

As we leave Judges, we must call attention to one great lesson that this book teaches. Israel's fortunes are clearly connected to her relationship to Jehovah. When Israel followed Him, all was well. When she did not, all was ill. So it always is for God's people. The pattern may not always be so clear because our blessing or oppression may be spiritual rather than physical. But it is an indisputable fact that obedience to God is the requirement for all blessing.

EXERCISES

Factual questions

1. The story of what period is begun in Judges?
2. What is the purpose of Judges?
3. When was Judges written?
4. What three facts are clearly taught in Judges?
5. What did the angel of Jehovah announce at Bochim? Judg. 2.
6. What pattern of Israel's history do we find in Judges?
7. Trace that pattern in Judges 3. It appears twice. Write the references where each step of the pattern is recorded.
8. Name the six most important judges and tell whom they conquered.
9. Why did Barak lose the glory of killing Sisera? Judg. 4:4ff.
10. How did Gideon show that he served Jehovah? Judg. 6:25ff.
11. Describe the means whereby Gideon defeated Midian. Judg. 7.
12. What evidence of strife between Israelites is seen in Judges 8?
13. What examples of Samson's great strength can be found in Judges 14-16?
14. What two sides of Israel's life are illustrated in Samson's life?
15. What did the Danites do to Micah? Judg. 18:14ff.
16. Why did Israel go to fight against Benjamin? Judg. 20:12ff.
17. What lesson should be learned from Judges?

Thought questions

1. Why is Ehud omitted from the list of names in Hebrews 11?
2. May we test God as Gideon did? Judg. 6.
3. What did Jephthah do to his daughter? (See a good commentary or Bible dictionary before answering this question.)
4. Divide the events of Samson's life into those which fit his position as Nazirite and those which betray his weak character.

Memory

1. Outline of Judges.
2. Judges 17:6.

Chapter 12

The Covenant Nation Contains a Faithful Minority

Ruth

PURPOSE

When we finish studying the book of Judges and turn to the book of Ruth, it is like turning from the field of a bloody battle to gaze at a quiet pastoral scene. There is a reason for this contrast. The book of Judges was designed to show us how desperate was the situation in which Israel found herself. Ruth is designed to show us that the situation was not hopeless. True piety was not dead. All respect for God and His law had not departed from Israel. God was still working in His people. He was even working in the hearts of heathen, bringing them within His covenant and making them faithful and true members of the covenant nation.

The book of Ruth is connected to Judges in another way. Judges showed us how badly the people of Israel needed a king. Ruth helps us to understand how God was preparing, even then, to give Israel a king who would truly reign for Him.

INTRODUCTION

It is not possible to date the book of Ruth precisely. From the fact that her descendants are traced to David and no further, it seems likely that the book was written after David began to rule and before Solomon received the throne.

The author of Ruth is also unknown to us. We do not even know if Ruth was written by a prophet. At present the Hebrew Bible includes Ruth in the Writings, which were written by non-prophets. But there is some evidence that Ruth was originally placed in the Hebrew Bible just where it is found in our Bible. Then it would belong to the Former Prophets.

There may be a simple explanation for this change of position in the Jewish canon. Part of the Writings is the Megilloth, or the Five Rolls. This group of books is read at the various Jewish feasts. Ruth is read at the Feast of Pentecost. So it may be that this book was originally included in the Former Prophets, but was later put into the Writings because of its liturgical use.

74

OUTLINE

ANALYSIS

Ruth's Character

The best-known words in the book of Ruth are surely those in which Ruth expresses her determination to remain with Naomi. "Entreat me not to leave thee, and to return from following after thee; for whither thou goest, I will go; and where thou lodgest, I will lodge; thy people shall be my people, and thy God my God; where thou diest, will I die, and there will I be buried: Jehovah do so to me, and more also, if aught but death part thee and me" (Ruth 1:16, 17). These words are filled with love for her mother-in-law. But they contain far more than that. The Moabitess will become an Israelitess, and the God of Israel shall be her God. This is the expression of a deep religious faith.

The depth of Ruth's faith is clearly shown by her conduct in Israel. She gave herself to caring for Naomi, in the spirit of the fifth commandment. In the few months of her stay in Bethlehem she became well known as a virtuous woman. Boaz knew how well she cared for Naomi. The elders of the city were ready to bless her when Boaz declared his intention to marry her. Her good works for which she quickly became known are evidences of the sincerity of her statement, "thy God [shall be] my God."

God's Law in Action

The book of Judges showed us a black picture of lawlessness. The book of Ruth presents a striking contrast. In it we see a high regard shown for God's law. To understand the events of the last two chapters of Ruth we must go back to the Mosaic law. Provision was made in the law for keeping the land received in Canaan within the family. If poverty rendered the sale of the land necessary, the closest relative (who was called the goel, or kinsman-redeemer) had the first privilege of buying the land. But there was also a duty placed on the goel. When there was a childless widow, the relative had a duty to marry her and raise a family, so that the husband's name would not die out in Israel. It was considered very important to keep family lines intact.

Ruth went to Boaz and asked him to carry out this duty. But there was a closer relative. So Boaz asked him, in the presence of the elders of the city, if he wished the privilege of buying Naomi's field. The man did. Boaz then pointed out that this involved the duty of marrying Ruth. This the man did not wish to do. Then Boaz was free to fulfill the duty of the law and marry Ruth. How strong a contrast we find between this careful observance of the law of God and the sinful character of the nation as a whole.

Ruth and the Theocracy

We must not forget that the development of the theocratic kingdom was the next step in God's plan. The story of Ruth fit into that plan. The theocratic kingdom was founded in David. And Ruth, the Moabitess who chose Jehovah as her God, became the ancestress of David, the king. And through her great-grandson David she became the ancestress of the great King, even Jesus Christ. Ruth "is the only instance in which a book is devoted to the domestic history of a woman, and that woman a stranger in Israel. But that woman was the Mary of the Old Testament" (Edersheim).

EXERCISES

Factual questions

1. What is the purpose of the book of Ruth?
2. When was Ruth written?
3. What may be the reason why Ruth is found in the Writings?
4. Why did Elimelech go to Moab? Ruth 1.
5. How did Ruth show that she had chosen Jehovah? Ruth 1:15-2:7.
6. In what ways did Boaz care for Ruth? Ruth 2:8ff.
7. On what law did Naomi depend when she advised Ruth as she did? Ruth 3.
8. Why did Boaz confer with other kinsman? Ruth 4.
9. Why is Ruth's history important? Ruth 4:13ff.

Thought questions

1. Was it wrong for Elimelech to take his family to Moab?
2. Was Ruth forward and immodest in asking Boaz to marry her?

Memory

1. Outline of Ruth.
2. Ruth 1:16, 17.

Chapter 13

The Covenant Nation Demands a King

Samuel

INTRODUCTION

The two books of Samuel were originally one book. Not only do they show every sign of being written by the same man, not only are the contents inseparably connected, but they are found as one book in the Hebrew manuscripts. So we will deal with them as one.

The book of Samuel was probably written after the division of the kingdom. The statement "Ziklag pertaineth unto the kings of Judah unto this day" (I Sam. 27:6), would scarcely make sense until the time when Israel and Judah existed as separate kingdoms. The evidence found within the book makes us think that it was written soon after the division of the kingdom. An unknown prophet who had access to written documents which came from the time of Samuel, Saul, and David used these documents and wrote this inspired book.

PURPOSE

The book of Samuel is not just a history book. In this it is like the other Former Prophets. The author chose various incidents which best served his purpose. Others, which may have been important from a different point of view, he excluded. He wove the story of these times in a way calculated to set forth the development of the theocracy.

The primary point which Samuel emphasizes is the means by which God established a theocratic king in Israel. A short continuation of the last days of the judges shows why Israel decided that a king was necessary. The story of Saul, who is the kind of king Israel wanted, teaches that a selfish monarch is not what Israel needs. Finally, the crowning of David provides the theocratic king, the king after God's heart.

But there is another point, closely connected to the first. The kingdom is always to be theocratic. God never abdicates as ruler of Israel. The king only serves under God. To provide direction for the kingdom God establishes an order of prophets, through whom He makes known His will. It is the purpose of Samuel to present the rise of these two institutions—the monarchy and the prophetic order.

OUTLINE

These three points in the outline of Samuel are also the three divisions under which the book of Samuel will be studied. The rest of this chapter deals only with the first point.

ANALYSIS

When Did Samuel Live?

In order to trace clearly the way in which God brought about the development of His kingdom in Israel, we should first examine the time when the events of I Samuel 1-8 took place. It is easy to assume, as we read through the Bible, that the order in which events appear on the pages of Scripture is the order in which they happened. Such is not always the case. The writers of Scripture were not interested in presenting events in chronological order. They often grouped similar events in order to make the lesson of those events clear. This lack of chronological order makes it necessary for us to study the Bible carefully so that we do not become confused.

Although some disagree, most biblical scholars believe that the events of I Samuel 1-8 occurred at the same time as the events of Judges 10-16. In other words, while Eli was the priest at the sanctuary at Shiloh, Jephthah was judging the eastern tribes and Samson was carrying on his one-man war against the Philistines. There is no reason why this cannot be so. The author of Judges was interested in showing the awful conditions in Israel and the temporary relief that God gave through judges. The author of Samuel is interested in showing how, in the same period, God was preparing the way for more permanent improvement of His people's lot.

The Good and Evil in Israel

The early chapters of Samuel provide a sharp contrast between the heights of faith and the depths of wickedness which existed side by side in Israel. The story of Samuel's mother reminds us of Ruth. In simple faith she seeks a child from Jehovah, and unselfishly promises that the child will be given as a Nazirite to Jehovah. When God answers her prayer there is no hesitation about fulfilling her vow. When Samuel is about three, he is brought to the tabernacle, there to serve God. (The tabernacle is referred to in the book of Samuel as the temple. But remember that the temple was built by Solomon, at least a century later. The use of the term "temple" probably indicates that the tabernacle received a more permanent structure when it was in Shiloh.

Since it was no longer moved from place to place, it became less a tent and more a house.)

Samuel and Samson were both Nazirites for life. They embody the differences existing in the religious life of Israel at this period. Samson was a Nazirite because God demanded it; Samuel was offered voluntarily as a Nazirite. Samson was a Nazirite outwardly, and was blessed with outward strength. Samuel was a Nazirite from his heart, and was blessed with strength of soul. It was Samuel, not Samson, who was used of God to deliver Israel from both the oppression of the Philistines and the sin which caused that oppression.

Against the beautiful picture of Hannah's faith we see the awful wickedness of Eli's sons. They despise the worship of Jehovah and His laws for conduct. By taking their portion of the sacrifice before the offering was completed, they acted as if the worship of Jehovah existed only to enrich them. They also committed adultery with the women who served at the door of the tabernacle. In every way they led the people away from Jehovah. What a dreadful picture! The piety of Israel is found in a humble woman; the sin of Israel centers in her priests.

God had blessed the pious Hannah, and he judged the wicked house of Eli. A prophet appeared to Eli and declared that his sons would both die on the same day, and that Eli's family would be cut off from being high priests.

Samuel the Prophet

In the days of Moses and Joshua God had revealed Himself to men. But for some time the word of God had come only rarely. Now God again began to reveal Himself through Samuel. He called Samuel one night and told him that the doom pronounced upon Eli's house would be fulfilled. From that time on "Jehovah was with him, and did let none of his words fall to the ground. And all Israel from Dan even to Beer-sheba knew that Samuel was established to be a prophet of Jehovah" (I Sam. 3:19, 20).

This call to the prophetic office explains the important part that Samuel played in the establishment of the monarchy. If the monarchy was to be theocratic, it must be God-directed. Samuel was God's instrument in guiding the establishment and development of the monarchy.

The Depth of Israel's Sin

How far Israel had departed from Jehovah is portrayed in the loss of the ark. Defeated by their enemies the Philistines, the children of Israel do not repent of their sin. Instead, they send to Shiloh for the ark, thinking that Jehovah has to be with them if they carry the ark to battle.

The sons of Eli bring it and carry it into the battle. But the ark is not a fetish. It possesses no magical powers. Jehovah cannot be forced to carry out the wishes of men. Israel is defeated, and the Philistines capture the ark.

But in order that the Philistines may know that this victory does not prove that their gods are greater than Jehovah, the ark causes them so much trouble that they soon send it back. The lesson is clear. Jehovah is not overcome by the power of heathen gods. He simply does not help unrepentant sinners.

Samuel as Judge

After twenty years had passed, Samuel issued a call to Israel to repent. And Israel heeded the call. God worked among them to raise them from the awful condition in which they were living. To express the national repentance, Samuel called for a national assembly at Mizpah. While Israel was thus gathered together, the Philistines attacked them. But now Israel was again a holy nation. Israel fought while Samuel prayed. And God fought for Israel. He sent a terrible thunderstorm upon the Philistines and they fled. This victory ended the Philistine oppression. From this time on Samuel judged Israel. Although he was recognized as a prophet by all Israel, he was probably judge only in the tribes of Judah, Benjamin, and Simeon.

Wanted — a King

When Samuel was old he called on his sons to help him judge. But they were not honest. They took bribes and perverted justice. So the elders of Israel came to Samuel "and they said unto him, Behold, thou art old, and thy sons walk not in thy ways: now make us a king to judge us like all the nations" (I Sam. 8:5). This displeased Samuel, and Jehovah declared that Israel was rejecting Him.

What was wrong with this request? We have stated that Judges was written to show that Israel needed a king. That need existed, and these elders recognized it. God had made provision for a king in the Mosaic law, even giving instructions how the king should conduct himself. What was wrong?

The motive was wrong. The people wanted a king "like all the nations." They had the wrong ideal for Israel. Israel was supposed to be different. It was supposed to be God's nation. He would rule His people. He had been ruling them. But His rule could be seen only by faith. The Israelites wanted to walk by sight. In this they were rejecting God. God planned for them to have a king who would rule under Him. Israel wanted a king to rule instead of God.

God told Samuel to warn the people what such a king would be like. He would oppress them for his own purposes. But that did not matter to them. So Samuel announced that they would get the type of king they wanted. They had learned that they needed a king. Now they must learn that the wrong kind of king is worse than none at all.

EXERCISES

Factual questions

1. When was the book of Samuel written?
2. What is the purpose of the book of Samuel?
3. Where does the life of Samuel fit in the history of Israel?
4. What promise did Hannah make? I Sam. 1:9ff.
5. Show how Samson and Samuel illustrate the differences in the religious life of Israel at this time.
6. List the sins of Eli's sons. I Sam. 2:12ff.
7. What did God threaten to do to Eli? I Sam. 2:27ff.
8. How did God call Samuel to be a prophet? I Sam. 3.
9. What happened to Eli when he heard of the ark's capture? I Sam. 4:12ff.
10. What happened to the Philistines while they had the ark? I Sam. 5.
11. How did they send it back? I Sam. 6:10ff.
12. What does the name Ebenezer mean? To what was this name given? I Sam. 7:12ff.
13. What was wrong with Israel's demand for a king? I Sam. 8.
14. How would a king treat the people? I Sam. 8:10ff.

Thought questions

1. To what king does Hannah refer in I Samuel 2:10?
2. What lesson can we learn from God's rebuke to Eli?
3. Was Eli a good or a bad priest?
4. What lesson can we learn from Israel's sin in seeking a king?

Memory

1. Outline of Samuel.

Chapter 14

The Covenant Nation under a Selfish King

Samuel

PURPOSE

The second part of I Samuel fits into the purpose of the book as a whole. We have seen how the anarchy in the time of the judges brought the people to the realization that they needed a king — but not a theocratic king. They wanted a king like the other nations. In this section we see what happened when they got what they wanted. From their sad experience under Saul, the people of Israel were made to realize that the theocratic nation needed a theocratic king. God was preparing His people for the theocratic kingdom under David.

In this part we also see the prophets becoming more prominent. Especially Samuel stands out in the narrative, although the other prophets are mentioned. They are always God's voice leading Israel toward a true theocracy.

ANALYSIS

Saul Anointed King

Israel had demanded a king. This in itself was not wrong. But Israel's motive was altogether wrong. The people wanted a leader they could see. It was not enough that they had Jehovah. They wished to walk by sight, and not by faith. Thus God declared that they were rejecting Him. Nevertheless He gave them the king they desired. But He chose their king and thus He indicated that He was still the ruler of Israel, even though Israel had rejected Him. By a series of providential circumstances He sent Saul to Samuel. Before Saul arrived He told Samuel that this man was to be Israel's king. So Saul received an honored reception from Samuel and was anointed to be king of Israel.

What Anointing Means

This act of anointing, by which Samuel made Saul king of Israel, is very important. It is one of the most important acts in the Old Testament. In studying Exodus you learned that the priests were anointed because they were called to serve God in the tabernacle. The king was anointed because he also was to serve God. The act of anointing was a symbol that the king was a servant of Jehovah. So, in spite of Israel's sinful motive, the kingdom is shown to be part of Jehovah's plan for Israel.

In the Old Testament, anointing symbolizes three things:

1. The person who is anointed is called by God to a certain office. In the case of Saul, he was called to be king.

2. God sends His Spirit upon the person anointed so that he will be able to fulfill the duties of his office. Thus we read that "the Spirit of God came mightily upon him [Saul]" (I Sam. 10:10). This gift of the Spirit does not refer to salvation. It is simply the gift enabling one to do God's work.

3. The person who is anointed is set apart, and is under God's protection. Therefore David would not harm Saul, even when Saul was trying to kill him, because Saul was "God's anointed."

That which was symbolized by anointing was realized in Jesus Christ. As the Anointed One of God and the great Servant of Jehovah, He received the offices of prophet, priest, and king. He is our chief Prophet, our great High Priest, and our eternal King. The Son of Man stands as the fulfillment of the Old Testament offices. They were simply types and shadows; He is the reality. They were imperfect; He is perfect. They were temporary; He continues forever.

This fact puts the Old Testament kingdom in its proper light. Although the monarchy was begun as the response to a sinful request, the kingship is not something opposed to God's plan and purpose. It was an important step in the development of the theocracy. It was a step which prepared for the fullness of the theocracy in and through Jesus Christ.

Saul Receives the Throne

Saul appeared to have all the qualifications for the throne. He stood head and shoulders above all the other men in Israel. When he was publicly chosen, most of Israel received him gladly as their king. He showed proper humility. He did not force himself upon the people. He awaited an opportunity to show himself as their leader. This came when he was called upon to rescue Jabesh-gilead from the Ammonites. After his victory he was charitable toward those who had not immediately accepted him. And he began a series of wars which freed most of Israel from her enemies. A striking figure, a bold warrior, a just ruler—what more could Israel ask in a king?

Saul Is Disobedient

One thing more could be asked—obedience to Jehovah. Here Saul failed. When he had ruled only two years, an attack by his son Jonathan

on a Philistine garrison at Geba brought the Philistine army into
Israel. Saul gathered his forces at Gilgal, and there they waited for
Samuel to come and offer sacrifices before the battle. But Samuel was
slow in coming. The seven days within which he had promised to
come had almost passed. So Saul himself offered a burnt offering.
As king, he rejected the sacred rules which God had set forth for His
worship, and took upon himself the task of priest.

This sin brought the first punishment upon Saul. Because of it,
he would not pass the kingdom along to his children. He had forfeited
for his family the right to rule over Israel, but he himself was not
rejected as king.

Another failure followed. Saul continued to fight against Israel's
enemies. The Amalekites, who dwelt south of Canaan, were among
Israel's worst enemies. They had fought against Israel at the time
of the Exodus. At that time God had declared that there would never
be peace between the two nations. Now, through Samuel, God told
Saul that the Amalekites were to be completely destroyed. None were
to be left alive nor any living creature taken as spoils. Saul went forth
and conquered the Amalekites. But he kept alive the king of Amalek
and the best cattle and sheep. This was disobedience, pure and simple.

When Samuel arrived he confronted Saul with his sin. To Saul's
claim that he had done this on religious grounds, Samuel replied, "Behold, to obey is better than sacrifice, and to hearken than the fat of
rams. For rebellion is as the sin of witchcraft, and stubbornness is as
idolatry and teraphim" (I Sam. 15:22, 23). What a majestic statement
of the essentials of true religion! It is heartfelt obedience that God
desires, not mere conformity to religious ceremonies. Samuel continued,
"Because thou hast rejected the word of Jehovah, he hath also rejected
thee from being king" (I Sam. 15:23).

Israel Receives a New King

The king whom Israel had desired, the king that was so representative
of the nation, had failed. He had been rejected, although the people as
a whole did not yet know it. A new king had to be chosen. God sent
Samuel to the city of Bethlehem to anoint David, the son of Jesse.
This was done secretly, lest Saul should discover it. From this time on
it is David not Saul, who is the chief character in Samuel. Saul may
still sit on the throne, but David is the true king. As evidence of
this "the Spirit of Jehovah came mightily upon David from that day
forward" (I Sam. 16:13), and "the Spirit of Jehovah departed from
Saul, and an evil spirit from Jehovah troubled him" (I Sam. 16:14).

David made no attempt to advance his claim to the throne. But God
in His providence brought him to a position of prominence. First as

the singer in Saul's court, then as the slayer of Goliath, then as the son-in-law of Saul and a leader in Saul's army, he was drawn more and more into the court life. In this way he received training for his future reign.

But David's growing fame also brought him increased danger. Saul, troubled by the evil spirit, was subject to fits of maniacal anger. In such fits he first threatened David, then tried to kill him. Eventually what Saul had attempted in madness he began to plot in his sane moments. David's rising fame and perhaps the rumors of his anointing by Samuel made him appear to Saul as a threat to the throne. Finally David had to flee the palace, and spend years in the rough wilderness of southern Judea and in the land of the Philistines, because the entire army of Saul was now turned to the task of killing this single fugitive. Yet even this was used of God, for at this time David gathered unto himself a band of followers who were to be his most loyal supporters when he came to the throne.

David's life during this period contains elements that are unpleasant. We must not think that the great sins of his later life are the only sins he committed. Lying, brutality, and deceit are all mentioned. But in spite of his sins, David was basically a man after God's heart. He believed firmly that God ruled Israel, and that God would raise him to the throne without scheming or rebellion on his part. Thus he refused to kill Saul when he twice had the opportunity. This utter dependence upon Jehovah is the characteristic of the theocratic king.

Saul's Downward Path

What a contrast is the life of Saul to that of David! It is not that Saul is a sinner and David is without sin. Both committed grievous sins. But there is a basic difference in their attitude toward sin. We might say that David sinned in spite of the fact that his heart was right before Jehovah. But Saul's sins were the result of a headstrong, self-centered nature that was not yielded to God.

The fact that the Spirit of Jehovah came upon Saul does not mean that he was converted. In the Old Testament, the Holy Spirit sometimes came upon men officially but not personally. That is, He would enable them to do the work to which God had called them, but would not change their hearts and lead them to salvation. His coming upon Saul was official only. We know this, because He departed from Saul when Saul was rejected as king. The Holy Spirit never leaves those whom He regenerates.

All God's people are sinners. But they are repentant sinners. They are sorry for sin. They try to overcome sin. They seek forgiveness for sin. There was no repentance in Saul. He sinned, and he continued in his sin. Finally his sin brought him to an awful end. He died by his own hand. "The wages of sin is death" (Rom. 6:23). Saul lived and ruled as a selfish, sinful king. He received his just wage.

The Rise of the Prophets

This period of Israel's history marks the introduction of a new order—the prophets. There had been prophets before. Abraham is called a prophet. Moses is the great prophet of the Old Testament. But now, under the leadership of Samuel, a prophetic order appears in Israel. This marks the beginning of an institution that continued until the coming of Christ.

A prophet is a man called of God to receive God's word and to communicate it to the people. This definition includes all that is essential to the biblical idea of a prophet. He is the mouthpiece of God. Through the prophets God reveals Himself to men.

The rise of the office of prophet (and with it the schools of prophets or "sons of the prophets") takes place at the same time as the beginning of the monarchy. There was good reason for this. God had ordained that Israel should have kings. But these were to be theocratic kings who ruled under God. Such kings had to know God's will. It was the task of the prophets to make God's will known to the kings. Most of the prophets were closely associated with kings. When the kings were true to their theocratic calling, the prophets were their counselors. But when the kings forsook Jehovah, the prophets were their opponents.

In this period it is Samuel who is the chief prophet. He announces God's will. He gives God's instructions to king Saul. He declares the king's sins to him, and boldly proclaims the punishment which God will bring. He anoints the new king. And when David flees from Saul he goes first to Ramah to consult with Samuel. Samuel is the first of many who will be God's voice to the kings of Israel.

EXERCISES

Factual questions

1. What is the purpose of this section of Samuel?
2. What is the threefold significance of anointing?
3. What signs did Samuel give to Saul when he anointed him? I Sam. 10.
4. By what means did Saul actually attain the kingship? I Sam. 11.
5. Write out some verses from I Samuel 12 to show that Samuel was still a prophet.
6. What sin of Saul is recorded in I Samuel 13:8ff?
7. What was the punishment? I Sam. 13:10ff.
8. What sin of Saul is recorded in I Samuel 15?
9. What was the punishment? I Sam. 15:17ff.
10. How did David expect to receive the kingdom?

11. How was David first introduced to Saul? I Sam. 16:14ff.
12. Why did Saul become jealous of David? I Sam. 18:6ff.
13. In how many ways did Saul try to kill David? I Sam. 18:10ff.; 19:8ff.; 20:30ff.
14. How did God protect David? I Sam. 18:10ff.; 19:12ff.; 20:35ff.
15. How did David escape from Achish? I Sam. 21:10ff.
16. How did David show that he did not seek Saul's life? I Sam. 24:8ff.
17. Why did David refuse to harm Saul? I Sam. 26:6ff.
18. What was Saul's sin before the battle with the Philistines? I Sam. 28:5ff.
19. What was Saul's final sin? I Sam. 31.
20. Describe Saul's attitude toward his sins.
21. What is a prophet?
22. Why were prophets so often associated with kings?

Thought questions

1. How would you feel if you were Saul and the events recorded in I Samuel 9:15-27 happened to you?
2. Does the fact that a vow is foolish make it less binding? I Sam. 14.
3. Does God command Samuel to tell a lie in I Samuel 16?
4. In the light of the purpose of the book, explain why the story of David and Goliath is included.
5. What do you think of David's conduct in I Samuel 27?

Memory

1. I Samuel 12:24.
2. I Samuel 15:22b.

Chapter 15

The Covenant Nation under a Theocratic King

Samuel

PURPOSE

We have traced the steps by which God brought Israel to the recognition of her need for a theocratic king. Now, in David, we see just such a king. Israel now becomes a truly theocratic kingdom, for the one on the throne acknowledges Jehovah as the king of Israel and rules as His servant.

Yet the picture is not all pleasant. David is not free from sin. And his sin is pictured that we might learn again that God rules over His people in mercy and in justice. He rules in mercy, for He forgives David's sin and does not depose him. He rules in justice, for sin is punished, even when it is committed by the man after God's own heart.

ANALYSIS

David Becomes King

While Saul lived, David was a fugitive. But when Saul died, God told David to go up to Hebron. Here he was anointed king over Judah. But the rest of Israel followed Ish-bosheth, a son of Saul. For seven and a half years David ruled in Hebron. During that time his kingdom grew stronger, while that of Ish-bosheth became weaker. When Ish-bosheth was assassinated by his servants, all Israel gladly claimed David as king.

When he was established as king of all the nation, David turned his attention to the capture of Jerusalem. This was still a stronghold of the heathen Jebusites. Although it was a fortress that seemed too strong to be captured, David conquered it and made Jerusalem his capital.

The Philistines, those perennial enemies of Israel, heard that David was made king of all Israel. Fearing a united Israel, they came up to fight against David. But their expedition led only to a decisive victory for David. This victory put David firmly on the throne.

David and Jehovah

David was a very religious man. We see this in the psalms he wrote. We see it also in his actions as king. He soon made plans to bring the ark of God to Jerusalem. Surrounded by thousands of rejoicing Israelites, the ark was moved. But David had not followed God's instructions for moving the ark, and its journey was interrupted by the death of Uzzah. This grieved David. But he learned his lesson, and when the ark was brought the rest of the way, it was carried by Levites. Thus, with much rejoicing, the symbol of God's presence was brought to Jerusalem. The Ruler of Israel and His servant the king dwelt in the same city.

But David was not satisfied. He had a fine house. God dwelt in a tent. He longed to build a house for God. God would not permit David to build Him a house. Instead He promised David, "Moreover Jehovah telleth thee that Jehovah will make thee a house. When thy days are fulfilled, and thou shalt sleep with thy fathers, I will set up thy seed after thee, that shall proceed out of thy bowels, and I will establish his kingdom. He shall build a house for my name, and I will establish the throne of his kingdom forever. I will be his father, and he shall be my son: if he commit iniquity, I will chasten him with the rod of men, and with the stripes of the children of men; but my lovingkindness shall not depart from him, as I took it from Saul, whom I put away from before thee. And thy house and thy kingdom shall be made sure for ever before thee: thy throne shall be established forever" (II Sam. 7:11b-16).

What a tremendous promise this is! God will build for David a house that will last forever. His descendants will be forever fixed on the throne of Israel. The fulfillment of this promise began with Solomon, for he is the one who built the temple. But it did not end with him. It continued on through the generations. The wicked kings were punished, but the line continued. Then the throne of David disappeared, but only that it might reappear in a spiritual sense, when the great Son of David came to occupy that throne eternally. Yes, this promise to David speaks of Christ. And through this promise the whole theocratic kingship points to Him, the eternal King.

David's Success as King

The reign of David was a time of greatness for Israel. Not only was the true religion central in the life of the nation, but the boundaries of Israel were expanded greatly. David conquered the heathen nations round about, who had so often oppressed Israel, until his domain stretched from the river Euphrates to the peninsula of Sinai.

David's greatness found expression also in deeds of kindness. Although as a warrior he was feared by all his enemies, yet in his rule there is none of cruelty and dictatorship so common in Eastern monarchs. His kindness to Mephibosheth is but one example of his love and mercy.

David's Grievous Sins

How wonderful it would be if we could present only the bright side of David's reign. But the Scripture is perfectly honest. In sharp contrast to his success as a warrior, his piety as a worshiper of Jehovah and his goodness as king over Israel stands the story of his great sin. When we read of his adultery with Bathsheba and the murder of Uriah we can only exclaim, "How are the mighty fallen." Perhaps this is what God would have us learn from this awful episode. None of us is immune to sin. If the man after God's heart could stoop to such sin, we dare not imagine that we are somehow beyond such sins. Let the one who thinks that he stands take heed lest he fall!

It is in connection with this sin that we again see the place of the prophets in Israel. Nathan, who had brought David the great promise of God, now stands before him to point the finger of God at the sinner on the throne. Like Saul before him, David has sinned against the King for whom he rules. But unlike Saul, David repents of his sin. The charge of sin brings forth confession of sin, and confession of sin brings forgiveness of sin. And out of the depths of this experience have come to us two beautiful psalms — 32 and 51.

Sin confessed is sin forgiven. But sin must be punished. God's justice demands it. The prophet spells out the punishment. As David slew Uriah by the sword, "the sword shall never depart out of thy house." Because David took the wife of Uriah secretly, another shall take David's wives in the eyes of all Israel. Though David shall not die for his sin, the child born of adultery shall die. From this point on the story of David is not the same. We see this punishment given to him.

We need not trace this punishment in great detail to see that the punishment fits the crime. David's lust is repeated in his son Amnon who disgraces his sister Tamar. The sword falls on David's house when Absalom avenges his sister by slaying Amnon. In neither case does David punish the offender as he should. Perhaps he recognizes how much his sons resemble their father. His poor handling of the offenders leads to the rebellion of Absalom, which almost costs David his throne. And in this David does not suffer alone. All Israel is affected. The country is torn by tumult. Only with difficulty is all rebellion suppressed and peace restored to Israel.

A Pause for Perspective

As we stand at this point in the Bible history and look back, we find ourselves on a vantage point from which we can survey all that has gone before. The Kingdom of God stretching behind us can be compared to three broad plateaus, each higher than the one before.

Farthest back and lowest we see the first plateau—the early days when the first theocracy was destroyed by sin and the knowledge of God was only barely kept alive. Perhaps this is more of a valley than a plateau. But then comes a rise and we see the second plateau—the plateau of promise, on which the patriarchs dwell. The tents which they pitched there are those of men who live only by faith in the promises of God. Dwelling as sojourners in the land of promise, they look for a better country, that is, a heavenly home.

Another rise brings us to the third plateau—the establishment of Israel as the covenant nation. The upward climb that leads to this plateau is marked by well-known events. The Exodus, the giving of the law, the wilderness wanderings, and the conquest of Canaan are milestones which mark the way. As we look back, we remember that the scenes on this plateau are not pleasant. The troublous time of the judges shows that much is yet lacking.

Directly below us there is another rise. We see the steps in the development of the Kingdom. And those steps bring us to the point on which we now stand—at the beginning of the high plateau of the theocratic kingdom. God has set on the throne of Israel one who rules for Him, and by His hand Israel has risen to a place of importance among the nations of the world. The nation is truly theocratic, for although there is still sin in the lives of the people and the life of the king, yet there is a recognition of Jehovah and a revival of true worship such as Israel has not seen since the time of Joshua.

But we cannot stop here. We must also look forward. The plateau of the Kingdom lies before us. That plateau must be traveled. The results of David's reign must bring about the prosperity of Solomon's. But we must also travel through much that will be discouraging. The story of the divided kingdom and the Exile is far 'rom pleasant. So even now we should lift up our eyes and look ahead. There in the distance is another rise. This plateau is not the summit. The Kingdom of God must develop still further. Though the sin of man may lead to apparent defeat for the purposes of God, He yet brings to pass His will. His kingdom is coming and will come. The Old Testament era is but preparation for the New. The Kingdom of God finds its perfection in Jesus Christ, the king who shall reign on the throne of David eternally.

EXERCISES

Factual questions

1. What is the purpose of the third section of Samuel?
2. What was David's reaction to the news of Saul's death? II Sam. 1:11ff.

3. What two murders ended the reign of Ish-bosheth? II Sam. 3:22ff.; 4:5ff.
4. What was David's sin in bringing up the ark? II Sam. 6.
5. What promise did God give David? II Sam. 7:12ff.
6. What did David do when he received this promise? II Sam. 7:18ff.
7. What did David do to Mephibosheth? II Sam. 9.
8. How did David try to hide his sin with Bathsheba? II Sam. 11:6ff.
9. How did Nathan show David his sin? II Sam. 12.
10. Why did Absalom hate Amnon? II Sam. 13:20ff.
11. How did he arrange to kill him? II Sam. 13:23ff.
12. How did David treat Absalom after this murder? II Sam. 14:21-24, 28-33.
13. How did Absalom prepare for his rebellion? II Sam. 15.
14. How did Hushai the Archite help David? II Sam. 15:32ff.; 17:5ff.
15. How was the rebellion ended? II Sam. 18:6ff.
16. Why did Sheba lead another rebellion? II Sam. 19:40 - 20:2.
17. How was Saul's violation of Joshua's treaty with the Gibeonites avenged? II Sam. 21.
18. What sin did David commit because Jehovah was angry with Israel? II Sam. 24.
19. From what three punishments could David choose? Why did he choose as he did? II Sam. 24:10ff.
20. How was the pestilence stopped? II Sam. 24:18ff.

Thought questions

1. Why did God not give David the entire kingdom as soon as Saul was dead?
2. Why did God give the great promise to David?
3. What lessons can we learn from David's sin against Uriah?
4. How did David fail, as king and father, in his duties to his sons?
5. What do we learn of David's character from his treatment of Shimei? II Sam. 16, 19.

Memory

1. II Samuel 7:16.

Chapter 16

The Poetry of the Covenant Nation

THE NUMBER OF POETICAL BOOKS

The Hebrews list Psalms, Proverbs, and Job as the poetical books. These three books are provided with a special system of accents (in the Hebrew) to bring out their poetical character. But these are not the only examples of Hebrew poetry. We find poetry scattered throughout the historical books. For instance, there is the song of Moses in Exodus 15, the song of Deborah and Barak in Judges 5, the song of Hannah in I Samuel 2, and the song of David in II Samuel 1. Also the Song of Songs and Lamentations are poetical in form. They were not included among the poetical books because they were read at certain Jewish feasts. Therefore they are placed in the Megilloth. But we may consider them as poetical books.

THE CHARACTERISTICS OF HEBREW POETRY
Parallelism

Hebrew poetry contains neither the rime nor the meter that is commonly used in English poetry, but emphasizes similarity of thought. All forms of Hebrew poetry are basically intended to teach. Since parallelism is a good teaching form, it became the chief characteristic of Old Testament poetry. Parallelism is the similarity of thought which exists between two or more lines of Hebrew poetry. We find a good example in Psalm 19:1:

> *The heavens declare the glory of God;*
> *And the firmament showeth his handiwork.*

It is easy to see that both lines of this verse speak about the same subject. They even say the same thing, but in different words. The three main types of parallelism are given below.

1. The synonymous parallelism is one in which the second line repeats the thought of the first line. This is the simplest type of parallelism. It is found frequently in the psalms. The one mentioned above is an example of this kind. Another example of synonymous parallelism is Psalm 24:1:

> *The earth is Jehovah's, and the fulness thereof;*
> *The world, and they that dwell therein.*

2. The antithetical parallelism is one in which the second line of the parallelism presents a contrast to the first line. In this kind the second line often begins with *but*. An example is Proverbs 15:1:

> *A soft answer turneth away wrath;*
> *But a grievous word stirreth up anger.*

3. The synthetic parallelism is one in which the second line completes the thought of the first line. This may be done in various ways. The second line may give reason for the first line, as in Proverbs 4:23:

> *Keep thy heart with all diligence;*
> *For out of it are the issues of life.*

The second line may also explain the result of the first line, as in Psalm 23:1:

> *Jehovah is my shepherd;*
> *I shall not want.*

The two lines may also make a comparison. This is usually indicated by the use of *as* and *so*. An example of this type is Psalm 125:2:

> *As the mountains are round about Jerusalem,*
> *So Jehovah is round about his people*
> *From this time forth and forevermore.*

Acrostic

Parallelism is a characteristic found in all Hebrew poetry. There is another characteristic which is found only occasionally. Hebrew poetry is sometimes arranged in acrostic fashion. In an acrostic the letters which begin each line form a pattern. In Hebrew poetry the usual pattern is alphabetic; that is, the first letters of the lines form the Hebrew alphabet. Thus the first line of an alphabetic acrostic in English would begin with *a*, the next with *b*, etc. Psalm 119 is an extended acrostic. It is divided into groups of eight verses. All the verses of the first group begin with *Aleph*, the first letter of the Hebrew alphabet. The verses of the next group begin with *Beth*, and so on. The American Standard Version marks this clearly by telling what letter begins each group.

THE VALUE OF HEBREW POETRY

We may be very grateful to God for including these poetical books in the Old Testament. Poetry often expresses the deepest feelings of men. Strong emotions easily bring forth poetical expression. So it is in the Old Testament. By means of the poetical books we gain an insight into the thinking and feelings of God's people in ancient times. We see them in joys and sorrows, in pain and pleasure, in blessing and punishment. And we learn to understand them better by means of their poetry.

But the poetry of the Old Testament does more than that. It gives us the revelation of God from a different point of view. Much of God's revelation is objective. It tells us what God has done and is doing for His people. But the poetical books show us the work of God in the hearts of His people. David's sorrow for sin, for example, is not simply an interesting study; it is God's revelation of how we should feel when we sin. Here is a revelation from God that reaches to the depths of our souls, that guides our emotions and our thoughts into Christian channels. How impoverished we would be if the Psalter was suddenly taken away from us. How we would miss the insights of Job, the practical wisdom of Proverbs. The poetical books are filled with choice blessings for us, if only we are willing to search for them.

EXERCISES

Factual Questions

1. Which books did the Jews count as poetical books?
2. What is parallelism?
3. Define the three main types of parallelisms.
4. In the following passages each verse may be considered as a complete parallelism. The strongest punctuation may be considered as the division between the two lines. Tell what type of parallelism each verse contains.

Psalm 1	Proverbs 16:1-3
Psalm 19:7-9	Proverbs 25:2-5
Psalm 24:1-5	

5. What is an acrostic?
6. What is the value of the poetical books?

Chapter 17

The Covenant Nation Sings of Its Sins

Psalms

INTRODUCTION

Date

The book of Psalms, or the Psalter, was not written at any one time. The various psalms were written over a period of about one thousand years. Within this time, there were three periods in which most of the psalm-writing took place.

1. The early period — the time of Moses
2. The classical period — the time of David and Solomon
3. The late period — during and after the Exile.

Of these three, the classical period is the most important. It was during the reigns of David and Solomon that the bulk of the Psalter was written.

Authors

Since the book of Psalms was written in these three periods, it is clear that the entire Psalter is not the work of one man. Rather there were many men who wrote the Psalms. David wrote more than anyone else. He wrote seventy-three psalms. Twelve were written by Asaph, who was David's choir director. Eleven were written by the sons of Korah, a family of Levites who helped with the singing in the temple. Two psalms were written by Solomon, one by Moses, and one by a man named Ethan. The remaining fifty are anonymous; that is, we do not know who wrote them. Actually, slightly less than half of the psalms are attributed to David. But since he wrote far more than anyone else, the Psalter is sometimes called the Psalms of David.

Use of the Psalter

The Psalter much resembles a hymnbook. We know that some of the psalms were sung by the people in their worship. Psalms 120-134 are called songs of ascents, because they were sung by pilgrims as they approached Jerusalem when they were coming to join in the religious festivals. Psalms 113-118 are called the hallel psalms. They were sung by Jewish families at the Passover. As a matter of fact, they are used in the same way even today. But it is likely that not all the psalms were written to be sung. Some psalms were intended to express the deep religious feelings of the psalmist's soul, and were not intended for singing.

Division of the Psalter

Whether or not we think of the Psalter as a hymnbook, it is clear that the Psalms have been divided into five books. According to an ancient Jewish tradition, each book in the Psalter is supposed to correspond to a book in the Pentateuch.

Book I	1- 41	(Genesis)
Book II	42- 72	(Exodus)
Book III	73- 89	(Leviticus)
Book IV	90-106	(Numbers)
Book V	107-150	(Deuteronomy)

At the end of the last psalm in each book is added a doxology of praise to God. Read Psalms 41:13; 72:18-19; 89:52; 106:48. Psalm 150 is a complete doxology, placed last to bring the Psalter to a fitting close.

PSALMS DEALING WITH SIN

The material of the Psalter can be divided in many ways. The three-fold division suggested by the Heidelberg Catechism—sin, salvation, and gratitude—fits the Psalter very nicely. In this chapter we will deal with the first section, the subject of which is sin.

The Psalms contain an outstanding description of man's sin in Psalm 14. The word "fool" in the first verse does not refer to one who is stupid or mentally deficient. It speaks of one who is blinded by the folly of sin. The description of the fool that is given in this psalm is used by Paul in Romans when he wants to present the sinfulness of the human race. This psalm tells us what man is like naturally, apart from God's saving grace.

The most important psalms that talk about sin, however, do not simply insist that man is sinful. They also portray sorrow for sin. We call them penitential psalms, because penitence means sorrow for sin. And these psalms truly present penitence. The writers are not sorry that they were caught sinning, nor are they sorry that they are liable to be punished. They are deeply sorry because they have sinned against God, and thereby have dishonored Him. The penitential psalms are 6, 32, 38, 51, 102, 130, and 143. Of these, the best known are Psalms 32 and 51.

Psalm 32 is a picture of God's forgiveness to the penitent sinner. Before repentance there was sorrow and punishment; with repentance the sinner receives forgiveness; after repentance comes blessing. Psalm 51 follows much the same pattern. But where Psalm 32 seems to be written from the viewpoint of one who is looking back on past forgiveness, Psalm 51 is the song of one who is receiving forgiveness in the present.

Psalm 73 is not listed as a penitential psalm but it also deals with sin. In it the psalmist traces the events which led him into sin—the sin of doubting God—and then explains how he was delivered from his sin. There are also many other psalms which present the sinfulness of man. Wherever the psalms speak of salvation there is usually some mention of sin.

EXERCISES

Factual questions

1. In what periods was the Psalter written?
2. Name the authors of the Psalms.
3. How is the Psalter divided?
4. What is found at the end of each division?
5. Who is a fool? Ps. 14.
6. Summarize the description of a fool in a few words. Ps. 14:1-3.
7. Will the fools always be able to oppress the righteous? Ps. 14:4-7.
8. Who is the blessed man? Ps. 32:1, 2.
9. What does the word "impute" mean?
10. What did David experience before he repented and confessed his sin? Ps. 32:3, 4.
11. How does David show that his experience (as recorded in Ps. 32) may be repeated in our lives? Ps. 32:8-11.
12. What is the difference between Psalm 32 and Psalm 51?
13. What made it possible for David to sin so grievously? Ps. 51:5.
14. What should we desire to do when God forgives our sins? Ps. 51:13-15.
15. What caused Asaph to doubt God? Ps. 73:3.
16. Where did he find the answer to his problem? Ps. 73:17.
17. What did he learn that he possessed that the wicked lack? Ps. 73:23-26.

Thought questions

1. Read II Samuel 11 and 12. How does this account help you to understand Psalm 51 better?
2. How does Psalm 51:13 explain why David wrote Psalm 32?
3. How does Psalm 14 help us to understand Matthew 5:22?

Memory

1. Psalm 51:14, 15.
2. Psalm 73:26, 27.

Chapter 18

The Covenant Nation Sings of Its Salvation

Psalms

The psalms by which the Old Testament people of God sing of their salvation can be divided into three types—the historical psalms, the imprecatory psalms, and the messianic psalms.

Historical Psalms

The historical psalms look back over the past history of the children of Israel. By means of this history the psalmist seeks to remind his people of the fact that God has truly been their saviour. Psalm 81 is a good example of this. In it the psalmist reminds Israel of the release from Egyptian bondage. But this is not done simply to recall past history. It is used as the basis for a commandment and a promise (Ps. 81:13-16). History, especially the history of God's people, is intended to teach later generations the truth about God. In a similar manner, Psalm 106 traces the history of Israel in the wilderness. It emphasizes Israel's rebellious actions and God's mercy to His people because of His covenant. Remembering that covenant faithfulness, the psalmist prays that God will still save His people (Ps. 106:47).

Imprecatory Psalms

The imprecatory psalms differ greatly from the historical psalms. In these psalms the writer asks God to destroy his enemies. These psalms sometimes sound very bloodthirsty. For instance, David prays about his enemies like this: "Let his days be few; And let another take his office. Let his children be fatherless, and his wife a widow. Let his children be vagabonds, and beg; And let them seek their bread out of their desolate places" (Ps. 109:8-10). These are harsh words. Because of these sentiments, some people say that Christians cannot agree with these psalms. They cannot sing them in worship. After all, they say, Christians are supposed to love their enemies. Rather than pray for their destruction, they should pray for their conversion. These statements are true. But they do not present the whole truth. Most of these psalms are by David. David was the anointed servant of God, and therefore he was under God's protection. Anyone who fought against David was fighting against God. His enemies were God's enemies.

> *Do not I hate them, O Jehovah, that hate Thee?*
> *And am not I grieved with those that rise up against Thee?*
> *I hate them with perfect hatred:*
> *They are become mine enemies.*
> — Ps. 139:21-22.

David's enemies have set themselves against God and His servant. In this way they place themselves under the wrath of a just God. David is really praying that God's justice may be displayed in the punishment of His enemies. And we as Christians can pray for the same thing, for God has promised to punish the wicked, both in this life and after death. Perhaps our imprecatory prayers cannot always be as specific as David's psalms were, but the spirit of our prayer can be the same as his was.

Messianic Psalms

By far the best expression of Israel's song of salvation is to be found in the messianic psalms. While the historical psalms point to God's salvation in the past, and the imprecatory psalms cry out for God's salvation at the present time, the messianic psalms look forward to the future perfection of God's salvation. These are psalms which speak about Christ. The word Messiah in Hebrew (from which the word "messianic" comes) means the same as the word Christ in Greek. Although the writers of these psalms did not know just who it was about whom they wrote, they were actually writing about Jesus Christ.

It is wonderful how much we can learn about Christ from these psalms. In Psalm 2 He is presented as the king given by God who will rule the entire earth. Psalms 45 and 72 also speak of His kingship. They emphasize the fact that it will be eternal. Psalm 110 shows another side of Christ's work—He will be a priest forever after the order of Melchizedek. In Psalm 22 we have a picture of the Crucifixion in amazing detail. And in Psalm 16 we find a prophecy of the Resurrection.

Since God's salvation was given to men before Christ appeared, we also find in the Psalms echoes of the psalmists' salvation. In fact, almost every time sin is mentioned, salvation is also mentioned. For the Old Testament saints as well as for us, salvation was not only historical, or something in the future. Neither was it simply deliverance from human enemies. Salvation was first of all deliverance from sin and its consequences. And echoes of this personal salvation ring throughout the Psalms.

EXERCISES

Factual questions

1. What is a historical psalm?
2. What is an imprecatory psalm?
3. What is a messianic psalm?
4. The following events from Israel's history are described in Psalm 105. Give references for each.

The promise to Abraham   The persecution by Pharaoh.
and Jacob   The plagues against Pharaoh.
The story of Joseph.   The Exodus.

5. Why did God do all these things for Israel? Ps. 105:45.
6. Name six sins of Israel that are listed in Psalm 106.
7. Why are these sins mentioned? Ps. 106:1-5, 47.
8. To whom is Psalm 109:8 applied in Acts 1?
9. When was Psalm 137 written?
10. Against whom does the psalmist pray in Psalm 137 and why?
11. List six references to the Crucifixion from Psalm 22.
12. Write out the verse from Psalm 16 which is quoted by Peter in Acts 2 to prove the resurrection of Christ.
13. Write out a verse which echoes personal salvation from:

Psalm 23   Psalm 91
Psalm 65   Psalm 95

Thought questions

1. What lesson can we learn from Psalm 105?
2. May Christians sing the imprecatory psalms?
3. Which petition of the Lord's Prayer is very much like the imprecatory psalms?
4. When did the anointing mentioned in Psalm 2:7 take place?

Memory

1. Psalm 2:7.
2. Psalm 110:4.

Chapter 19

The Covenant Nation Sings of Its Gratitude

Psalms

No one who has been made aware of his great sin and misery and who has received God's wonderful salvation can stop there. Salvation always results in thankfulness. And those who are thankful want to show their gratitude in every way possible. Every true Christian prays:

> *Fill thou my life, O Lord, my God, in every part with praise,*
> *That my whole being may proclaim Thy being and Thy ways.*
> *Not for the lip of praise alone, nor even the praising heart*
> *I ask, but for a life made up of praise in every part.*
> —Horatius Bonar.

The Old Testament people of God knew this gratitude and they expressed it in their psalms. Most of the psalms contain echoes of a thankful heart. This is to be expected. A person who is truly thankful cannot keep it to himself. But there are several types of songs in which this thankful spirit is especially evident. These are the theocratic psalms, the hallel psalms, the songs of ascents, and the hallelujah psalms. To these we will add Psalm 119 as another song of gratitude.

Psalms 95-100 are called the theocratic psalms. They receive this name because of the many times they refer to the sovereign rule of God. Because God reigns, these psalms call on us to worship Him, and to sing His praises. Indeed, all the earth is exhorted to praise the sovereign God. Here the gratitude of Israel breaks forth in songs of praise.

Psalms 113-118 are the hallel psalms. Like the theocratic psalms, they also bring praise to God. In fact, the word "hallel" means praise. But these psalms form a separate group because of their use. These were the psalms sung by the Israelites during the Passover. Psalms 113 and 114 were sung before the paschal meal, and Psalms 115 and 118 after the meal. The themes of these psalms are appropriate for remembering and celebrating the Exodus.

Psalm 119 is another psalm which expresses gratitude. It deserves separate mention because of its unique structure. Psalm 119 has 176 verses, divided into 22 stanzas of 8 verses each. Each stanza is marked by the fact that all of the eight verses in it begin with the same letter of the Hebrew alphabet. These stanzas are arranged consecutively. Verses 1-8 begin with *a;* 9-16 begin with *b;* and so on throughout the Hebrew alphabet. This type of psalm is called an acrostic. The difficulty of this type of writing is easily discovered if one will only try to think of a group of words which refer to the same object, one beginning with each letter of the alphabet. The writer of Psalm 119 began each verse in a stanza with the same letter of the alphabet. But he did more than that. He also centered every verse except two about the Word of God. It is this emphasis on God's Word that makes this an expression of gratitude. The Word of God is a means to a holy life, and a holy life is a life of gratitude to God. Every student should be familiar with stanzas *B* (vs. 9-16), *M* (vs. 97-104), and *N* (vs. 105-112).

The songs of ascent (Pss. 120-134) are psalms which were supposedly sung by pilgrims coming up to Jerusalem to worship at the feasts. In these psalms there is much said about the temple, the sanctuary, and the mountain of God. These terms all refer to the Old Testament house of God. Worshiping God in His holy place is the chief expression of thankfulness in these psalms.

The hallelujah psalms (Pss. 146-150) end the Psalter. They receive their name from the fact that each one begins with the word hallelujah. This is translated "praise ye Jehovah." It is therefore obvious that in these psalms praise is the chief form of gratitude. This group comes to its climax in Psalm 150, which is a complete doxology of praise. Every line in this psalm speaks of praise to God. It is a fitting finale to the Psalter.

EXERCISES

Factual questions

1. What are the theocratic psalms?
2. What are the hallel psalms?
3. What are the songs of ascents?
4. What are the hallelujah psalms?
5. What expressions of gratitude are recommended in:

Psalm 95:6	Psalm 96:3
Psalm 96:2	Psalm 97:10

6. What reasons for gratitude are presented in:

Psalm 95:7	Psalm 98:9
Psalm 96:3	Psalm 99:9
Psalm 97:1	Psalm 100:3

7. What method of expressing gratitude is taught in Psalm 116:13?
8. Write out three verses from Psalm 119 which show that God's Word helps us to attain a holy life. See especially sections *B* (vs. 9-16), *M* (vs. 97-104), and *N* (vs. 105-112).

9. Find the theme of Psalm 121 and show how it expresses gratitude.
10. In what period was Psalm 126 written?
11. Find the theme of Psalm 133 and show how it expresses gratitude.
12. What reasons for praising God are given in:

    Psalm 147:2, 3   Psalm 148:13
    Psalm 148:5, 6   Psalm 149:4

Thought questions

1. Why is Psalm 114 appropriate in the Passover celebration?
2. How does the contrast between God and idols in Psalm 115 express gratitude?
3. What would be the proper way for us to obey the psalmist's command to "pray for the peace of Jerusalem" (Ps. 122:6)?

Memory

1. Psalm 95:6, 7.
2. Psalm 100.
3. Psalm 119:11.

Chapter 20

The Wisdom of the Covenant Nation

Proverbs

INTRODUCTION

Authors

The very first verse of this book deals with authorship: "The proverbs of Solomon the son of David, king of Israel." With this before us there can be no doubt in our minds that Solomon must be counted among the authors of this book. But it is equally certain that the entire book is not by Solomon. Some of the proverbs are said to be those of the "wise men" (Prov. 22:17; 24:23). These wise men are possibly more ancient than Solomon. Then too we are told that Agur and Lemuel (concerning whom we know nothing) are the authors of the last two chapters of Proverbs. The book is a collection of wise sayings from various sources. But the majority of the sayings are by Solomon, the king who received wisdom from God.

Collection

These proverbs, written by different men at different times, had to be collected into the book of Proverbs as we know it. The book itself tells us when part of this collecting activity took place. "These also are proverbs of Solomon, which the men of Hezekiah king of Judah copied out" (Prov. 25:1). Beyond this we know nothing about the work of collecting the proverbs. But we may be sure that God inspired the collectors as well as the writers, so that only His inspired Word is included in our collection.

ANALYSIS

The Nature of Proverbs

Proverbs is a poetical book. It may not look like poetry to us, but it has all the marks of good Hebrew poetry. It is written in parallelisms, and parallelism is the outstanding characteristic of Hebrew poetry.

The poetry of the ancient Hebrews, just like poetry in our own language, contains great variety. As English poetry may range from two line verses to long epic poems, so Hebrew poetry may include short sayings, poems of some length, and acrostics. We find all of these in Proverbs. Proverbs 10-15, for instance, are composed of short sayings which contrast the righteous and the wicked. Proverbs 2 is a long poem in praise of wisdom. In Proverbs 31:10-31 we find an acrostic in praise of a virtuous woman.

Outline of Proverbs

The book of Proverbs cannot be outlined according to ideas. The only practical outline is that which shows the various collections of Proverbs which the book contains.

I.	The praise of wisdom	Proverbs 1: 1- 9:18
II.	Proverbs of Solomon	Proverbs 10: 1-22:16
III.	The words of the wise	Proverbs 22:17-24:34
IV.	More proverbs of Solomon	Proverbs 25: 1-29:27
V.	The words of Agur	Proverbs 30
VI.	The words of Lemuel	Proverbs 31: 1- 9
VII.	Acrostic—A virtuous woman	Proverbs 31:10-31

Dividing Proverbs

Proverbs has been called "Laws of Heaven for Life on Earth." In order to consider the teachings of Proverbs systematically, we need some method of division. Let us use the words of Jesus when He summarized the law of God. He told us to love God with every aspect of our personalities, and to love our neighbors as ourselves. In these words we find three kinds of duties—to self, to others, and to God. Let us examine Proverbs under these heads.

Our Duties to Ourselves

The Bible never suggests that man was made to be unhappy. Man was made to be happy. But true happiness is found in obedience to God's rules for our conduct. Proverbs is a mine laden with gems of practical wisdom. Some are given below. You should dig out many more for yourself.

Here are some of our duties to ourselves:
1. To be diligent, not slothful (Prov. 6:6-11).
2. To avoid sexual impurity (Prov. 7).
3. To gain wisdom and receive instruction (Prov. 2).
4. To avoid the danger of strong drink (Prov. 23:29-35).
5. To avoid entangling ourselves in someone else's financial problems (Prov. 6:1-5).
6. To avoid excessive luxury (Prov. 21:17).

Our Duties to Others

On an equal plane with ourselves we should put our fellow men. Our dealings with them are to be governed by the law of love. Proverbs

gives many practical applications of the law "Thou shalt love thy neighbor as thyself." Some of these are:
1. Honesty in all our business dealings (Prov. 11:1; 28:8).
2. Tact and kindness in our speech (Prov. 15:14; 25:11).
3. Mercy to those in need (Prov. 11:25, 26; 19:17).
4. Fairness and justice without respect of persons (Prov. 28:20, 21).
5. Training our children properly (Prov. 13:24; 19:18).
6. Helping friends who are in need (Prov. 17:17; 27:10).

Our Duties to God

Above and beyond all our duties to ourselves and to others is our duty to God. Our chief purpose in life is to glorify Him. Proverbs also provides sound advice in regard to this. For instance:
1. We are to trust in Jehovah (Prov. 3:5).
2. We are to give our offerings to Him (Prov. 3:9).
3. We are to fear Jehovah (Prov. 10:27).
4. We are to run to Him in time of trouble (Prov. 18:10).
5. We are to put Him before anything else (Prov. 30:7-9).

Promises of Proverbs

If we should think that Proverbs consists merely of one strict requirement after another, we would be badly mistaken. Proverbs does not only present our duties but it also speaks of the blessings that come to those who fulfill their duties, and the misery that comes to those who live in wickedness. Proverbs is a practical book from beginning to end. It points us to the proper way of life, and by its promises stirs us up to walk in that way.

EXERCISES

Factual questions
1. Who are the authors of Proverbs?
2. When were the proverbs collected into a book?
3. Why did Solomon write his proverbs? Prov. 1:1-6.
4. Proverbs 3:5-12 lists four obligations toward Jehovah. List them, and tell what reason or promise is given for each.
5. What benefits does wisdom confer on those who have her? Prov. 4:5-9.
6. Write out four statements from Proverbs 10 about fools.
7. Write out two verses from Proverbs 20 to show that Jehovah is interested in honest business dealings.
8. Write out the instructions for bringing up children found in Proverbs 22 and 23.
9. Write out two warnings against strong drink from Proverbs 23.
10. Romans 12:20 is a quotation of what verses from Proverbs 25?

Thought question

1. Some people believe that the wisdom mentioned in Proverbs 9:1-12 is really Christ. What reasons for or against that belief can you find?

Memory

1. Proverbs 3:5.   3. Proverbs 14:12.
2. Proverbs 4:18.   4. Proverbs 30:7-9.

Chapter 21

The Covenant Nation Sings of Love

Song of Solomon

INTRODUCTION

Author

There is no question about the authorship of this book. It is "the Song of Songs, which is Solomon's" (Song of Sol. 1:1). And since there are references to Solomon as king it must have been written during the forty years of his reign.

Interpretation of the Book

Every passage of Scripture has been interpreted in different ways. But the Song of Solomon has been especially subjected to a variety of interpretations. Dr. Edward J. Young lists at least eight different types of interpretations of the Song. But amid this wide variety there are really only two interpretations which have found great favor among evangelical Christians.

The first view holds that this book really speaks of the love of Christ for His church and of the Church for Christ. This view is very popular. It has been defended by competent scholars, and is reflected in the chapter headings which are often found in the King James version of the Bible. According to this view Solomon represents Christ and the bride represents His church. The expressions of love reflect the deep and mutual love of Christ and the Church.

In favor of this view it may be said that it gives the book a religious meaning. This makes it easier to explain why God put this book in the Old Testament. Also, some of the messianic psalms seem to reflect the Song of Solomon. This would be additional support for this view.

But some scholars maintain that the Song should not be interpreted in this way. They point out that this method of interpretation leads to all sorts of fanciful conclusions. According to these scholars, the book should be interpreted literally. It is just what it seems to be—a picture of the beauty and purity of true love. God has included it in the Old Testament to help safeguard the purity and sanctity of marriage.

The purpose of the Song does not end with human love, however. By pointing out the wonders of pure love, it points to a higher love that is altogether pure and beautiful. In this way the Song of Solomon is like a parable about the love of God, and specifically the love of Christ.

ANALYSIS

It is very difficult to analyze the Song of Solomon. In general, we may say that the Song is like a conversation, in which the bride and the bridegroom sing to each other and about each other. The following outline may help in understanding the book.

 I. The bride and groom sing to each other Song of Sol. 1: 1-2:7
 II. The bride sings the groom's praises Song of Sol. 2: 8-3:5
 III. The marriage; the bride is praised Song of Sol. 3: 6-5:1
 IV. The bride sings of her love
    and the groom's beauty   Song of Sol. 5: 2-6:9
 V. The beauty of the bride   Song of Sol. 6:10-8:4
 VI. The beauty of love   Song of Sol. 8: 5-14

But no outline can do justice to this book. Even quotations are unsatisfactory. This book must be read and reread, preferably at one sitting. And it should be read often. Its beauty is a fitting garb for its wonderful message of love.

(The outline above is adapted from *An Introduction to the Old Testament* by Edward J. Young. It is not designed to be memorized. But the reader may find it helpful to mark the divisions in his Bible as an aid to his reading.)

EXERCISES

Factual questions

 1. Who is the author of the Song of Songs?
 2. Explain the two best interpretations of the Song.

Thought question

 1. How would you explain that the Song of Solomon may be considered a picture of Christ and His church?

Chapter 22

The Covenant Nation Examines Suffering

Job

PURPOSE

The book of Job presents a question which has been asked by men in every age—why do the righteous suffer? Job also provides an answer to that question. It denies that all suffering is punishment for open sin. It does not even admit that all the suffering of the righteous are chastisements, intended to remove our sins and make us better Christians. Sometimes suffering is God's means of testing His people, so that their faith will be clearly demonstrated to be genuine.

INTRODUCTION

Author

The author of Job is unknown. It is most likely that he was a man who had himself passed through great sorrows and had been forced to think about the question of suffering. God might well use such a man to provide the divine answer to this important question. Although scholars have presented many different views about the time of writing, it seems most likely that it was written during the time of Solomon. Two facts favor this: (1) This problem required deep thought, and such meditation is most likely to occur in a time of peace and leisure, as was Solomon's reign. (2) The book of Job is very much like Proverbs and Song of Solomon, which were written about this time.

Who Is Job?

The name Job means "the much persecuted." Some have thought that Job was not an actual person, but simply a picture of sufferers. But in Ezekiel 14:14 and 20 he is mentioned in connection with Noah and Daniel, who were actual persons. And in James 5:11 his patience is set forth as an example for us. These references demand that we accept Job as a historical person. But when and where did he live? The fact that he is not presented as an Israelite, and the absence of any mention of the law of Moses make it necessary to place him at a very early date. He is probably a contemporary of the patriarchs of Genesis.

111

Perhaps he even comes before them. In the early days of the history of mankind the knowledge of God was spread abroad widely. Only as men rejected that knowledge and turned away from God was He hidden from all men except those whom He chose for His own people. Job is something like Melchizedek. He is a non-Israelite who worships the true God.

Job lived in the land of Uz. No area in the Middle East is known by that name today. Tradition locates the area where Job lived somewhere in the modern kingdom of Syria.

I.	Prologue—the cause of Job's suffering	Job	1,2
II.	Conversation with friends—Job is being punished	Job	3-31
III.	Speeches of Elihu—Job is being chastised	Job	32-37
IV.	Words of Jehovah—Job is being tested	Job	38-41
V.	Epilogue—the result of Job's suffering	Job	42

ANALYSIS

The book of Job approaches the problem of the suffering of the righteous in several steps. First we are shown the true cause of Job's suffering. Then we have various explanations set forth. Finally God Himself provides the proper answer.

Job's Enemy

The suffering of Job is caused by Satan, who desires to do away with Job's righteousness. For Job is righteous. God Himself says so. But Satan's actions are limited by God's permission, and it is only within the limit of God's permission that Satan can bring evil upon Job. At first Job passes the test with flying colors. Neither Satan's attack on his possessions nor the attack on Job himself turns him from his righteousness.

Job's Comforters

Then Job's "friends" arrive to "comfort" him. For seven days they sit in silence. Finally their presence leads Job to curse the day of his birth.

> *Let the day perish wherein I was born,*
> *And the night which said, There is a man-child conceived.*
> *—Job 3:3.*

This is really cursing the God who caused him to be born. With this the three friends begin their conversation with Job. All three of them take the same position. Suffering is always punishment for sin.

> *Remember, I pray thee, who ever perished, being innocent?*
> *Or where were the upright cut off?*
> *According as I have seen, they that plow iniquity,*
> *And sow trouble, reap the same.*
> *—Job 4:7, 8.*

The more suffering, these friends reason, the greater the sin being punished. Therefore they conclude that Job must be a great sinner. And they assume, since they are not punished by suffering, that they are not great sinners. No wonder that Job says of them:

> *No doubt but ye are the people,*
> *And wisdom shall die with you.*
> *—Job 12:2.*
> *Miserable comforters are ye all.*
> *—Job 16:2.*

Job's Victory

At first Job agrees with the reasoning of his friends, but insists that he is innocent. As a result he is led to attack God's justice. But as the friends continue their charges against him, Job begins to doubt the truth of their position. He comes to full confidence in God his redeemer.

> *But as for me I know that my Redeemer liveth,*
> *And at last he will stand up upon the earth:*
> *And after my skin, even this body, is destroyed,*
> *Then without my flesh shall I see God;*
> *Whom I, even I, shall see, on my side,*
> *And mine eyes shall behold, and not as a stranger,*
> *My heart is consumed within me.*
> *—Job 19:25-27.*

From this point on Job becomes more bold. He continually asserts that he is not the sinner that his friends assume him to be. He denies that they speak the truth. He shows them that their principle is false, for the wicked often prosper. And while he still cannot understand why he suffers, he no longer complains against God.

Finally, Job reduces his friends to silence. He gives a last speech of his own. Wisdom is not to be found in man's principles, but in God. "The fear of the Lord, that is wisdom; and to depart from evil is understanding" (Job. 28:28). After contrasting his former blessed state with his present misery, Job again declares his righteousness. But here his words end. He cannot arrive at the answer to his problem.

Elihu's Challenge

Now another speaker comes to the fore. Elihu has kept silence because the others are older. But now he speaks, angered at both Job and his friends. Job, he says, justifies himself at the expense of God. The friends have no answer to the problem. Elihu's answer is this. Job is indeed suffering because of sin. But his suffering is chastisement, not punishment. He is chastised because he is self-righteous. Elihu is even more severe with Job than the three friends were.

Surely thou hast spoken in my hearing,
And I have heard the voice of thy words, saying,
I am clean, without transgression;
I am innocent, neither is there iniquity in me : . . .
Behold, I will answer thee, in this thou art not just;
For God is greater than man.
                                          —*Job 33:8, 9, 12.*

God's Answer

Then Jehovah speaks out of the whirlwind. He speaks to these men about the universe, with all its mysteries which are too great for man to understand. In this way He shows them that they cannot understand the ways or the purposes of the infinite God. Therefore it is folly to think that they can explain the reasons for God's actions. God cannot be measured by man's logic. These words of God stir Job up to greater faith. He sees that God is sovereign, and that his sufferings are part of God's plan for him. Therefore he repents of his complaining words.

I have heard of thee by the hearing of the ear;
But now mine eye seeth thee:
Wherefore I abhor myself,
And repent in dust and ashes.
                                          —*Job 42:5, 6.*

Finally, God accepts Job's integrity. His righteousness is again declared. And the three friends are required to make sacrifices and have Job pray for them in order that they may be forgiven. God gives Job blessings even greater than those that he had before his time of testing.

The Problem of Suffering

The words of God at the end of the book do not give a definite answer to the problem that faced Job and his friends. He does not explain precisely why Job suffered. He simply points out that neither Job nor his friends are able to provide all the answers about this problem of suffering. There are reasons for suffering which are hidden from them.

But this does not mean that the book of Job does not provide an answer to the question which it raises. It both provides an answer and shows us the proper attitude to take when we must suffer. We must remember that God has revealed to us something which was not revealed to Job. We have in chapters 1 and 2 of the book of Job the story of what happened in Heaven. We know how Satan challenged the righteousness of Job and we know that God permitted Satan to test Job by suffering, so that Job's faith would be clearly demonstrated. So when God tells Job and his friends that Job's suffering was caused by something that they could not know about, we know what that cause was. Job's suffering was neither punishment nor chastisement, but testing. The reason Job suffered is not the most important point made in this book. The words of God give us the proper attitude toward suffering. From them we learn that there are many reasons why people suffer. It is not for us to ask why we must suffer. We cannot know. God's purposes are too great for us, as they were too great for Job. Therefore we must not question. Above all, we must not doubt the righteousness of God. We must leave the reason with God, and trust Him completely to use our suffering for His glory and for our good.

Factual questions

EXERCISES

1. What is the purpose of the book of Job?
2. When was Job written?
3. When did Job live? Where?
4. How did Job show his righteousness when he was afflicted? Job 1, 2.
5. What does his vision tell Eliphaz about man? Job 4:12-19.
6. In what way does Eliphaz' vision answer the questions in Job 4:7?
7. Where does Bildad find the source of his authority? Job 8:8-10.
8. On what principle do all three friends agree?
9. What does Elihu tell Job? Answer with words from Job 33.
10. What is the final answer to the question of Job's suffering?
11. What does the book of Job teach us about the proper attitude toward suffering?

Thought questions

1. How could Job's attitude in Job 1 be applied to your own troubles?
2. Can Satan appear before God today to accuse us? See Luke 10: 18 and Revelation 20:2, 3.
3. How does the fact that man can know so little about the universe help us to understand the problem of suffering?
4. How would you use the book of Job in visiting a shut-in?

Memory

1. Outline of Job.
2. Job 19:25-27.

PART FOUR

THE PERIOD OF
THEOCRATIC DECLINE

Chapter 23

The Covenant Nation in Its Time of Decision

Kings

The history that is recorded in Kings brings us to a new period, the period of theocratic decline. This term may require some explanation. It does not mean that Jehovah has given up His plan for the advancement of His kingdom. His plans and purposes do not change. But on the surface we come to a time of decline. There is a decline of theocratic feeling in the hearts of Israel's kings and people. That is, there is less and less recognition that Jehovah is ruler of Israel. There is a corresponding decline in the monarchy. From the glory of Solomon to the shame of captivity—this is the path traced out in Kings.

But this decline does not frustrate or change the plan and purpose of God. By His prophets He points the way to that which lies ahead. He draws in bold strokes the picture of that spiritual kingdom where the eternal King reigns in glory from the throne of David.

INTRODUCTION

The book of Kings, like that of Samuel, is one book which has been divided into two. Kings is the last of the Former Prophets. Like the other books in this group, it is anonymous.

Since the book of Kings traces the history of Israel until the Babylonian captivity, it is obvious that it must have been written after that time. The standpoint from which the events of the final chapters are viewed makes it most likely that the author was one of those who had been carried away to Babylon. An ancient Jewish tradition says that Jeremiah is the author. But he was taken to Egypt, not Babylon. It was probably written by another prophet who was a captive in Babylon.

The events mentioned in Kings cover a span of more than four centuries, from 973 B.C. to 560 B.C. Therefore it is obvious that the author could not have firsthand information about all that he relates. He had to rely on earlier documents. As a matter of fact, this book mentions such documents more than any other Old Testament writing. Reference is made to "the book of the acts of Solomon" (I Kings 11:41), "the book of the chronicles of the kings of Judah" (I Kings 14:29), and "the book of the chronicles of the kings of Israel" (I Kings 14:19). These earlier documents were probably public records of the kingdoms. They were probably not inspired writings. But the prophetic writer of Kings was inspired of God as he selected his material from these documents, so that our book of Kings contains the inspired (and therefore infallible) revelation of Jehovah.

PURPOSE

The book of Kings traces the story of the monarchy from the accession of Solomon to the Babylonian captivity. But it is not simply a factual recording of the events by which this decline and fall occurred. It is prophetic. It is designed to show the cause of this tragedy. The kingdom declined and fell because it ceased to be a theocratic kingdom. Beginning with the latter days of Solomon's reign the people turned away from Jehovah. By rejecting Him who had redeemed them for Himself and who was pleased to be their ruler, they were destroying the foundation on which their nation was built.

The book of Kings also stresses the position of the prophets. Special attention is given to Elijah and Elisha. There are two possible reasons for this. First, these two prophets had left no written record. (Most of the Latter Prophets had been written by the time Kings was written.) Second, these two had stood in a most critical time in Israel's history. No prophetic record of this period would be complete without the story of Elijah and Elisha.

OUTLINE

I. The united kingdom under Solomon   I Kings   1-11
II. The divided kingdom of Judah and Israel I Kings 12-II Kings 17
III. The remaining kingdom of Judah   II Kings 18-25

ANALYSIS

Solomon's Rise to Power

Kings begins with the last days of David, for the events of those days were of great importance to Solomon. David's failure to discipline his children had had disastrous effects in the lives of Ammon and Absalom. The same failure precipitated a crisis during David's final days. Adonijah, his oldest living son, determined to steal the throne for himself, even though David had promised it to Solomon. This promise was based on a divine command. But it required quick, decisive action on the part of Nathan, Bathsheba, and David to bring that promise to fulfillment. Important leaders like Joab the general and Abiathar the high priest had taken sides with Adonijah. But God's plan could not be foiled.   Solomon was crowned king and the would-be usurpers scattered.

When David was dying he gave Solomon his blessing and some final advice.   Solomon was to punish Joab and Shimei for their crimes.   Not only were they criminals, but they represented those who might again attempt to seize Solomon's throne.   In accordance with David's advice, Adonijah, Joab, and Shimei were executed.   Abiathar was deposed as high priest.   By these measures Solomon gained firm control of the kingdom.

The Wisdom of Solomon

Solomon reaped the benefits of David's victories.   He ruled a large kingdom, situated at the crossroads of the East.   One sign of his importance was his marriage to the daughter of Pharaoh, which united the two countries in an alliance.   But the size and importance of his kingdom brought problems also.   Solomon was a young man, and his task was a great one.

Shortly after his inauguration, God appeared to Solomon when he went to Gibeon to worship, and asked him what He should give him.   The reply of Solomon, that he sought wisdom to rule the people, pleased God. He promised Solomon honor and riches as well as wisdom.

The wisdom of the East is very practical.   It is contained in the solving of problems and the uttering of proverbs.   In this Solomon excelled.   His decision regarding the child claimed by two women spread his fame throughout the land, and his wisdom in all spheres of learning brought men from far and near to hear him.

The Temple of Solomon

Solomon did not forget that his kingdom and his wisdom came from God.   He recalled the promise God had made to David that his son should build the temple which David had desired to build.   With the aid of Hiram, king of Tyre, Solomon began the building of the temple.

The building of the temple was an event of tremendous importance for Israel.   As far as worship was concerned, the temple could provide nothing that was not already present in the tabernacle.   The presence of God in the midst of His people and the proper approach to God were truths clearly symbolized in the tabernacle and its worship.   But the tabernacle was a tent.   It was designed for travel.   Therefore it could not symbolize the rest which God had promised to His people.   This was symbolized by the building of the temple.   God had established His people in the promised land.   He had given them a theocratic king who had made them a great nation.   Now it was time to establish the worship of Jehovah in a temple which would be a symbol of the rest which Israel would have as long as she was faithful to God's covenant.

There is something fitting about the fact that Solomon built the temple. David was a man of war, but Solomon was a man of peace. His reign was one of peace and prosperity for Israel. He himself was a symbol of God's blessing on His covenant nation. And he might be marked as one who typified the coming Prince of Peace.

The temple defies description. This is partly because the author of Kings gives us insufficient information for a description, and partly because the amounts of gold, silver, and precious stone used are beyond our powers of imagination. We do know that the outside of the temple was stone. Inside, the stone was covered with wood paneling. This was carved, and then overlaid with gold encrusted with precious stones of all kinds. The temple must have been gorgeous, a fitting dwelling place for the Ruler of Heaven and earth.

And yet the important fact about the temple was not its beauty nor its costliness. It was rather that God dwelt therein. That is the emphasis of Solomon's prayer of dedication. This temple is the center of worship. This is the place where God will hear prayer, and the source from which help will come. Perhaps there is no more glorious scene in Israel's history than this dedicatory ceremony when, amidst the rejoicing and the sacrifices of all the people, the cloud of God's glory filled the holy of holies, and flame from on high lighted the fire on the great altar.

The Wealth of Solomon

God had promised to give Solomon riches and honor in addition to wisdom. That promise was abundantly fulfilled. Our imaginations are staggered by the revenue which poured into Solomon's court and the luxury which surrounded him. Nor were the riches all retained in the court. The people also knew a time of prosperity unlike any other in Israel's history. How clearly God pictured to His people the blessings that would be theirs if only they would be faithful to His covenant.

This was brought again to Solomon's attention. After the dedication of the temple God appeared to him again, and promised to be with him if he were faithful. But this time there was an extended warning of the results of unfaithfulness. It was as if God were counseling him against the danger which lay ahead.

The Sin of Solomon

When Solomon was old, he departed from serving Jehovah. He married many wives. Perhaps this was partly to make alliances with other nations. But his wives were heathen, and they brought their heathenism with them. Solomon was affected by it. He permitted them to worship their gods. He even built places of worship in Jerusalem for them. It is not certain that Solomon himself worshiped these false gods. But he aided the false worship of his wives.

David had been a sinner. His sins had been grievous. But never had he been guilty of idolatry or toleration of idolatry. This was the fundamental sin. This was rebellion against the Ruler of Israel. This was the denial of the theocracy. So God appeared to Solomon and announced the division of the kingdom.

The kingdom would not be divided in Solomon's day. But in his time the seeds of division were sown. God raised up adversaries in Edom and Syria who would reduce the boundaries of Israel. And in the tribe of Ephraim—which had always been a tribe that coveted leadership in Israel—there was a man named Jeroboam who "lifted up his hand against the king." God told Jeroboam, through the prophet Ahijah, that the rule of ten tribes would be his after the death of Solomon. Solomon had caused the division of the kingdom by his sin. Now God set the stage for that division to occur. Solomon's reign had been a time of decision. In spite of the glory, the wealth, the blessing, it had been a reign in which the wrong decision had been made.

EXERCISES

Factual questions

1. Where and when was Kings written?
2. How did the author learn about earlier events?
3. What is the purpose of the book of Kings?
4. How did Adonijah expect to get the throne? I Kings 1:5ff.
5. Whose example did he follow? I Kings 1:5ff.
6. Why was Adonijah killed? Joab? Shimei? I Kings 2:13ff., 28 ff., 36ff.
7. Why did Solomon ask for wisdom? I Kings 3:4ff.
8. Taking a cubit as 18 inches, how large was the temple? the porch? I Kings 6.
9. How long did it take to build the temple? I Kings 6:37ff.
10. According to Solomon's prayer, what place was the temple to have in Israel's worship? I Kings 8.
11. What warning did God give Solomon? I Kings 9.
12. How did Solomon compare with the rulers of other nations? What was his annual income? I Kings 10:14ff.
13. What led Solomon away from Jehovah? I Kings 11.
14. What was the punishment for Solomon's sin? I Kings 11:9ff.
15. What adversaries did God raise up? I Kings 11: 14ff.

Thought questions

1. In what ways may Solomon be likened to Christ?
2. Was it wrong for Solomon to kill his enemies?
3. Using I Kings 7 and II Chronicles 3, 4 for information, try to describe Solomon's temple in your own words.

4. Why is the queen of Sheba important to people in the New Testament age? Matt. 12:38-42; Luke 11:29-32.

Memory
1. Outline of Kings.

Chapter 24

The Covenant Nation
in Its Time of Division

Kings

PURPOSE

We noticed before that the purpose of Kings is to show how the decline and fall of Israel was caused by Israel's failure to be true to its theocratic character. In Solomon's reign we noted the blessing which God poured out on Israel, but also the fatal error which entered in the last years. In the section before us we see the first unfolding of God's judgment. In this period of the divided kingdom, our attention will be focused more on Israel, the northern kingdom, than on Judah, the southern kingdom. The kingdom of Israel came into being because of sin. From its beginning it forsook the theocratic principle. Its history shows us the awful results of such apostasy.

ANALYSIS

The Revolt of the Ten Tribes

The end of Solomon's life was marked by compromise with idolatry. Having received the theocratic throne, Solomon so far departed from serving God that he built altars for other gods in Jerusalem. As a result of this, God told him that the kingdom would be divided in the days of his son. And the only reason why he would not lose it entirely was God's promise to David.

When Solomon died and Rehoboam reigned, the threatened split became a reality. Motivated by tribal jealousies, the northern tribes promised allegiance to Rehoboam only if he would reduce the oppressive levies of money and man power that Solomon had introduced. Rehoboam foolishly refused, and the northern tribes rejected him as king. Instead they chose Jeroboam who had "lifted up his hand against the king [Solomon]" to be their king. This too was a fulfillment of prophecy.

Jeroboam's Sin

This revolt could hardly lead to friendly terms between the two kingdoms. The time of the divided kingdom can be separated into three periods. At first there was a time of enmity, which was the natural outcome of the rift. This was followed by a period of harmony, when the two royal families intermarried. Finally there was a second period of enmity, which lasted until the captivity of Israel in 722 B.C.

The enmity between Israel and Judah did not affect their religious unity. The people from both kingdoms worshiped Jehovah, and the temple in Jerusalem was the center of worship. In this Jeroboam saw a threat to his kingdom. Unity in religion would lead to a desire for political unity. The people of the north would again accept the rule of David's family, and government and religion would both be centered at Jerusalem. In order to keep this from happening, Jeroboam resorted to the ancient heresy of Israel. He made golden calves, like the one Aaron had made at Sinai, and introduced them to his people with words like those of Aaron, "behold thy gods, O Israel, which brought thee up out of the land of Egypt" (I Kings 12:28). These calves he set up at Dan and Bethel and established around them a new, national religion.

This departure from the true religion was soon condemned by God. A prophet denounced Jeroboam's altar at the height of the ceremony of dedication. His denunciation was accompanied by a sign — the altar split and the ashes poured out. But this solemn warning was not heeded. Jeroboam continued his false worship. And every king of Israel followed in the sin of Jeroboam and continued this false worship.

This religion introduced by Jeroboam was a complete denial that Israel was a theocratic nation. The king had declared independence from Jehovah, and the people had willingly followed him. Such apostasy was bound to bring judgment upon the northern kingdom.

The First Period of Enmity

The history of Israel during this period is in striking contrast to that of Judah. In Judah there was order, and for most of the time a king who was true to Jehovah sat on the throne. But for Israel this was a time of near anarchy. Jeroboam had been promised that if he obeyed God his family would continue to rule. But Jeroboam disobeyed from the start, and the kingdom did not long remain with his family. His son Nadab ruled two years and then was slain by his general Baasha. Baasha became king, and his son Elah followed him. Elah reigned two years and was killed by Zimri. Zimri ruled for seven days before he perished. Then Israel was divided four years between Tibni and Omri. Omri finally did away with his rival and established himself as sole king. All these kings had been wicked, but Omri "dealt wickedly above all that were before him" (I Kings 16:25). And his son and heir was Ahab, the most wicked king of Israel.

In Judah this period began with the reign of Rehoboam. He turned away from Jehovah, and his son Abijam followed in his footsteps. But these two together reigned less than twenty years, and they were followed by Asa, who ruled for forty years. Asa was a good king. He put away the idolatry and wickedness in Judah. He led the people back to Jehovah. He was a theocratic king.

The Difference Between Israel and Judah

We might pause at this point to notice how different the religious histories of the two nations are. Israel began in sin and continued uninterruptedly in sin. Never was the sin of Jeroboam cast aside. As a result Israel went into captivity more than a century before Judah.

The history of Judah, religiously speaking, is checkered. While there were wicked kings in Judah, there were also some who were very good kings. Even when the wicked kings introduced the worship of false gods into Judah, idolatry never became as firmly established as it did in Israel. Edersheim points out three reasons for this:

1. The temple in Jerusalem was a continual influence for good. This place where God dwelt among His people was a hindrance to the introduction of idolatry and an inspiration to true worship.
2. The wicked kings, who imported other gods, were always followed by good kings, who swept away the idolatry of their fathers.
3. The reigns of the evil kings were always brief as compared to the reigns of the good kings.

On the one hand, this greater faithfulness to the worship of Jehovah explains the longer life of the kingdom of Judah. On the other hand, we must not forget that it is God who keeps this people more faithful to Himself, in order that the promise to David might be fulfilled.

The Period of Harmony

The time of harmony between Israel and Judah began in the reigns of Ahab and Jehoshaphat. Ahab, the son of Omri, is rightly known as the worst king of Israel. His father had been worse than those who went before, but Ahab far outstripped his father in wickedness. His marriage to Jezebel, the heathen daughter of the king of Sidon, was a wicked act which caused much more wickedness. Jezebel was an ardent worshiper of Baal. Under her influence, Ahab made the worship of Baal the official worship of Israel. A systematic attempt to wipe out the worship of Jehovah was begun. The prophets were killed, and the faithful worshipers persecuted.

The Ministry of Elijah

In this critical hour God raised up Elijah the Tishbite. He was a strange figure, but a mighty prophet of God. To him and to his successor Elisha God gave the power to work miracles. This power is not often displayed in the Scriptures. Many miracles had accompanied the establishment of the theocratic nation in the days of Moses and Joshua. But since then there had been few, if any. But now the theocracy was threatened by heathenism. If Baal worship was successfully established in Israel, the harmonious relations existing between Israel and Judah would surely have spread it to the southern kingdom also. As the power of Jehovah had been displayed against the gods of Egypt, it must now be set forth against the false god Baal. Jehovah must be shown to be the true and living God, while the gods of the heathen are but dumb idols. It is for this reason that Elijah and Elisha work miracles.

Elijah is the prophet of judgment. He is the "John the Baptist" of the Old Testament, calling the people to repentance. His first appearance is to Ahab. He pronounces that there will be no rain except at his command. Then he disappears. For three years Israel suffers without the life-giving rain. Elijah's reappearance is equally sudden, and results in the famous contest on Mount Carmel. The miraculous outcome of this contest turns the people from their idolatry. Jehovah is acknowledged as the true God. The priests of Baal are slain. Even Ahab is a changed man for a short time, and receives aid from Jehovah in his battle against the Syrians. But Jezebel is unchanged, and her evil influence turns Ahab again to iniquity. It is Elijah who pronounces God's judgment upon Ahab and his family.

Elijah's life ends as spectacularly as it began. Without tasting death, he is carried into Heaven in a whirlwind. Elisha is left to take his place. But Elisha's task is not the same as Elijah's. For Elijah was not unsuccessful. His call to repentance, presented in powerful words and supported by powerful deeds, had been heeded. Although the influence of the evil Jezebel still lingered, Elisha faced a people who had repented. Baal worship still existed, but it had lost much of its hold on the people. The tide had been turned by this mighty servant of God, Elijah the Tishbite.

The Work of Elisha

The story of Elisha's life is not presented in chronological order. Although the author of King presents Elisha's ministry as though it all occurred within the short reign of Ahaziah, we should remember that he lived through the reigns of six kings. The recorded events probably occurred over a period of many years, but were gathered together in this way in order to tell of his ministry more effectively.

The ministry of Elisha is primarily one of mercy rather than judgment. Special emphasis is placed upon his miracles. By these miracles the ministry of Elisha is connected with that of Elijah. But at the same time the two ministries form a contrast. Elijah was the prophet of judgment; Elisha is the prophet of mercy. Elijah called the nation to repentance; Elisha leads a repentant people. Elijah fought against evil within the nation; Elisha helps the nation against evil from without. Taken together, their ministries present a balanced picture of the workings of Jehovah in the midst of His covenant nation.

The End of Harmony

In this period of harmony most of the attention is focused on Israel. Here the theocratic principle is most sharply challenged. In Judah, on the other hand, the nation is led by godly king Jehoshaphat. His long reign follows that of Asa, who was also godly. All seemed well for Judah. But the very act which brought about harmony between the two kingdoms was the seed of evil in Judah. Jehoshaphat gave his son Jehoram in marriage to Athaliah, the daughter of Ahab and Jezebel. Athaliah was like her mother, and caused Jehoram to walk "in the ways of the kings of Israel." Their son Ahaziah, who reigned after Jehoram, was also wicked.

In the northern kingdom the influence of Jezebel was felt in the reigns of her sons. Ahaziah followed in Ahab's steps. Jehoram was not as bad, but he still led Israel into sin. In order to fulfill the prophecy which Elijah had spoken to Ahab, Elisha sent a prophet to anoint Jehu to be king. This bloody man wiped out the family of Ahab completely. Ahaziah, king of Judah, who was visiting his uncle Jehoram, was also killed. This murder of Judah's king by the one who became king of Israel naturally ended the harmony which had existed. Judah's enmity was increased by Athaliah's attempt to kill all the royal seed so that she could usurp the throne. Jehoash was rescued from her and hidden in the temple by Jehoiada the high priest and his wife. After six years on the throne Athaliah was killed, and the influence of Jezebel perished in Judah.

Judah in the Second Period of Enmity

Again in this period we find a contrast between the two kingdoms. After the death of Athaliah the kings of Judah were true to Jehovah. Yet they were not completely faithful to Him. Jehoash departed from Jehovah toward the end of his reign. Amaziah compromised with idolatry. Uzziah, who had a long reign, was a faithful servant of God. He extended the kingdom and gave it a new time of glory. But he intruded into the priest's office and burned incense in the temple. For this he became leprous. His son Jotham also followed Jehovah. For a century the people of Judah were led by kings who were basically theocratic. Although they were not without sin, they considered themselves servants of the Ruler of Israel.

This time of good kings was interrupted by Ahaz, who turned Judah to idolatry. He shut up the door of the temple and placed a heathen altar in the court. He sought to replace the worship of Jehovah with his heathen worship.

But Ahaz ruled only sixteen years. And after his death, the throne went to Hezekiah, of whom it is said, "He trusted in Jehovah, the God of Israel; so that after him was none like him among all the kings of Judah, nor among them that were before him" (II Kings 18:5). God continued to bless the kingdom of Judah with good kings. Yet the people of Judah were not deeply devoted to Jehovah. The evil kings had no trouble leading the nation astray. But the good kings often found it difficult to reform the nation. God's blessing is of grace, not of merit. Judah's favored condition rested upon God's promise to David.

Israel in the Second Period of Enmity

This is the last period of Israel's history. From the beginning the kings of Israel have followed the sin of Jeroboam. In the reign of Ahab it was necessary to defend the truth against heathenism with mighty miracles. Jehu had ended the threat of Baal worship. But he did not follow Jehovah. He continued in the sin of Jeroboam. This led again to strife and virtual anarchy. Zechariah, great-great-grandson of Jehu (II Kings 10:30), was murdered by Shallum. Shallum in turn was slain by Menahem. Menahem passed the throne on to his son Pekahiah, who was killed by Pekah. Pekah in turn died at the hand of Hoshea.

During this period the sins of Israel continued to grow. The work of Jehu had been a check on Israel's sin. But the effects of that check were short-lived. During Hoshea's reign Israel was a vassal state, paying tribute to Assyria. But Hoshea attempted to rebel and in 722 B.C., after a three-year siege, Samaria fell to the Assyrians. The Israelites were carried into captivity, and the land of Israel repopulated with other captive nations. This was the end of the northern kingdom. This was God's punishment for her sins.

The inspired writer explains the reason for Israel's downfall. In II Kings 17 he spells it out carefully. Because "the children of Israel had sinned against Jehovah their God" (vs. 7), because "the children of Israel did secretly things that were not right against Jehovah their God" (vs. 9), because "they would not hear [His prophets], but hardened their neck" (vs. 14), because they "sold themselves to do that which was evil in the sight of Jehovah, to provoke Him to anger" (vs. 17), therefore "Jehovah was very angry with Israel, and removed them out of His sight: there was none left but the tribe of Judah only" (vs. 18).

God's Voice to His People

God did not leave Himself without a testimony during this period. As Elijah and Elisha proclaimed God's will during the period of harmony, other prophets now arose to speak His words. But these prophets also committed their prophecies to writing. Their books form part of the Old Testament. We shall study them shortly. During this period Joel, Isaiah, and Micah brought God's word to Judah. Israel also heard the word of Jehovah. Amos and Hosea eloquently called that rebellious people to repentance. But they would not hear, and the wrath of God fell upon them.

A Note on Chronology

The chronology (dating of events) of this period is most difficult. It was once thought to be comparatively simple. One had only to add the figures given in the scriptural record to arrive at the proper dates. Many chronologies were set up on this basis. Today these are called "long chronologies." They generally ascribe a total of 390 years from the division of the kingdom to the destruction of Jerusalem.

More recently, scholars have been able to compare a few events in Scripture with the same events in Assyrian and Babylonian history. These peoples had a different method of dating events. Some of their writers make mention of eclipses and other natural events which can be precisely dated. By the use of such material, the sciences of astronomy and archaeology can combine to give accurate dates for some events. These dates form a framework for the rest of the scriptural account.

The application of this knowledge to the chronology of this period has shown that the old chronology was about fifty years too long. The conclusion is obvious. The writer of Kings was not interested in providing a chronology. He only wished to show how the kings of Israel and Judah were related to each other. Consequently he ignored such matters as coregencies (when two kings rule together).

Most scholars are willing to admit that we cannot provide a chronology which will solve all the difficulties. Our present information is insufficient. We must be willing to admit that we do not have all the

---

Notes on the chart of

THE KINGS OF JUDAH AND ISRAEL
(See opposite page.)

1. The dates given are approximate, since it is still impossib'e to achieve certainty on most Old Testament dates.

2. The prophets whose names are in parentheses did not write. The line below a prophet's name shows the length of his prophetic ministry.

3. Tibni and Omri were both contenders for the throne. In 883 B.C. Omri defeated his rival and began his undisputed reign.

THE KINGS OF JUDAH AND ISRAEL

JUDAH		Prophets	ISRAEL	
Rehoboam	933-917	(Ahijah) (Shemaiah)	Jeroboam	933-912
Abijam	916-914			
Asa	913-873	(Jehu)	Nadab	912-911
			Baasha	911-888
			Elah	888-887
			Zimri	887
			Tibni	887-883
			Omri	887(883)-877
Jehoshaphat	873-849	(Elijah) (Micaiah)	Ahab	876-854
		(Elisha)	Ahaziah	854-853
			Jehoram	853-842
Jehoram	848-842			
Ahaziah	842		Jehu	842-815
Athaliah				
(Queen)	842-836			
Jehoash	836-797			
		Joel (?)	Jehoahaz	814-798
Amaziah	797-779		Jehoash	798-783
		Amos	Jeroboam II	783-743
Uzziah	779-740	Isaiah Hosea		
			Zechariah	743
			Shallum	743
Jotham	740-736	Jonah Micah	Menahem	743-737
			Pekahiah	737-736
Ahaz	736-728		Pekah	736-730
			Hoshea	730-722
Hezekiah	727-699			
			Fall of Samaria	722
Manasseh	698-643	Obadiah (?)		
Amon	643-641	Nahum (?)		
Josiah	640-609	Jeremiah		
Jehoahaz	609	Zephaniah Habakkuk (?)		
Jehoiakim	609-598	Daniel		
Jehoiachin	598			
Zedekiah	598-586	Ezekiel		
Destruction of				
Jerusalem	586			
Gedaliah	586			

answers. Therefore the dates given on the accompanying chart are approximate dates. However, they are the dates most widely accepted by modern scholars.

Factual questions
EXERCISES

1. What is the purpose of the second part of Kings?
2. What did the people ask Rehoboam? I Kings 12.
3. What answer did he give? I Kings 12:6ff.
4. Why did Jeroboam set up the golden calves? I Kings 12:25ff.
5. What did the prophet prophesy about Jeroboam's altar? I Kings 13.
6. Give three reasons for Judah's better resistance to idolatry.
7. What did Asa do to purify the land? I Kings 15:9ff.
8. Name some of Ahab's sins. I Kings 16:29ff.
9. List four miracles of Elijah in I Kings 17-II Kings 2.
10. What test did Elijah propose between Jehovah and Baal? I Kings 18:20ff.
11. What message did Elijah receive at Sinai (Horeb)? I Kings 19:9ff.
12. How did Ahab get Naboth's vineyard? I Kings 21.
13. What punishment was prophesied by Elijah? I Kings 21:17ff.
14. Why was it significant that Elisha saw Elijah ascend into Heaven? II Kings 2:9ff.
15. List eight miracles of Elisha in II Kings 2 - 7.
16. How did Jehu end the house of Ahab? II Kings 9:21-10:11.
17. How did Jehu end the worship of Baal? II Kings 10:18ff.
18. How did Jehoiada the high priest reform Judah? II Kings 11:17-12:16.
19. How did Menahem save Samaria from the Assyrians? II Kings 15:17ff.
20. How did Ahaz seek relief from Syria and Israel? II Kings 16:7ff.
21. What idea did Ahaz get in Damascus? How did he put it into practice? II Kings 16:10ff.
22. What happened between Assyria and Israel in Hoshea's reign? II Kings 17.
23. Why was Israel sent into captivity?

Thought questions
1. Why was Jeroboam so unaffected by the word of the prophet that he continued his false worship?
2. Write a character sketch of Elijah.
3. How much influence did Jezebel have on her family?
'4. How could a godly king like Jehoshaphat enter into an alliance with a wicked king like Ahab?

5. Why was the contest on Mount Carmel so important?
6. How was Deuteronomy 18:21, 22 fulfilled in I Kings 22?
7. Why did Elijah destroy the soldiers sent to bring him to the king? II Kings 1.
8. What is a "double portion"? II Kings 2:9.
9. Show why Israel deserved her punishment.

STOP !

Chapter 25

The Covenant Nation
in Its Time of Disintegration

Kings

PURPOSE

It is the purpose of these closing chapters of Kings (II Kings 18-25) to show how Judah, like Israel departed from the ideal of being a theocracy. Jehovah was rejected as their ruler. As a result Judah was also taken into captivity.

ANALYSIS

A Spiritual Awakening

Ahaz was one of the most wicked kings of Judah. He was followed by Hezekiah, one of the best kings of Judah. Here we see again what we noted earlier — that God blessed Judah by giving her godly kings to overcome the effects of the evil kings.

Hezekiah led the people in a religious reform. The idols which Ahaz had permitted and promoted were removed. The altar which Ahaz had placed in the court of the temple was removed and the temple, which had been closed, was reopened. There was a great rededication of the temple and a Passover feast. This was an awakening on the part of the people as well as the king. The people themselves called for a second seven-day feast after the Passover was completed. These events took place before Samaria fell to Assyria. They marked a new high in the religious life of Judah.

The time of Hezekiah was turbulent. In his reign Israel was taken captive. Assyria, the dominant power at that time, also troubled Judah. Sennacherib led his hosts in a campaign which was designed to bring all Palestine under his control and remove the threat of Egyptian power from his borders. In this campaign he attacked the walled cities of Judah and laid siege to Jerusalem. But Hezekiah took the plight of Jerusalem to God in prayer. "And it came to pass that night, that the angel of Jehovah went forth, and smote in the camp of the Assyrians a hundred fourscore and five thousand [185,000] : and when men arose early in the morning, behold, these were all dead bodies. So Sennacherib king of Assyria departed" (II Kings 19:35, 36a).

134

The final story about Hezekiah recorded in Kings tells how he was granted fifteen additional years of life in answer to his prayer. Isaiah the prophet also assured him that God would deliver Jerusalem from the Assyrians. (It is likely that this answer to prayer actually occurred before the siege of Jerusalem mentioned above.) As a sign, God made the shadow on the sundial of Ahaz to go backward.

Hezekiah's remarkable recovery brought messengers from the king of Babylon to congratulate him. Perhaps they also came to seek an alliance against Assyria. Hezekiah welcomed them and showed them his treasures. God condemned this action through Isaiah the prophet. He declared that all these treasures would be taken to Babylon. Here we see the importance of ordering all our actions rightly. Even the godly Hezekiah was partly responsible for the Babylonian captivity.

Return to Idolatry

When Hezekiah died, his son Manasseh ascended the throne. The reign of Manasseh was a long one — fifty-five years — but it was one of great wickedness. Not only did he restore the idolatry of his grandfather Ahaz, but he "shed innocent blood very much, till he had filled Jerusalem from one end to another" (II Kings 21:16).

As a result of Manasseh's sins, God declared through a prophet, "Behold, I bring such evil upon Jerusalem and Judah, that whosoever heareth of it, both his ears shall tingle. And I will stretch over Jerusalem the line of Samaria, and the plummet of the house of Ahab; And I will wipe Jerusalem as a man wipeth a dish, wiping it and turning it upside down" (II Kings 21:12, 13). The people of Judah would be punished as Israel had been punished.

We must remember that the people of Judah were guilty along with Manasseh. He may have permitted and encouraged idolatry, but they engaged in it. The nation of Judah would not have gone down to captivity if the people themselves had been faithful to Jehovah. But they were ever prone to follow the evil example of wicked kings.

The writer of Chronicles tells us that Manasseh was carried into Babylon as a captive, and there repented of his sins. As a result of this repentance, God caused him to be released and restored to his throne. After this he tried to undo some of his wrongs. But the author of Kings must have considered this unimportant. Manasseh's later repentance did not undo the results of his early wickedness.

Manasseh was followed by his son Amon, who ruled two years. He walked in the path of his wicked father, and led Judah down the road to destruction.

A National Reform

After Amon's death Josiah received the throne of Judah. Only eight years old when crowned, Josiah became one of Judah's best kings. At first he was guided by older men, but when he began to rule alone he started a great reform. He ordered the temple repaired, since the preceding kings had allowed it to fall into disrepair. During the repair work, a copy of the law of God was found. When this was read to the king it sparked a great reformation.

Josiah, aware that Judah had not obeyed this law, sent messengers to Huldah the prophetess. He wished to know from Jehovah what would result from this disregard for God's law. God's answer is instructive. There is no promise that the nation will be spared. The curses which God had pronounced upon His people if they were disobedient are to be experienced by Judah. The sincere repentance of king Josiah only brings the promise that the punishment will not come in his day.

Josiah led the people in a great reformation. The law was read to all the people, that they might know how to live before God. Then the king began removing all the signs of idolatry. Not only in Jerusalem was this done. Josiah even went into Israel. (There was no king in Israel now. The Captivity had already taken place.) At Bethel Josiah fulfilled the words which the prophet had spoken to Jeroboam (I Kings 13:2). He burned bones on the altar and defiled it. The heathen priests were killed. Then Josiah led the people in a great Passover celebration.

The Pangs of Death

The reforms of Josiah did not touch the hearts of the people. There was outward worship of Jehovah, but their hearts were still idolatrous. They still walked in the sinful ways of Manasseh. For centuries God had preserved Judah by giving her godly kings. But Josiah was the last one. He died in battle against Pharaoh-necoh, king of Egypt. Jehoahaz succeeded his father. He reigned only three months, and then was taken captive into Egypt, where he died.

The king of Egypt put Jehoiakim on the throne. He too was wicked. In 606 B.C., three years after his accession, Nebuchadnezzar, king of Babylon, came to Jerusalem and plundered it. He also carried away some captives. This was the first part of the Babylonian captivity. Jehoiakim was allowed to remain on the throne as a vassal king. But he rebelled against Nebuchadnezzar.

Jehoiakim died and Jehoiachin received the throne. He reigned only three months, for the Babylonians came because of his father's rebellion. Jehoiachin was taken captive into Babylon, and many of the upper classes with him. This second captivity took place in 597 B.C.

Nebuchadnezzar now put Zedekiah on the throne. But he, who had pledged his support to Nebuchadnezzar, rebelled. As a result the Babylonians laid siege to Jerusalem. After a terrible siege lasting three years, the city fell in 586 B.C. Zedekiah was captured, the city was burned completely, and all Judah was carried into captivity except the poorest people. They were left to cultivate the land.

A man named Gedaliah was appointed governor of those who remained. But after two months he was assassinated. Those who remained then fled to Egypt for fear of Nebuchadnezzar.

The book of Kings does not end with disaster. The author records that Jehoiachin, after thirty-seven years in prison, was given a place of honor in the Babylonian court. This is prophetic of what lies ahead for the people.

A Note about Prophets

We must not forget that God spoke to Judah during these dark days through His prophets. Zephaniah and Habakkuk belong to this period. Jeremiah, Ezekiel, and Daniel all belong to the time of captivity. Daniel was one of those deported in 606 B.C. Ezekiel was taken to Babylon in 597 B.C. and prophesied to the captives in Babylon. Jeremiah suffered through the destruction of Jerusalem, and was carried into Egypt with the fugitives.

CONCLUSION

We have come to the end of the covenant nation. Although Israel was established as the theocratic nation by God Himself, although God gave her a theocratic king to rule her, yet because of her constant apostasy God fulfilled the curses pronounced on disobedience. The decline and fall of Israel and Judah has been a black picture indeed.

But we need to note two facts. First, the history of God's people has not ended. In Israel and Judah there was a remnant that was true to Jehovah. And God had promised that this captivity would not be permanent. Although the theocratic nation would never rise again, this group would be the theocratic people from whom would come the great spiritual Kingdom of God.

Second, we need to recall again that God's purposes are never defeated. The decline and fall of the kingdoms was not a defeat for God. It was part of His plan. It was part of the preparation for the coming of Christ. The Captivity purified Israel as fire purifies fine metals. Idolatry disappeared in Israel. And other developments helped to pave the way for the golden era which lay ahead.

EXERCISES

Factual questions

1. What is the purpose of the third part of Kings?
2. What reforms did Hezekiah introduce? II Kings 18.
3. Why did Rabshakeh say that Jehovah could not deliver Jerusalem from the Assyrians? II Kings 18:26ff.

4. What did God say would happen to Sennacherib? II Kings 19:29ff.
5. How was this fulfilled? II Kings 19:35ff.
6. What sign was given to Hezekiah to show that he would recover? II Kings 20:8ff.
7. What sins did Manasseh commit? II Kings 21.
8. What was the result of his wickedness? II Kings 21:10ff.
9. What was Josiah's first act of reform? II Kings 22:3ff.
10. How did Josiah fight against idolatry? II Kings 23:4ff.
11. How did Josiah fulfill the prophecy of I Kings 13:2? II Kings 23:15ff.
12. How was Jehoiachin treated by the Babylonians? II Kings 24:10ff; 25:27ff.
13. How was Zedekiah punished? II Kings 25.
14. What happened to Gedaliah? II Kings 25:22ff.
15. Did the downfall of Judah end God's plans? Why?

Thought questions

1. Why was it wrong for Hezekiah to show his treasures to the Babylonian messengers? II Kings 20.
2. Trace the role that Assyria, Egypt, and Babylon played in the history of Judah in this period.
3. Why was Manasseh's reign a turning point in Judah's history?

Memory

1. Dates of Judah's three captivities and the name of the king ruling her at the time of each captivity.

Chapter 26

The Lesson of the Covenant Nation's History

Chronicles

INTRODUCTION

Historical Books in the Writings

You will remember that the Old Testament is divided into three sections — the Law, the Prophets, and the Writings. Thus far all the historical books that we have studied (with the possible exception of Ruth) have been from the Law or the Prophets. Chronicles, Esther, Ezra, Nehemiah, and Daniel are historical writings that belong to the third section of the canon.

The Writings contain all the inspired books that were not written by prophets. These historical books which we will study differ from those that we have studied in that they are non-prophetic. What is the difference between the prophetic and non-prophetic histories? The prophetic viewpoint takes in the whole sweep of the history of God's people. This does not mean that the prophet records everything that happens. But he selects his material from the whole of Israel's history, and uses that material to show how God is working out the development of His kingdom. The non-prophetic writers are more limited in their designs. They "take single parts out of the history of the people of God and treat those parts from individual points of view" (Keil).

We should not judge that this difference in purpose makes the non-prophetic histories inferior to the prophetic. Each has a function in God's revelation. Both are valuable. By including both, God has given us a better over-all picture of His kingdom. The prophetic writings may be compared to a picture taken from a high mountain. Such a picture enables us to understand the broad outlines of the area pictured. The non-prophetic writings are more like close-up pictures of interesting and important sections of that landscape. They present valuable details which the other picture does not show.

Chronicles

Chronicles, which like Samuel and Kings was originally one book, must have been written after the return from the Babylonian captivity.

The book ends with a brief record of the decree of Cyrus, king of Persia, which allowed the Jews to return to Jerusalem. This could not have been recorded before it happened. So we conclude that this book was written for Jews who had returned to Judah from the Exile.

Ezra begins with the same edict with which Chronicles closes. In addition, there are many similarities between the two books. Some scholars believe that both books were written by Ezra. Jewish tradition has always named him as the author of Chronicles. Certainly Ezra, who was a priest and a scribe, was a person well qualified for the task.

The author of Chronicles had access to many old documents. Some of these are named. These documents made it possible for one writing in the fifth century B.C. to relate accurately genealogies which go back to Adam and events which took place five hundred years before.

OUTLINE

I.	Genealogies	I Chronicles 1- 9
II.	The reign of David	I Chronicles 10-29
III.	The reign of Solomon	II Chronicles 1- 9
IV.	The history of Judah to the Exile	II Chronicles 10-36

ANALYSIS

Genealogies

The nine chapters of genealogies in Chronicles make dry reading for the average person. But these lists were given for a reason. In the first place they form a foundation for the rest of the book. They link Israel to the rest of the world. And the genealogies of the tribes show how they received their land as a heritage from Jehovah.

In the second place, these genealogies were tremendously important to the people who had returned from the Captivity. "The genealogies which occupy the first nine chapters had for their immediate object the resettling of the land according to the public records. Those who had returned from the Captivity were entitled to the lands formerly held in their own families. The genealogies showed the people's title to land and office" (Halley).

History of the Kingdom

Since the greater part of Chronicles is parallel to the books of Samuel and Kings, we do not want to repeat all that history. Rather, we should notice the differences between Chronicles and the prophetical histories. These differences will help us to understand why Chronicles was written.

1. The book of Chronicles does not record those incidents in the lives of the kings which are strictly personal. In the life of David, no mention is made of the years David spent as a fugitive from Saul. Nor is there any record of his sin against Uriah or of the troubles in his family which were the result of that sin.

2. The book of Chronicles emphasizes those incidents which are connected with faithfulness to the covenant, and especially those which are connected with the temple and its worship. It records the preparations that David made for building the temple, and his speech in which he called upon the people to aid in that task. It tells of the Levites and singers who were appointed by David to aid in the temple worship. It records the building of the temple in more detail. It emphasizes the ceremonies in the days of Solomon, Hezekiah, and Josiah. It enumerates the offerings which were brought. Time and again the worship in the temple is brought to the fore.

3. Chronicles utterly disregards the kingdom of Israel. The kings of Israel are mentioned only when they fight against or make alliances with the kings of Judah.

4. Those sins of Judah's kings which affected the nation are presented more fully in Chronicles. Kings does not mention the idolatry of Amaziah, but Chronicles does. This is also true of Uzziah's attempt to intrude into the priestly office by offering incense. In the opposite vein, the repentance and reforms of Manasseh are neglected in Kings, but found here.

PURPOSE

This description of differences brings us to the purpose of Chronicles. It is clear that the writer omitted many matters and added others. He must have had some basis on which the selection was made. What was it? The author of Chronicles has turned his attention to *those times* especially in which Israel's religion dominated the people and their leaders and brought them prosperity; and to *those men* who had endeavored to give a more permanent house for the worship of God, and to restore the true worship of Jehovah: and to *those events* in the history of worship which were important.

These things were emphasized in order to make clear to the returned exiles the lesson which should be learned from the past history of God's people. Faithfulness to God's covenant brought blessing. Faithfulness to God's covenant involved the proper use of the worship that God had ordained. So proper worship was necessary to receive God's blessing, and departing from this worship brought God's curse upon His people. This point Chronicles makes clear — the theocratic nation can be blessed only when God is her ruler, and when the Ruler of Israel is the object of her worship.

EXERCISES

Factual questions

1. Explain the difference between the prophetic and non-prophetic histories.

2. When was Chronicles written? By whom?

3. Why are the genealogical tables found in Chronicles?

4. Explain the main differences between Chronicles and the books of Samuel and Kings.

5. What is the purpose of Chronicles?

6. How did David prepare for the building of the temple? I Chron. 22:2ff.

7. What was the work of the Levites? I Chron. 23:24ff.

8. Where did the pattern of the temple come from? I Chron. 28:11ff.

9. What did the people contribute? I Chron. 29:6ff.

10. From whom did Asa seek help against Ethiopia? Against Israel? II Chon. 14:9 ff.; 16.

11. How was Jehoram punished for his idolatry? II Chron. 21:11ff.

12. What did Joash do when Jehoiada died? II Chron. 24:15ff.

13. How did Uzziah sin? II Chron. 26:16ff.

14. How was he punished? II Chron. 26:19ff.

15. Whom did Hezekiah invite to the Passover? Who came? II Chron. 30.

16. How did the revival under Hezekiah help the priests? II Chron. 31:2ff.

17. Trace briefly the history of Manasseh. II Chron. 33.

18. With what does Chronicles end? II Chron. 36:22ff.

Thought questions

1. Why do we have both Chronicles and the books of Samuel and Kings in the Old Testament?

2. List evidences from Chronicles that the author considered temple worship important.

3. Why does Chronicles ignore the kingdom of Israel?

Memory

1. Outline of Chronicles.

2. II Chronicles 7:14.

Chapter 27

God's Voice to His Covenant Nation

WHAT IS A PROPHET?

We have asked this question at various times in the course of our study of the Old Testament history. We have given the same answer each time. A prophet is a man who is called of God to receive God's word and communicate it to the people. There are three parts to this definition:

1. A prophet is called by God to his particular task.
2. A prophet receives a revelation from God.
3. A prophet is charged with the task of bringing the revelation he has received to the people.

All three of these ideas are necessary to the biblical idea of a prophet.

This definition may be considered a technical one. That is, it explains the precise meaning of the office of prophet. This office was very important in Israel. All the writers of the prophetic books were prophets in this technical sense. They had been called to the office of prophet. But we should recognize that the word "prophet" is sometimes used in a more popular sense. Abraham and Daniel are called prophets (Gen. 20:7; Matt. 24:15). Yet neither of these occupied the office of prophet.

THE HISTORY OF THE PROPHETS

The Early Prophets

Strictly speaking the office of prophet began in Samuel's time, but the idea of prophet goes back much further. We find it already in Abraham's time. There it seems to refer to one who has a close acquaintance with God. In Genesis 20:7 Abimelech is told to restore Abraham's wife, "for he is a prophet, and he shall pray for thee, and thou shalt live."

By the time of Moses the term appears to designate one who speaks for God. At this time there were prophets in Israel. But they were inferior to Moses, through whom God spoke most frequently. The difference is expressed in Numbers 12:6-8. "If there be a prophet among you, I Jehovah will make myself known unto him in a vision, I will speak with him in a dream. My servant Moses is not so; he is faithful in all my house: with him will I speak mouth to mouth, even manifestly, and not in dark speeches: and the form of Jehovah shall he behold." The difference was in directness and clarity of God's revelation. But He did speak through prophets as well as through Moses. That these prophets were the spiritual leaders of Israel is clear from the desire expressed by Moses, "Would that all Jehovah's people were prophets, that Jehovah would put his Spirit upon them" (Num. 11:29).

The Institution of the Prophetic Office

With Samuel something new occurred in Israel. A prophetic order was established. Samuel is often called the first of the prophets. That title is well given. He is the first of a line of prophets who continued throughout the rest of Israel's history as the theocratic nation. These men were prophets in the technical sense. They were called to the prophetic office, even as today God calls men to the office of minister of the gospel. These men were God's special servants, chosen by Him to be His ambassadors through whom He would make known His word.

What brought about this new prophetic movement? The institution of the prophetic office is closely connected with the institution of the office of king. The establishment of the monarchy in Israel is the occasion for the rise of the prophets. Samuel, the first of these prophets, was given the task of anointing Saul and David for the kingly office. The establishment of the monarchy gave rise to the office of prophet.

The connection between kings and prophets is important. That there is a connection is clear from the Old Testament history. The prophets appear before and address the kings far more than the people. Some of them, like Isaiah and Jeremiah, were in very close contact with the palace. But why? Because the kingdom in Israel was a theocratic kingdom. The kings of Israel were to be theocratic kings. When He established the kingdom, God did not thereby resign as ruler of Israel. He simply ruled through the kings. It was the duty of the theocratic kings to rule the people according to the will of God. And it was the duty of the prophets to set forth clearly what the will of God was.

The prophets were never servants of the kings. Both prophets and kings were servants of God. When the kings were truly theocratic, then the prophets acted as their counselors. Thus we see Nathan advising David, and Isaiah counseling Hezekiah. But when the kings forsook their theocratic task and sought to rule without God, the prophets did not hesitate to speak out boldly against them. What Ahab said about Micaiah ("He doth not prophesy good concerning me, but evil." I Kings 22:8) expresses the relation between the evil kings and the prophets.

The Change in the Prophetic Outlook

If we study the history of the prophets carefully, we will discover two different stages in the activity of the prophets. The first stage includes the earlier prophets, who did not write their messages. These prophets were interested in the erection and the maintenance of the theocratic kingdom. They helped the good kings, sounded the alarm against sin and apostasy, and called for repentance. They were the watchdogs of the theocratic kingdom. Their task was to preserve the existing order.

In the eighth century B.C. a new type of prophetic activity came to the foreground. This type is found in those prophets who wrote their messages as well as spoke them. Here we find a change of emphasis. There is still an urgent call to repentance. But these later prophets do not really expect that their call to repentance will be heeded. We find in their prophecies an increased emphasis on the judgment which will fall on the people of God. And they point beyond the judgment to a wondrous work of mercy. They point to a new era, to the dawning of a new day. Instead of preserving the existing order, the later prophets look forward to the establishment of a new and better order. More and more the finger of prophecy points to the coming of Jesus Christ.

THE MESSAGE OF THE PROPHETS

The various prophets all had different messages, each adapted to the needs of the audience. And yet there are several themes which run through all the messages of the prophets.

1. Jehovah is presented as the only living and true God, whose glory fills the heavens, but who is ever close to His people Israel.

2. The relationship between God and the people of Israel is always based on that covenant made at Sinai, by which God promised to be Israel's God.

3. The sin of Israel is considered as a breaking of the covenant relationship.

4. The result of this sin is judgment from God. But this is not final. There is also a restoration of God's people to His favor and the blessings of His covenant.

These themes are presented in many different ways. Differing figures of speech, differing expressions, and differing approaches are all to be found. And yet this same message underlies all the variety of the prophetic messages, because it is one God who speaks through them all.

EXERCISES

Factual questions

1. What are the three essential parts in the definition of a prophet?
2. In what ways is the word "prophet" used?
3. What were prophets like before the time of Samuel?

4. What brought about the institution of the prophetic office?

5. How was the work of the prophets related to the kings?

6. What two changes took place in the activity of the prophets?

7. What themes do the prophets develop?

Chapter 28

God's Prediction of His People's Future

Joel

INTRODUCTION

Author

Of Joel the prophet we know nothing except the little we can learn from his book. He identifies himself as the son of Pethuel. We infer from the frequent mention of Judah and Jerusalem that he prophesied in Jerusalem.

Date

To determine precisely when Joel prophesied is extremely difficult, since he does not supply much information about the time in which he lived and worked. But we are quite sure that he was the earliest of the writing prophets. Two facts point in that direction.

1. The Jews placed Joel, along with Hosea and Amos, at the beginning of the Minor Prophets. Although the order in the Minor Prophets is not strictly chronological, the books are grouped together in a rough chronological order. So the Jews (who were in a position to know) considered Joel to be an early prophet.

2. Joel is quoted frequently by the other prophets. This means that the prophecy of Joel was considered to be Scripture at the time when these men wrote. Since Amos (one of the earliest writing prophets) quotes Joel, Joel must have been written early.

While this does not give us an exact date, some reliable scholars think that Joel probably prophesied during the reign of Jehoash, king of Judah (836-797 B.C.).

PURPOSE

The ministry of Joel was intended to turn the sinful people of the southern kingdom back to God. To this end he showed them that God's judgments were intended to chastise, not to destroy. If His people would return to Him, God would abundantly bless them. For this reason the future blessings of God's people occupy an important place in Joel.

147

OUTLINE
I. The present plague of locusts   Joel 1: 1-2:27
II. The future blessing of Israel   Joel 2:28-3:21

ANALYSIS

The Plague of Locusts

The book of Joel begins with a description of a terrible plague of locusts. The prophet cries out, "Hear this, ye old men, and give ear, all ye inhabitants of the land. Hath this been in your days, or in the days of your fathers?" (Joel 1:2) Never, as far back as the traditions of the people go, has there been a locust plague such as this one. All men are affected by it, from the drunkards to the priests.

Some students of the Bible have thought that Joel is using the locust plague as a parable. That is, he is not describing a real plague of locusts. He is using the locusts as a symbol of the heathen nations. If this were so, then the whole prophecy would deal with the future. The "locust plague" would not actually take place until the Assyrians came down into Judah, in the days of King Hezekiah.

But Joel is describing something which is taking place at the time when he speaks. His language is that of a man who is talking to a people who are in actual distress. We are most likely correct if we take his words literally, as describing an actual plague of locusts.

The Day of Jehovah

Joel calls this plague the day of Jehovah. He also uses the phrase "days of Jehovah" to describe the final judgment of the nations (Joel 3). This phrase, which Joel introduces, becomes a common expression in the Bible. Other prophets use it. The New Testament writers use it also. And they give it the same meaning that it has in Joel 3. The day of Jehovah is the day of judgment, when God will judge the nations.

If the day of Jehovah is the day of God's judgment, which is still in the future, how can the plague of locusts be connected to it? To understand that we must learn about the "prophetic perspective." And perhaps we can best understand that if we use an illustration. If you stand on a plain, and look at a hill, behind which is a mountain, it will look as if the hill and the mountain are close to each other. The hill may even seem to be the first rise of the mountain. But when you climb the hill, you discover that between the hill and the mountain there are valleys and other hills. You were fooled because of your perspective. Now, we are not to think that the prophets were fooled. But in their prophecies they often ignore the valleys of time and look only at the hills and mountains of God's redemptive actions. So they bring together events which are actually separated in time.

In Joel we have an example of this prophetic perspective. The plague of locusts is the beginning of a series of events, actually far separated in time, which culminate in the final judgment of God. Joel does not show the lapse of time. He simply shows how they are connected. After all, prophecy is primarily intended to tell *what* God is going to do, not *when* He will do it.

The Results of the Plague

To Joel, the plague of locusts was a judgment from God. And so he preached. He called the people, one and all, to a solemn assembly where they might pray to God for deliverance from this plague.

"Then was Jehovah jealous for his land, and had pity on his people" (Joel 2:18). Through Joel He gave a promise that He would destroy the locusts and bless the land so that it would produce again. The people would have plenty, and would know that Jehovah is indeed their God.

The Promise of Pentecost

This blessing leads to the promise of a greater blessing. God promises to pour out His Spirit upon all flesh, so that they will prophesy. He will do great wonders in heaven and earth before the great day of Jehovah comes. And at that time, "whosoever shall call on the name of Jehovah shall be delivered" (Joel 2:32).

This prophecy was quoted by Peter on the day of Pentecost (Acts 2:17-21). He declared that this prophecy was fulfilled at that time. Not all of it, of course. The signs and wonders in heaven and earth will come just before the day of Jehovah. But God did send His Spirit. And He did open the way of salvation to all who call upon Him.

The Final Judgment

This promise leads Joel to another prophecy. God will judge the nations. Joel speaks in figurative terms. But the thought is clear. All those who oppress God's people will be judged. And God will bless His people with abundant blessings. The day of Jehovah will mean judgment upon the heathen, but it will be the fullness of blessing for the people of God.

EXERCISES

Factual questions

1. Give two reasons why Joel is thought to be the earliest of the Latter Prophets.
2. What is the purpose of the book of Joel?
3. List five statements from Joel 1 which show how bad the locust plague was.
4. What is prophetic perspective?
5. To what does the prophet compare the locusts? Joel 2:4-11.
6. How does Joel picture the judgment of the heathen? Joel 3:9ff.
7. How does Joel picture the blessing of God's people? Joel 3:18ff.

Thought question
1. How was Joel 2:28-32 fulfilled on Pentecost?

Memory
1. Outline of Joel.
2. Joel 2:28, 29.

Chapter 29

God's Denunciation of Israel's Sins

Amos

INTRODUCTION

Author

The book was written by the prophet Amos, whose name it also
bears. He was from Tekoa, a small town about five miles southeast
of Bethlehem, in the kingdom of Judah. He was by occupation a
shepherd and a dresser of sycamore trees. Previous to the call to
bring these prophecies to Israel he was not a prophet, nor one of
those known as "the sons of the prophets." He prophesied to the
people of the northern kingdom during the reign of Uzziah, king of
Judah, and Jeroboam II, king of Israel. The book was written more
than two years after the prophecies were spoken (Amos 1:1).

PURPOSE

Amos was sent to the kingdom of Israel. The Israelites were a
people who had departed from the true worship of Jehovah, who
worshiped the golden calves made by Jeroboam I, who lived in
wickedness and violence, and who yet thought that they were safe
from calamity because they were the chosen people of God. It was
the purpose of Amos' prophetic ministry to destroy this illusion by
warning of the judgment of God which would be visited on them
because of their sins.

OUTLINE

	I.	God's judgment against the nations	Amos 1,2
	II.	God's judgment against Israel	Amos 3-6
	III.	Visions of the coming judgment	Amos 7-9

ANALYSIS

God's Judgment Against the Nations

Amos begins his prophecy with a quotation from Joel. "Jehovah
will roar from Zion, and utter his voice from Jerusalem; and the pas-
tures of the shepherds shall mourn, and the top of Carmel shall wither"
(Amos 1:2; also see Joel 3:16). With this introduction Amos begins to

151

predict the woes that God will bring upon the nations. This section is a piece of practical psychology. He begins with those nations farthest away from Israel. Then he mentions the nearer nations, which are also distantly related to Israel. He comes then to Judah — Israel's sister nation and southern neighbor. As Amos spoke of God's judgment on one after another of Israel's traditional enemies, the people must have shaken their heads in agreement. Even the judgment against Judah was agreeable to them. But step by step Amos draws closer to Israel itself. Finally he boldly denounces the sins of his audience and announces the Exile which will be their punishment. "Thus saith Jehovah: For three transgressions of Israel, yea, for four, I will not turn away the punishment thereof; because they have sold the righteous for silver, and the needy for a pair of shoes — they that pant after the dust of the earth on the head of the poor, and turn aside the way of the meek: and a man and his father go unto the same maiden, to profane my holy name: and they lay themselves down beside every altar upon clothes taken in pledge; and in the house of their God they drink the wine of such as have been fined" (Amos 2:6-8).

God's Judgment Against Israel

Amos declares boldly what God has decreed. The punishment will be so severe that only a remnant will escape. "Thus saith Jehovah: As the shepherd rescueth out of the mouth of the lion two legs, or a piece of an ear, so shall the children of Israel be rescued that sit in Samaria in the corner of a couch, and on the silken cushions of a bed" (Amos 3:12). This punishment comes because they have not returned to Jehovah. He has chastised them for their sins time after time, but never have they repented. Thus their final punishment must come.

Visions of Coming Judgment

In the last section of Amos we find five visions which picture the judgments which are coming upon Israel. The plague of locusts and the fire which devours the great deep symbolize the final judgment. Both of these visions picture the terrible destructiveness of that judgment. But God's mercy is also pictured. After each of these visions the prophet prays for his people. And God promises to spare them.

The next two judgments represent the captivity of Israel by Assyria. Here there is no intercession by the prophet, nor any promise that God will spare Israel. The vision of the plumb line signifies that God has drawn the line of judgment in the midst of His people. He will no longer spare Israel. Even the royal family will be destroyed. The basket of summer fruit shows that Israel is ripe for judgment.

The final vision, the breaking of the temple upon the heads of the people, illustrates again that God will bring judgment upon Israel.

And yet this is not the end of Amos' prophecy. Jehovah is still the covenant God, faithful to all His promises. He promises to "raise up the tabernacle of David that is fallen" (Amos 9:11). He will again show mercy upon His people. This promise is quoted in Acts 15:16-18 by James, the leader of the Jerusalem Council. He quotes it in order to prove that God has prophesied that the Gentiles will have a place in His church. Therefore we know that this promise of God has been fulfilled through the work of our Lord Jesus Christ. This is a characteristic that is not uncommon in the prophets. When they pronounce judgment upon the covenant nation, they also announce blessings that will come through Christ. In this way they remind the reader that the destruction of the covenant nation will not end the Kingdom of God. The theocracy will continue. More than that, it will attain new heights of glory.

EXERCISES

Factual questions

1. Who was Amos? When and where did he prophesy?
2. What is the purpose of the book of Amos?
3. Against what nations does Amos prophesy in Amos 1 and 2?
4. What chastisements has God brought upon Israel in the past? Amos 4:6ff.
5. Describe those "that are at ease in Zion." Amos 6.
6. For what social sins does Amos condemn Israel? Amos 5:10-13; 8:4-6.
7. What visions did Amos receive as symbols of the coming judgment? Amos 7-9.
8. What does each vision teach?
9. When was the final prophecy of Amos fulfilled?

Thought questions

1. Why does God hate the feasts and solemn assemblies of Israel? Amos 5:21.
2. How do Amos 1:2; 3:8; 3:12 reflect the background of Amos' former occupation?
3. Why are God's people punished for their sins more severely than other people? Amos 3:2.

Memory

1. Outline of Amos.
2. Amos 9:11, 12.

Chapter 30

God's Indictment of His Unfaithful People

Hosea

Author

The author of this book is Hosea, the son of Beeri. Of him we know nothing except that which can be learned from his book.

The Times of Hosea

Hosea tells us that he prophesied in the reigns of Uzziah, Jotham, Ahaz, and Hezekiah, kings of Judah, and Jeroboam II, king of Israel. Jeroboam II must have been the first king of Israel in whose reign he prophesied. But his ministry did not end there. He probably prophesied until the time of the fall of Samaria. His ministry in the northern kingdom paralleled that of Isaiah in the kingdom of Judah.

The ministry of Hosea (and of Amos, whose work began about the same time as Hosea's) began shortly after the death of Elisha. By Hosea and Amos God's call to the northern kingdom was continued. At this time Israel was in a period of prosperity and grandeur. Jeroboam II had extended her borders from the Dead Sea to the Euphrates River. But this was also a time of great sin. The outward splendor of the times was a cloak for the inward corruption that was eating at Israel's heart. Despite the present prosperity, the nation was deserving of judgment. And that judgment was beginning to take shape. On the eastern horizon Assyria was beginning to grow into a world empire. And Assyria was the rod that God would use to punish His unfaithful people.

PURPOSE

The northern tribes had been given many opportunities to return to Jehovah. But they had continued in sin, especially the sinful worship of the golden calves. To them had come Amos with words of judgment. Hosea brings them a message of God's love. In the light of that love, Israel's unfaithfulness is exceedingly sinful. That sin must be punished. And yet after the punishment will come blessing. The punishment will be a time of refining, and then God's mercy will again be shown.

OUTLINE

ANALYSIS

God told Hosea to marry a very sinful woman, a harlot, and have children who would be known as "children of harlotry." These children were given symbolic names. The first was named Jezreel. This was a sign that God would destroy the family of Jehu, which was then ruling. The second child was named Lo-ruhamah, which means "that hath not obtained mercy." This was God's message that "I will no more have mercy upon the house of Israel, that I should in any wise pardon them" (Hos. 1:6). And when the third child was born God said, "Call his name Lo-ammi [meaning "not my people"] : for ye are not my people, and I will not be your God" (Hos. 1:9). The three children thus became God's message to Israel.

This object lesson leads to a strong condemnation of Israel's sin. Israel is personified as a faithless wife who commits adultery continually in spite of her husband's love. Behind this figure of speech lies a thought which runs through Hosea. Israel is married to God by the covenant at Mount Sinai. She is pledged to be faithful to Him. So all idolatry is adultery. The idolatrous Israelites, who have never put aside the golden calves of Jeroboam I, but have even worshiped the gods of the heathen, are portrayed by the adulterous wife.

This figure provides a beautiful background on which God's mercy is displayed. God is the loving husband who is willing to receive the adulterous wife back into His love. He promises to receive His people again, even though they must be punished for their sins. Hosea is also commanded to symbolize this. He is told to love an adulterous woman. He buys her as his wife for half the price of a slave. Many scholars believe that this is the same woman Hosea married as recorded in Hosea 1. But now he does not immediately take this woman as his wife. For a time she is isolated. This is to symbolize the captivity which must overtake Israel before God's mercy will again be manifested.

Was Hosea's Marriage Real?

There are two schools of thought about Hosea's marriage. Some scholars believe that he actually married a harlot, or that he married a wife who became a harlot after her marriage. Others believe that this is a prophecy or vision which was told to the people but never actually occurred.

There are good reasons why some scholars have taken this literally. It reads like history. Even the names of his wife and children are given. One writer says, "The whole account bears the stamp of reality;

indeed, only as real history would the prophet's words have any effect. For his domestic experience served as a living mirror of Israel's unfaithful relation to Jehovah" (Robinson).

Nevertheless, there is another side to the story. There are problems raised by this marriage that cannot be ignored. Would not the prophet lose his reputation as a servant of God by marrying a harlot? And, if the children were born about a year apart, would not the lessons of their names lose its effect because of the lapse of time? These questions, and others of a technical nature, have caused many scholars to conclude that the marriage is an allegory, not an actual fact.

In both views the lesson of the marriage is the same. It demonstrates the great love of God for His people, and the exceedingly great sinfulness of their unfaithfulness to Him. It provides a backdrop for the message which Hosea proclaims.

The Sins of Israel

The latter section of Hosea consists of prophecies uttered by the prophet. There is no clear division of material here. Hosea is more emotional than logical. But he points to certain sins of Israel. Robinson lists the following sins that Hosea condemns:

1. Lack of knowledge — "My people are destroyed for lack of knowledge" (Hos. 4:6).

2. Pride — "And the pride of Israel doth testify to his face" (Hos. 5:5).

3. Instability — "For your goodness is as a morning cloud, and as the dew that goeth early away" (Hos. 6:4).

4. Worldliness — "Ephraim, he mixeth himself among the peoples; Ephraim is a cake not turned" (Hos. 7:8).

5. Corruption — "They have deeply corrupted themselves, as in the days of Gibeah" (Hos. 9:9).

6. Backsliding — "My people are bent on backsliding from me" (Hos. 11:7).

7. Idolatry — "And now they sin more and more, and have made them molten images of their silver, even idols according to their own understanding" (Hos. 13:2).

These sins are like the unfaithfulness of Hosea's wife. And idolatry is the worst, for it is spiritual adultery. It is breaking God's covenant with Israel.

God's Judgment and Mercy

As the picture of Hosea's marriage did not omit a beautiful portrayal of God's love, so the message that Hosea preached included mercy as well as judgment. The emphasis is necessarily on judgment. Israel's sins must bring judgment from a righteous God. "For they sow the wind, and they shall reap the whirlwind" (Hos. 8:7). God declares, "They shall not return into the land of Egypt; but the Assyrian shall be their king, because they refused to return to me" (Hos. 11:5). And yet even in judgment the mercy of God shines forth. "How shall I give thee up, Ephraim? how shall I cast thee off, Israel? . . . my heart is turned within me, my compassions are kindled together" (Hos. 11:8).

It is on this love of God for His unfaithful people that Hosea bases his call to repentance. Hosea 14:1-3 contains a beautiful plea to Israel to repent. And after this comes a final promise of forgiveness from the God who loves His people so much (Hos. 14:4-8).

EXERCISES

Factual questions

1. In what kind of era did Hosea live?
2. What is the purpose of the book of Hosea?
3. Explain the symbolic meaning of the names given to Hosea's children. Hos. 1.
4. Explain the two views about Hosea's marriage.
5. What does the marriage teach?
6. What sins of Israel does Hosea condemn?
7. How is Israel to be punished? Hos. 11:5ff.
8. What will happen after Israel is punished? Hos. 11:10ff.; 14:4ff.

Thought question

1. Trace the history of the theocratic nation as it is symbolically portrayed in Hosea 1-3.

Memory

1. Outline of Hosea.
2. Hosea 14:7

Chapter 31

God's Promise of Judah's Deliverance

Isaiah

INTRODUCTION

Author

The first verse of this book states that it is "the vision of Isaiah the son of Amoz, which he saw concerning Judah and Jerusalem, in the days of Uzziah, Jotham, Ahaz, and Hezekiah, kings of Judah." This verse is the introduction to the entire book. It sets forth the statement that Isaiah, the prophet of Jehovah who lived in the eighth century B.C., wrote the prophecies that this book contains.

The View of the Higher Critics

For twenty-five centuries practically no one thought to question this statement. But about two hundred years ago the Higher Critics began to raise many questions about the Bible. The belief that Isaiah 1:1 is true, and that the prophet Isaiah really wrote this book, was seriously questioned. At first there was only one chapter that was thought to be the product of another author. But soon the entire second section of Isaiah (chap. 40-66) was said to be the product of a great unknown prophet who lived in Babylon during the time of the Exile. Since nothing was known about him, this prophet came to be called Second Isaiah. Critics acclaimed him as the greatest prophet who ever lived.

At the end of the last century the Critics decided that Second Isaiah had not written all of chapters 40-66. Now it was claimed that he had written only chapters 40-55. The rest of the book was written by a man who lived in Judah during the time of Nehemiah. He came to be called Third Isaiah. Many Higher Critics have followed this point of view. But no theory has been able to answer all the questions. No theory has been accepted by all the Critics. The Critics violently disagree with one another. But they all agree that Isaiah was not written by one man. They view it as a collection rather than a single work.

The Biblical Evidence

We have seen that the Higher Critics are willing to disregard the statement of Isaiah 1:1 concerning authorship. Do they do this because other parts of the Bible support their theories? No, indeed. On the contrary, all the biblical evidence points to the prophet Isaiah as the author of the book that bears his name. Over twenty times the New Testament quotes from this book and names Isaiah as the author of the quoted words. The passage in John 12:37-41 is especially significant. In this passage John says that the unbelief of the people is a fulfillment of Isaiah 53:1, which he calls "the word of Isaiah the prophet." The reason for this unbelief is also found in Isaiah 6:10. Then John adds, "These things said Isaiah, because he saw his glory; and he spake of him" (John 12:41). John quotes from "Isaiah" and "Second Isaiah" and says that the same man, Isaiah, spoke these words. The New Testament knows only one author of the book of Isaiah. That author is the prophet of the same name.

Why the Critical View?

With this evidence before us, we might well ask why the Critics think it necessary to devise theories which multiply the authors of the book. The Critics have several rules of interpretation to which they would point. But one main rule underlies all the rest — prediction is impossible. The Critics do not believe that a prophet can foretell the future. Since the second part of Isaiah is clearly a portrayal of future events, they do not believe that Isaiah could have written it. The author must have been a man who lived much later. He did not write actual prophecy. He recorded events which had already happened as if they were still to happen in the future.

Why do the Critics deny that the prophets can predict the future? Because they do not believe that the Bible is the Word of God. They believe that the prophets wrote their own ideas. Of course, no man can foretell the future. And since they think that the book of Isaiah is the work of man, they do not believe that the prophet Isaiah could have written the predictive passages.

The Important Question

This brings us to a very important question. What is the Old Testament? Is it truly God's Word? Is God the author of it? The Christian Church has always insisted that the whole Bible is the Word of God. God is the true author, though He used men to record His Word. To this the New Testament testifies (II Tim. 3:16; II Peter 1:21). And the Holy Spirit, who dwells in the hearts of all God's people, convinces us that the Bible is the Word of God. Such conviction the Higher Critics seem to lack.

It is important for us to remember the real difference between those who believe that Isaiah wrote the book of Isaiah and those who do not. The view of the Higher Critics is often presented as if it were the only scholarly view. Anyone who believes that Isaiah is actually the author is scorned, and considered to be uneducated. But that is not necessarily the case. The Higher Critics' view is not the most scholarly. It does not face all the facts. It does not consider that the Bible is the Word of God. When the Holy Spirit witnesses to us that the Bible is God's Word, then we will gladly confess that the New Testament statements about this book are true. We will believe that God spoke through the prophet Isaiah.

Isaiah and His Times

Isaiah's ministry in the kingdom of Judah paralleled that of Hosea in the kingdom of Israel. However, Isaiah apparently lived and prophesied longer than did Hosea. When Isaiah began his ministry the nation was at the height of its prosperity. The reign of Uzziah was the closest approach to the glory of Solomon that Judah had ever experienced. But the outward prosperity was no sign of inward prosperity. The spiritual health of the nation was none too good. While Uzziah and Jotham reigned, the leadership exercised by these kings held the forces of evil and decay in check. But when Ahaz came to the throne, he led the people of Judah away from Jehovah. He also drew Judah into an alliance with Assyria that was to have disastrous consequences. When Hezekiah came to the throne he sought to undo his father's folly and lead the people back to God. He was partly successful. But Ahaz had set in motion some forces that could not be reversed. The latter days of Isaiah's ministry were quite a contrast to the prosperity which marked the beginning of his work. Judah was declining, and God's judgment upon her sin was beginning to appear on the horizon.

OUTLINE

    I. The sins of God's people   Isaiah 1-12
    II. The judgments of God   Isaiah 13-27
    III. The future of Judah   Isaiah 28-35
    IV. The crises of Hezekiah's reign   Isaiah 36-39
    V. The blessings of God's church   Isaiah 40-66

PURPOSE

The whole book of Isaiah teaches the grand lesson that salvation is completely a work of grace. The first chapter of Isaiah speaks of redemption. "Come now, and let us reason together, saith Jehovah: though your sins be as scarlet, they shall be as white as snow; though they be red like crimson, they shall be as wool" (Isa. 1:18). That theme is enlarged upon throughout the entire book. At times redemption is expressed in national terms, as salvation from hostile nations. But more often redemption is the salvation of man from the penalty and power of sin. Especially in the latter part of Isaiah, the redemption of God's church is the chief subject of the prophet's message.

ANALYSIS

The prophecies of Isaiah cannot be catalogued strictly according to subjects. They are like sermons. As a sermon on sin may and should contain material about salvation from sin, so Isaiah's prophecies include sin, judgment, and salvation. In a sense, many of these prophecies may be considered as sermons preached to the people of Judah. But a good sermon has a theme. And Isaiah's prophecies have various themes. On the basis of the themes we can catalogue his prophecies. But we should remember that each section will also contain material on other topics.

The Sins of Judah

The first section of Isaiah deals with the sins of the people of Judah. Isaiah 1 is an introduction to the prophecies of Isaiah. It also introduces us to the sins of Judah. Two sins receive special attention: Judah's refusal to repent when chastened by God, and Judah's formal continuance of religious ceremonies when the hearts of the people were far from God.

Isaiah does not hesitate to spell out the sins by which Judah has provoked God. In addition to lack of repentance and formalism in worship, he points to the importation of foreign customs (Isa. 2:5, 6), idolatry (Isa. 2:8), oppression of the poor (Isa. 3:13-15), love of luxurious finery by the women (Isa. 3:16), greediness (Isa. 5:8), and love of strong drink (Isa. 5:11, 12).

Isaiah does not stand apart from the people in their sins. His vision (Isa. 6) in which he sees the holiness of the Lord, includes also his confession of his personal sins and his responsibility for the sins of the nation. Thus, when he is told to prophesy to people who will not hear, but will continue in sin until God's judgment falls, he is able to proclaim God's word with a sympathetic heart.

Prophecies of the Messiah

To Isaiah was given the blessed privilege of prophesying about the coming of the Messiah of God more than any of the other prophets. His message included both predictions about the Messiah Himself and descriptions of the glorious Messianic Age that He would usher in. These are found throughout the book of Isaiah. But the reign of Ahaz appears to have been a time when many such prophecies were given to Isaiah to proclaim. The peculiar circumstances of that time provided an apt occasion for such prophecies. During Ahaz' reign Syria and Israel united to fight Assyria. When Judah would not join them they turned against her. God sent Isaiah to Ahaz with messages of assurance that Judah would be spared. As a sign to the unbelieving king God gave the wonderful prophecy of the virgin birth of the Christ (Isa. 7:14-17). But Ahaz preferred to trust in man, and called for help from the king of Assyria. This led to other prophecies of punishment for Judah, of the Assyrian captivity of Israel, and of the final destruction of Assyria. Among these are found prophecies of the birth and reign of the Messiah. Isaiah 9:1-7 is a beautiful example of such messianic prophecies. It emphasizes the kingly work of Christ. It shows that God's kingdom will in the future come to its perfect expression when God sends the eternal King to be born as a man.

Judgment on the Nations

Isaiah is primarily interested in Judah — her sins, her judgment, her salvation. But the age in which Isaiah lived was like our own. No nation lived to itself. Judah was involved with many other nations, some of whom were her enemies. Isaiah's prophecies include oracles of judgment against these nations.

What the Future Holds

The prophecies of Isaiah often speak of the future. Sometimes this is done in general terms, as in Isaiah 24-27. In these chapters we have a picture of the judgments which God sends upon the earth. In these judgments the people of God are involved. But they are judged in order that they may be purified from their sins. On the other hand, the judgments which visit the enemies of God destroy them completely.

The future is also presented in more concrete terms, as in the prophecy in Isaiah 28-35. Here the relations of Judah and Assyria are discussed. Assyria was the dominant power of the day. Judah feared that Assyria would attack her. There was a party in Judah that counseled seeking aid from Egypt. Isaiah denounces the folly and sin of trusting in Egypt. He announces that Assyria will indeed come against Judah, but will be destroyed by the hand of God. While the enemies of God's people face total destruction, the future of the people of God is pictured in glowing terms. "And the ransomed of Jehovah shall return, and come with singing unto Zion; and everlasting joy shall be upon their heads: they shall obtain gladness and joy, and sorrow and sighing shall flee away" (Isa. 35:10).

The Reign of Hezekiah

Isaiah 36-39 is a historical section which forms a bridge between the two sections of Isaiah. These chapters tell of two events, both of which are also recorded in Kings. The destruction of Sennacherib's army is related first, probably to illustrate the fulfillment of the prophecy against Assyria contained in the previous section. Then the story of Hezekiah's sickness is related. This probably occurred before the invasion of Sennacherib, but it is told last so that it can form an introduction to the second part of the book. Isaiah 40-66 assumes that Israel is in captivity in Babylon and will be delivered. But that captivity had not yet occurred when Isaiah wrote. So the story of Hezekiah's sickness is told, with emphasis on the messenger from Babylon. Chapter 39 ends with a prediction of the Babylonian captivity, and thus prepares for the rest of Isaiah.

EXERCISES

Factual questions

1. Who, according to the Critics, is "Second Isaiah"? "Third Isaiah"?
2. What does the New Testament say about the authorship of the book of Isaiah?
3. Why do the Critics question the authorship of Isaiah?
4. In what kind of times did Isaiah live?
5. What is the purpose of the book of Isaiah?
6. Write out six verses from Isaiah 1-5 that point out Israel's sins.
7. What was Isaiah commissioned to proclaim? Isa. 6:6ff.
8. What was the sign of the virgin-born child intended to teach Ahaz? Isa. 7:1-17.
9. What titles are given to the Messiah? Isa. 9:1-7.
10. How was Hezekiah responsible for the Babylonian captivity? Isa. 39.

Thought questions

1. Why is the Higher Critics' view of the authorship of Isaiah a denial of the inspiration of the Bible?
2. How would you feel about receiving a call to preach like that which Isaiah received in Isaiah 6?

Memory

1. Outline of Isaiah.
2. Isaiah 1:18.

Chapter 32

God's Promise of Messianic Salvation

Isaiah

INTRODUCTION

Isaiah's Beautiful Message

The second section of Isaiah (chap. 40-66) ranks among the most sublime literature in all the Sacred Writings. For breadth of vision, for beauty of expression, and for presentation of New Testament truths these chapters from Isaiah's pen stand out among all the Old Testament writings. It is still true, for example, that we go to Isaiah when we want a clear, beautiful, expressive description of the meaning of Calvary. Isaiah, more than any other Old Testament writer, speaks directly to the New Testament Christian.

Because there is so much of the New Testament in this part of Isaiah, there is a temptation to assume that these chapters have no connection with the times in which Isaiah lived. Nothing could be more misleading. These prophecies of Isaiah play an important part in the development of the theocracy. They are a link between Israel in the days of Hezekiah and the Church of Jesus Christ.

Isaiah's Pertinent Message

Joseph A. Alexander points out four sins of which the people of Judah were guilty—idolatry, formalism, spiritual pride, and unbelief. The first two of these sins had to do with the ritual of worship. Idolatry was a perversion of the worship of the true God. Formalism was a misuse of the ritual arising from the idea that God would accept anyone who carried out the ritual, even if his heart was not in it. The second set of sins revolved around the fact that Israel was the covenant nation. Spiritual pride was evidenced by the prevalent belief that all Jews would be saved and all Gentiles damned. The particular form of unbelief that was very common was the thought that the Kingdom of God was doomed to destruction. Men saw that Israel must be punished for her sins. They thought that the Kingdom of God was inseparably connected to the covenant nation, and that God's purposes were being defeated by the sins of His people.

The latter prophecies of Isaiah deal with these four sins and errors. Both idolatry and formalism are denounced, and the punishment of those who indulge in them is set forth. And throughout the section there is clear expression of the fact that apostate Israel will be punished, but the true worshipers of God will be blessed. Not only so, but the fact that the Kingdom will be separated from the nation when the Messiah comes is expressed, and is presented as the source of great blessing for God's people.

Isaiah's Messianic Message

This section of Isaiah meets the needs of the people of Isaiah's time. But at the same time it looks forward to the blessings of the Messiah's reign. In this way Isaiah is God's instrument in preparing His people for the great change that was to take place in the theocracy. In Isaiah's time the nation was beginning its final decline and the Exile was clearly visible on the horizon. The Spirit of God enabled Isaiah to look beyond the Exile and to bring to his people the glorious picture of the Messianic Age.

ANALYSIS

The Salvation of True Israel

This passage, beginning with the beautiful "Comfort ye, comfort ye my people, saith your God" of Isaiah 40:1, speaks to the true Church, the spiritual Israel within the sinful nation. The comfort of the Church lies in the coming of God, who will "come as a mighty one, and his arm will rule for him . . . He will feed his flock like a shepherd . . . and will gently lead those that have their young" (Isa. 40:10-11). This God is the one before whom all the nations are as nothing, and the idols of the heathen as less than nothing. Therefore Israel may rest assured that, although the heathen should seek to overthrow God's church, they shall not succeed. Israel's comfort lies in the assuring voice of God, "Thou art my servant, I have chosen thee and not cast thee away; fear thou not, for I am with thee; be not dismayed, for I am thy God; I will strengthen thee; yea, I will help thee; yea, I will uphold thee with the right hand of my righteousness" (Isa. 41:9b, 10).

In Isaiah 42 we learn of the Servant of Jehovah. He is here introduced as the Saviour of mankind, whose work will be accomplished with the greatest patience and tenderness. But He is also the head of Israel, and the sinful nation has been unfaithful to its head. Therefore, the prophet turns to denunciation of Israel's sin. But he does not stop here. For the nation of Israel contains that spiritual Israel that is the delight of Jehovah, and so the prophet breaks out with promises of protection and deliverance. "When thou passest through the waters, I will be with thee; and through the rivers, they shall not overflow thee. . ." (Isa. 43 :2). As God once delivered the Iraelites from Egypt, now He will destroy Babylon for their sake. But above all He will redeem them from sin. "I, even I, am he that blotteth out thy transgressions for mine own sake; and I will not remember thy sins" (Isa. 43:25).

The Exile and Restoration

In Isaiah 44-48 the restoration from the Babylonian exile is clearly in view. We have in these chapters a marvelous prediction that Cyrus is to be the shepherd of God who will "perform all [Jehovah's] pleasure, even saying of Jerusalem, She shall be built; and of the temple, Thy foundation shall be laid" (Isa. 44:28). Even the heathen rulers are under the sovereign hand of God. As a sign of God's sovereignty the defeat of Babylon's idols and the fall of that great and wicked city are predicted. These predictions are held before the sinful nation to call her to repentance.

But since God has uttered predictions before, and Israel would not hearken, and since Israel now will not turn from her sin, God will put her in the fire of adversity. Israel will suffer because of her sins, but will come out of exile with rejoicing.

The Servant of Jehovah

In Isaiah 42 we were introduced to the figure of the Servant of Jehovah, who will save mankind. In Isaiah 49-53 this figure is brought to the fore several times. Each time we learn more about Him, until the fullest description of the Servant and His work is presented in Isaiah 53. In Isaiah 49 the Servant is told by God that His work will not be limited to the salvation of Israel. He is also to be a light to the Gentiles, "that thou mayest be my salvation unto the end of the earth" (Isa. 49:6). In Isaiah 50 the Servant speaks of His sufferings, but with no indication of the reason for those sufferings. This leads us to the greatest "Servant" passage — Isaiah 52:13-53:12. This passage is a song, consisting of five stanzas of three verses each. Each stanza is essential to the full understanding of the passage. The thought may be best understood if we set forth the teaching of these stanzas in order.

1. The Servant will be exalted in spite of His great suffering, which is for the salvation of the nations (Isa. 52:13-15).

2. The Servant is rejected by men who see no beauty in Him. (Isa. 53:1-3).

3. The Servant suffers as a substitute who bears our sins and purchases our salvation (Isa. 53:4-6).

4. The Servant's suffering extends even to a substitutionary death (Isa. 53:5-9).

5. The Servant through His suffering will justify His people and earn His own exaltation (Isa. 53:10-12).

This passage presents to our gaze the work of the Servant of God, Jesus Christ. There is none other to whom this can refer. One might almost think that it was written by someone who stood at the foot of the Cross, rather than by one who lived centuries before. Even today, with the wealth of New Testament teaching at our disposal, we turn to this passage when we want to describe the work of Christ. Here we see how God enabled Isaiah to bridge the gap of time and to present to the ancient Church of God the assurance that Jehovah would provide perfect salvation for His people.

The Blessings of the Church Through Christ

This wonderful prophecy of Christ naturally leads the prophet to a description of the blessings that He will bring to His church. Immediately he turns to a description of the glories which will come to the Church, and the confidence that God's people may have that God will never forsake them. Then the prophet utters a word of invitation which shows that the Servant will open the doors of the Church to the entire world. "Ho, every one that thirsteth, come ye to the waters, and he that hath no money; come ye, buy, and eat; yea, come, buy wine and milk without money and without price" (Isa. 55:1). No more shall there be a distinction between Jew and Gentile. All who love God, whether Jew or Gentile, shall be blessed, and all who disobey God, whether Jew or Gentile, shall be punished.

God's Dealings with the Jews

Isaiah again turns to the relationship of God to the Jews. He spares nothing to demonstrate that the sinful nation will be destroyed. The Jews are especially guilty of hypocrisy. They perform the religious ceremonies, yet continue to engage in all sorts of evil practices. As a result God turns away from them. "Behold, Jehovah's hand is not shortened, that it cannot save; neither his ear heavy, that it cannot hear: but your iniquities have separated between you and your God, and your sins have hid his face from you, so that he will not hear" (Isa. 59:1, 2). Therefore destruction will rush upon them. But for the true Israel, the Church of God within the wicked nation, "a Redeemer will come to Zion, and unto them that turn from transgression in Jacob, saith Jehovah" (Isa. 59:20).

The Character of the Messianic Age

Isaiah ends his prophecy by portraying the blessings that await God's people in the coming age. In that age God will greatly glorify Zion, causing all the nations to come to her. The Servant will be the one through whom this will be accomplished. It is through His ministry that blessing comes to Zion. But at the same time the Messianic Age will be a time of destruction for the enemies of God. And the prophet must face the fact that Israel as a nation has broken the covenant God made with her. The Jews therefore are rejected, although God's blessings upon His people are presented in the picture of the new heavens and the new earth.

CONCLUSION

These latter chapters of Isaiah's prophecy bring us closer to the New Testament than any other comparable portion of the Old Testament. Indeed, we might say that they place us in the New Testament. We need not be at all amazed that Christians have found these chapters so precious. Martin Luther said that every Christian, at any cost, ought to memorize Isaiah 53. God marvelously used Isaiah, the son of Amoz, to present graphically the truth that the Old Testament exists to point men to the New.

Isaiah's message also points up the future of the Kingdom of God. In his day Judah was declining. The Captivity was drawing near. Isaiah predicted the Exile. He realized that it would mean the destruction of Israel as a nation. But he was not pessimistic about the future of God's kingdom. In the nation Israel he recognized a godly minority who were the true people of God. They were the Kingdom of God within the covenant-breaking nation. They would not be destroyed. And some day, in God's time, the Messiah would come to bring the Kingdom of God into a new and glorious era.

EXERCISES

Factual questions

1. What sins and errors are dealt with in Isaiah 40-66?
2. How does this section prepare Israel for the future of the theocracy?
3. According to Matthew 3, to whom does Isaiah 40:3-5 refer?
4. What work has Jehovah given to His Servant? Isa. 42:1-9.
5. What do we learn about the Servant of Jehovah in Isaiah 49? In Isaiah 50?
6. Explain in your own words what the five stanzas of Isaiah 52:13-53:12 teach us about the Servant.
7. Write out a verse from Isaiah 55 which promises salvation to those who call upon God. (Do not use verse 1.)
8. List the characteristics of the new heavens and the new earth. Isa. 65:17ff.

Thought questions

1. Why is Christ presented as a servant?
2. What is the connection between Israel and the Church?

3. Is the picture of the new heavens and new earth in Isaiah 65 to be understood literally or figuratively?

Memory
1. Isaiah 41:10.
2. Isaiah 53:4-6.
3. Isaiah 55:10, 11.

Chapter 33

God's Promise of Mercy After Judgment

Micah

INTRODUCTION

The Prophet

This book is the work of Micah, a resident of Moresheth-gath, which is a village about 20 miles southwest of Jerusalem. He should not be confused with the other prophet Micaiah (for Micah and Micaiah are different forms of the same name) who prophesied to king Ahab on the eve of the battle against Ramoth-gilead. Micah prophesied in Judah during the reigns of Jotham, Ahaz, and Hezekiah. He was a contemporary of Isaiah, although he began his ministry slightly later than did Isaiah and probably ended his ministry somewhat earlier. Thus he faced the same type of situation as that faced by Isaiah.

The Nature of the Book

The book of Micah is probably a condensation of the message which Micah proclaimed throughout his ministry. The book is composed of three parts, each of which begins with the word "Hear" (Mic. 1:2; 3:1; 6:1). In each part the same general thoughts occur. There is a denunciation of Israel's sin, a warning of judgment which is to come as punishment for that sin, and a promise of mercy after the judgment has been fulfilled. But each part has a different emphasis. The first section emphasizes judgment, with only a short promise of mercy at the end. The second emphasizes the blessings which will come in the latter days, when "the mountain of Jehovah's house shall be established on the top of the mountains, and it shall be exalted above the hills; and peoples shall flow unto it" (Mic. 4:1). The third part places the emphasis upon a call to repentance.

The Sins of Judah

Micah preached to the same people as did Isaiah. He therefore held before Judah the same sins that Isaiah unveiled. Biting denunciation of the sins of the people came from Micah's lips. Hear his exposé of oppression: "And they covet fields, and seize them;

and houses, and take them away: and they oppress a man and his house, even a man and his heritage. . . . The women of my people ye cast out from their pleasant houses; from their young children ye take away my glory forever" (Mic. 2:2, 9). Hear his denunciation of the perversity of the people: "If a man walking in a spirit of falsehood do lie, saying, I will prophesy unto thee of wine and of strong drink; he shall even be the prophet of this people" (Mic. 2:11). The grasping prophets of the times are pictured: "Thus saith Jehovah concerning the prophets that make my people to err; that bite with their teeth, and cry, Peace; and whoso putteth not into their mouths, they even prepare war against him" (Mic. 3:5). Nor does he spare the wicked shopkeepers and the rich who are quick to do evil. Where sin is found in Judah, Micah is there to denounce it. However, he seems to have kept himself aloof from political matters. Isaiah was the prophet to the kings; Micah is called to reprove the people.

God's Judgment on Sinful Judah

Micah does not only point out Israel's sin. He also warns of the judgment of God upon Israel and Judah because of their sins. "Therefore I will make Samaria as a heap of the field, and as places for planting vineyards; . . . For her wounds are incurable; for it is come even unto Judah; it reacheth unto the gate of my people, even to Jerusalem" (Mic. 1:6, 9). "Therefore shall Zion for your sake be plowed as a field, and Jerusalem shall become heaps, and the mountain of the house as the high places of a forest" (Mic. 3:12). This is the first prophecy that Jerusalem will be destroyed. Although the prophecy of Micah contains great strains of mercy, there is no indication that God's mercy will overlook the sins of His people. Before the final mercy is sent, Israel must receive her just punishment.

The Latter Days

In the fourth chapter of Micah we have a beautiful picture of the blessings that will spring forth from the Messianic Age. This picture is presented in the Old Testament language. It speaks of Zion and Jerusalem. But the thoughts it presents are New Testament thoughts. The Kingdom of God is for all people. God will judge all nations. Peace shall be universal. God will bring together the outcasts of the world. This is the Kingdom of Christ—a kingdom which is not of this world. It is a kingdom of joy and blessing and peace which reaches to the spiritually poor and needy of all nations. It is the goal toward which the Old Testament theocracy ever presses.

The first verses of Micah 4 are also found in Isaiah 2:2-4. It is most probable that Micah originally uttered these words, and that

Isaiah quoted them, using them as a text for his prophecy. From this we learn that the words of the prophets were recognized as the Word of God, and could be quoted as authority.

The Birth of Christ

The best-known prophecy from Micah is that in Micah 5:2. "But thou Beth-lehem Ephrathah, which art little to be among the thousands of Judah, out of thee shall one come forth unto me that is to be ruler in Israel: whose goings forth are from of old, from everlasting." This prophecy of the birthplace of Christ led the Magi to Him many centuries after it was first spoken. In it we see that the Messiah is human, because His birthplace is mentioned. We see also that He is divine, because He is eternal.

From this prophecy Micah develops his picture of what Messiah will do. "And he shall stand, and shall feed his flock in the strength of Jehovah, . . . And this man shall be our peace" (Mic. 5:4, 5). Through the work of the Messiah the blessing of God shall come upon the people of God.

The Call to Repentance

The prophet of God is not satisfied simply to uncover sin, to warn of judgment and to promise mercy. As a true servant of the God who loves Israel he must call to repentance. That call is touching. It comes from the very mouth of God, pleading with His sinful people to consider His works on their behalf. "O my people, what have I done unto thee? and wherein have I wearied thee? testify against me" (Mic. 6:3). This leads to the question of how God's people shall come before Him. Does He seek many offerings and great actions of atonement? "He hath showed thee, O man, what is good; and what doth Jehovah require of thee, but to do justly, and to love kindness, and to walk humbly with thy God?" (Mic. 6:8) This is one of the grandest, most sublime statements of the nature of true religion that we find anywhere in Scripture.

OUTLINE

We can now see that an outline of Micah is difficult to make. The best we can do is show the various emphases of each section.

    I. Prophecy emphasizing judgment   Micah 1-2

    II. Prophecy emphasizing the reign of Christ Micah 3-5

    III. Prophecy emphasizing repentance   Micah 6-7

PURPOSE

The purpose of Micah's short book is to show God's complaint against the sin of Israel and Judah, to warn of the judgment that will come because of this sin, and to point beyond the judgment to the salvation that God will provide through His Messiah.

EXERCISES

Factual questions

1. Identify the author of Micah.
2. What does each section of Micah emphasize?
3. Give four of Israel's sin's condemned in Micah 2.
4. What judgment will God bring upon His sinful people? Mic. 1: 5ff.; 3:9ff.
5. In what terms does God describe the blessings of Messiah's reign? Mic. 4.
6. What historical examples does God use in calling Israel to repentance? Mic. 6.
7. What is the purpose of Micah?

Thought question

1. The term "latter days" in the Old Testament refers to both the New Testament age and the time after the return of Christ. Show how "prophetic perspective" (see page 148) explains this broad use of the term.

Memory

1. Outline of Micah.
2. Micah 5:2.
3. Micah 6:8.

Chapter 34

God's Picture of the Universal Saviour

Jonah

AUTHOR

This book was written by the prophet Jonah, the son of Amittai Although it does not make this claim, it everywhere bears marks of being the record of a personal experience. The Jews considered it the work of a prophet. In fact, the only people who have denied that Jonah wrote this book have been the Higher Critics, who seek to explain away the miracles which the book contains.

The author, Jonah, is also mentioned in I Kings 14:25, where we learn that he prophesied that Jeroboam II would restore the ancient boundaries of Israel. From this we conclude that the prophet lived and reigned during the middle of the eighth century B.C. Many scholars believe that the trip to Nineveh came rather late in the prophet's career, and that the book was written shortly after the trip ended.

PURPOSE

The book of Jonah is unique among the Minor Prophets. It records very little actual prophecy. Rather, it deals with the history of the prophet. But the history of Jonah's mission to Nineveh is prophetic history. The story is designed to bring out two lessons.

1. The mission to Nineveh resulted in repentance on the part of the heathen. This was intended to teach Israel that God did not always limit his grace to the nation of Israel. In this way it pointed forward to the day when the gospel of grace would break all national barriers and go to all men.

2. Another purpose of the book of Jonah is "to show that Jonah being cast into the depths of Sheol and yet brought up alive is an illustration of the death of the Messiah for sins not his own and of the Messiah's resurrection" (Young). This purpose is closely connected to the first. It is through the death and resurrection of Christ that the gospel goes to all nations.

OUTLINE

ANALYSIS

Jonah's Disobedience

The book of Jonah opens with a startling picture. God calls a prophet to preach, and the prophet runs away. How can this action of Jonah be explained? Jonah himself answers in Jonah 4:2, "I pray thee, O Jehovah, was not this my saying, when I was yet in my country? Therefore I hasted to flee unto Tarshish; for I knew that thou art a gracious God, and merciful, slow to anger and abundant in lovingkindness, and repentest thee of the evil." Because he feared that Nineveh would repent and therefore God in His mercy would not destroy the city, he ran away. Jonah is a picture of the Israelites of his day. The Jews were sure that God's kingdom and the nation of Israel were identical. The feeling that the Jews and only the Jews could receive God's blessings was strong and was growing stronger. Jonah's actions after Nineveh was spared, which may almost be described as a childish temper tantrum, show how strong that feeling was. But it was precisely this feeling that needed to be destroyed. The Jews had to learn that the Kingdom of God could come to expression outside the covenant nation. And it was to destroy that feeling that God sent Jonah to Nineveh.

The Sign of Jonah

The story of Jonah and the whale (or great fish, since it was probably not a whale) has been the object of a great deal of scoffing and ridicule. Unbelievers have pointed to it as an example of things in the Bible which cannot be true. The rescue of Jonah from death by drowning was a miracle, and unbelievers are certain to stumble over it. But it is precisely this miracle which is of utmost importance in the book of Jonah. Jesus pointed to it and applied it to Himself, "For as Jonah was three days and three nights in the belly of the whale; so shall the Son of man be three days and three nights in the heart of the earth" (Matt. 12:40) The experience of Jonah is a type which is to point us to the death and resurrection of Him who would save both Jews and Gentiles.

The Repentance of Nineveh

When Jonah finally went to Nineveh and proclaimed God's message there, the results were startling. All Nineveh from the king to the lowliest peasant repented in sackcloth and ashes. The whole city mourned, and the people turned from their evil ways. There is evidence that this repentance was only temporary, and that after a short time Nineveh returned to its old ways. But there is no doubt that the repentance was real.

Jesus also pointed to this repentance. He said to the scribes and Pharisees, "The men of Nineveh shall stand up in the judgment with this generation, and shall condemn it: for they repented at the preaching of Jonah; and behold, a greater than Jonah is here" (Matt. 12:41). The reaction of the heathen Ninevites to the preaching of Jonah stood in contrast to the stark unbelief of Israel both in the time of Jonah and in the time of Christ.

EXERCISES

Factual questions

1. Identify the author of the book of Jonah.
2. What is the purpose of the book of Jonah?
3. How did Jonah try to avoid the call to prophesy? Jonah 1:2.
4. How was his sin discovered? Jonah 1:4ff.
5. How did the people of Nineveh display their repentance? Jonah 3:5ff.
6. How did God teach Jonah not to be angry about Nineveh being spared? Jonah 4:6ff.
7. How does Jonah point to Christ?
8. How is the Greek word for "whale" in Matthew 12:40 translated in the marginal notes of the American Standard Version of the Bible?

Thought question

1. Does Jonah's psalm in Jonah 2 ask for deliverance from the stomach of the fish or does it thank God for deliverance from drowning?

Memory

1. Outline of Jonah.
2. Matthew 12:40.
3. Luke 11:30.

Chapter 35

God's Guarantee of Covenant Faithfulness

Obadiah

AUTHOR

There are many Obadiahs mentioned on the pages of the Old Testament. But the writer of Obadiah, except for his very brief prophecy (one chapter), is completely unknown. We do not even know when he lived. Some believe that he was the earliest of the writing prophets, living in or shortly after the days of Elisha. Some Critics believe that he is a very late prophet, perhaps from the time of Ezra and Nehemiah. Most likely the truth is somewhere in the middle. It seems certain that Jeremiah quoted from him, so he must have lived and prophesied before the Exile.

If we could identify exactly the invasion of Judah to which Obadiah refers in the opening verses we could date him more precisely. But there are several invasions which could explain Obadiah's words. Both the identity and the time of this prophet remain a mystery.

PURPOSE

The short prophecy of Obadiah deals with the judgment which will come upon Edom because of Edom's hatred to Judah in Judah's time of need. But Obadiah's vision is not limited. He sees the coming punishment of Edom as part of the day of Jehovah in which all the nations will be punished and God's people will be blessed. By the use of this specific example Obadiah again reminds the people that God is faithful both to bless His covenant people and to punish their enemies.

ANALYSIS

Obadiah begins by predicting doom to the proud inhabitants of the rocky citadel Petra, the capital of Edom. The reason for the punishment which will come is clear. When Judah was invaded and the invaders were spoiling the land and the people, Edom would not help. (Remember that Edom and Judah are related through Esau and Jacob.) On the contrary, Edom cheered the invaders on and helped to make life miserable for the Jews. As a result, God says, "As thou hast done, it shall be done unto thee; thy dealing shall return upon thine own head" (vs. 15).

Obadiah connects the punishment of Edom with the day of Jehovah (vs. 15). This is the day when the nations, that is, the heathen, are punished. But that same day of Jehovah is a time of blessing to God's people. "But in mount Zion there shall be those that escape, and it shall be holy; and the house of Jacob shall possess their possessions. And the house of Jacob shall be a fire, and the house of Joseph a flame, and the house of Esau for stubble, and they shall burn among them, and devour them; and there shall not be any remaining to the house of Esau; for Jehovah hath spoken it" (vs. 17, 18). The covenant faithfulness of God shall abide upon His people to the end. The people of God shall be blessed, but the enemies of God shall be destroyed.

EXERCISES

1. What do we know about the author of Obadiah?
2. What is the purpose of the book of Obadiah?
3. Write out a verse from Obadiah showing the pride of Edom.
4. Write out a verse from Obadiah showing the cruelty of Edom.
5. Write out a verse from Obadiah showing the punishment of Edom.
6. Prove that Israel will be saved. See vs. 17-21.

Chapter 36

God's Warning From Nineveh's Destruction

Nahum

AUTHOR

Of Nahum, the author of this little book, we know practically nothing. He is simply called Nahum the Elkoshite. "Elkoshite" probably refers to the town from which he came, but no one knows certainly where that village was located.

The prophecy of Nahum must probably be dated somewhere between 664 B.C. and 612 B.C. In 664-663 B.C. Thebes, or No-amon, the capital of Egypt, was conquered by the Assyrians. Nahum mentions this fall of No-amon in Nahum 3:8. And in 612 B.C. the fall of Nineveh which Nahum predicted came to pass. So it seems likely that Nahum prophesied sometime during the reign of Josiah.

BACKGROUND

Behind this prophecy of Nahum lies a long history of Assyrian oppression of the people of God. Assyria first appeared as a power to be feared in 738 B.C., when Menahem, king of Israel, paid tribute to the king of Assyria. During the reign of Pekah the Assyrians invaded Israel and took the people of Naphtali captive. Also during the reign of Pekah, Ahaz, king of Judah, called upon the Assyrians for aid when he was attacked by Israel and Syria. In 722 B.C. the Assyrians came down upon Israel, captured Samaria, and took the people of the northern kingdom into captivity. In 701 B.C. the Assyrians under Sennacherib again invaded Palestine. This time it was the remaining kingdom of Judah that felt their wrath. Hezekiah had to give a great ransom to purchase peace. And that peace was only temporary, for in a short time the forces of Sennacherib returned. But this time the Assyrian was destroyed by the hand of God.

The destruction of Sennacherib's army did not destroy Assyria. It remained on the horizon, always a potential source of trouble. Nahum's word about the fall of Nineveh arises, humanly speaking, out of years of misery.

179

PURPOSE

The prophecy of Nahum sets forth the coming downfall of Nineveh as a demonstration of God's justice and as a comfort to the oppressed covenant nation. In this book we see a practical expression of God's covenant faithfulness, as He destroys the proud enemy of His people.

OUTLINE

I.	A psalm praising God's justice	Nahum 1
II.	A description of Nineveh's ruin	Nahum 2
III.	An explanation of Nineveh's ruin	Nahum 3

ANALYSIS

The Honor of God

At first reading, the book of Nahum seems to be a narrow rejoicing at the downfall of an enemy. It seems to be motivated by petty patriotism. But on closer examination we see that Nahum rises to much greater heights. His entire discourse is based upon the honor of God. The key to Nahum's thought is found in Nahum 1:7, 8. "Jehovah is good, a stronghold in the day of trouble; and he knoweth them that take refuge in him. But with an over-running flood he will make a full end of her place, and will pursue his enemies into darkness." God is a God of mercy and justice. He will provide shelter for His people, but will scatter His enemies.

The Destruction of Nineveh

From his psalm the prophet turns to a description of the fall of Nineveh. In stark, strong language he pictures the desolation that will overtake her. And the reasons why God thus deals with Nineveh are listed in Nahum 3. It is obvious from this that the repentance in Jonah's day was short-lived. Nineveh was a city, and Assyria a nation, that deserved the wrath of God.

The Message to God's People

In Nahum there is little said about Judah. Yet the covenant nation is mentioned. The destruction of Nineveh is presented as the cause of Judah's safety. The great enemy has been destroyed. The prophet's name, which means comfort, aptly describes the message he brings to the people of God. Nineveh, after all, is only one of the enemies of God's kingdom. And like Nineveh, all the enemies shall be destroyed, and the covenant people shall find safety in God Himself. However strong the enemies may appear, they can never overthrow the Kingdom of God. Even the gates of Hell shall not prevail against it.

EXERCISES

Factual questions

1. Identify the author of Nahum.
2. Why was the fall of Nineveh so important to the Jews?
3. What is the purpose of the book of Nahum?
4. What do the prophets Nahum and Jonah have in common?
5. Approximately how much time elapsed between the prophecies of Jonah and Nahum? See chart on page 131.
6. Find in Nahum 1 evidence of God's wrath against sin and mercy toward His people.

Thought question

1. How is the book of Nahum like the imprecatory psalms?

Memory

1. Outline of Nahum.
2. Nahum 1:7.

Chapter 37

God's Warning of Coming Wrath

Zephaniah

AUTHOR

Zephaniah, the author of this prophecy, identifies himself by tracing his ancestry back to the fourth generation. This is unusual, since the prophets usually named only their fathers. The reason for this genealogy seems to be that the Hezekiah who was the great-great-grandfather of Zephaniah was the great and good king of Judah. If this is so, Zephaniah was of the royal line, and would have had easy access to the palace.

Zephaniah prophesied in the reign of Josiah. Josiah, you will remember, inherited the corruption and idolatry of the two previous reigns, those of Manasseh and Amon. He also inherited many problems due to the fact that the previous kings had become involved in the affairs of foreign nations. There was little that Josiah could do about the problems of foreign policy. Indeed, he died in a battle that was due, at least in part, to the position which he held as a vassal of Assyria. But he was able to do something about the religious situation. He inaugurated sweeping reforms which removed the outward evidences of idolatry from the land. But he could not change the hearts of his people, and therefore his reforms were effective only as long as he reigned.

We do not know whether Zephaniah prophesied before or after the reforming work of Josiah was begun. In either case his message of God's wrath against sin would have helped Josiah in his program of reform.

PURPOSE

Zephaniah is God's voice proclaiming the doom which shall come upon the nation. He also pictures the great day of God's wrath and promises God's people that they will be delivered.

OUTLINE

I. The warning of coming judgment	Zephaniah 1:1-2:3
II. The recipients of coming judgment	Zephaniah 2:4-3:7
III. The results of coming judgment	Zephaniah 3:8-20

ANALYSIS

The Day of Jehovah

Zephaniah's opening words point to the theme of his message. "I will utterly consume all things from off the face of the ground, saith Jehovah" (Zeph. 1:2). The prophet goes on to indicate what that means for Jerusalem and Judah. Both man and beast will be consumed. The idols and those who worship them will be destroyed, and all the wicked will be searched out and punished. From this picture of the judgment which lay before Judah, Zephaniah turns to the great day of Jehovah, which he describes in language that is beautiful and forceful. "That day is a day of wrath, a day of trouble and distress, a day of wasteness and desolation, a day of darkness and gloominess, a day of clouds and thick darkness, a day of the trumpet and alarm, against the fortified cities and against the high battlements" (Zeph. 1:15, 16).

The judgment of God which is coming leads the prophet to call the nation to repentance. "Seek ye Jehovah, all ye meek of the earth, that have kept his ordinances; seek righteousness, seek meekness: it may be ye will be hid in the day of Jehovah's anger" (Zeph. 2:3).

Judgment on the Nations

The thought of judgment coming to the theocratic nation turns the mind of the prophet to the surrounding heathen nations, whose sin before God is also great. And so he pronounces doom upon these also. Nineveh is especially marked out as a city that will receive the judgment which it so richly deserves. But Zephaniah cannot stop there. Judah must not think that God will judge only the heathen. Again the prophet points to the sins of Jerusalem, sins which are as great as those of Nineveh. Therefore the judgment of God will be poured out on all the nations.

God's Blessing on His People

The judgment of God will mean destruction for the heathen. But when the judgment of God falls on the covenant nation it will act like a purifying fire that will leave a small but pure remnant. The nation will be destroyed, but this remnant will continue the Kingdom of God. "In that day shalt thou not be put to shame for all thy doings, wherein thou hast transgressed against me; for then I will take away out of the midst of thee thy proudly exulting ones, and thou shalt no more be haughty in my holy mountain. But I will leave in the midst of thee an afflicted and poor people, and they shall take refuge in the name of Jehovah" (Zeph. 3:11, 12). In that day the daughter of Zion will sing, because God is with her and He will save.

EXERCISES

Factual questions

1. Identify the author of the book of Zephaniah.
2. In what circumstances did Zephaniah prophesy?
3. What is the purpose of the book of Zephaniah?
4. List those people of Judah who are especially singled out for punishment by God. Zeph. 1:4ff.
5. Write out the prediction of the punishment that will come to Nineveh. Zeph. 2.
6. For what sins does God's punishment come to Jerusalem? Zeph. 3.
7. Give two reasons why the daughter of Zion may sing. Zeph. 3:8ff.

Memory

1. Outline of Zephaniah.
2. Zephaniah 1:15, 16.

Chapter 38

God's Explanation of Coming Punishment

Habakkuk

AUTHOR

Of Habakkuk we know nothing except his name. We cannot even tell precisely when this prophecy was uttered. In Habakkuk 1:5, 6, God speaks of raising up the Chaldeans. This probably points to a date in the time of Manasseh just before the Babylonians overthrew the Assyrian empire. Both Kings and Chronicles tell of God raising up prophets at that time who warned of the evil to come to Judah because of Manasseh's sins. Habakkuk may have been one of these prophets.

OUTLINE
    I. Habakkuk's conversation with God   Habakkuk 1, 2
    II. Habakkuk's prayer to God   Habakkuk 3

PURPOSE

Habakkuk's little prophecy presents beautifully the absolute right-eousness of God in His government of the nations. He is a God who punishes iniquity without partiality. Though it may seem to men that the great King is acting unjustly, the course of events will prove the justice of His government. It is this absolute righteousness and justice of God that gives the Christian true comfort and confidence in Him.

ANALYSIS

Habakkuk's Questions and God's Answers

Habakkuk has been called a philosopher. If a philosopher is one who asks questions about life and wants to understand why things happen as they do, then Habakkuk is a philosopher. He looks at his people. He sees the sinfulness of the nation. He cries out to God. "O Jehovah, how long shall I cry, and thou wilt not hear? I cry out unto thee of violence, and thou wilt not save" (Hab. 1:2). God answers Habakkuk. "Behold ye among the nations, and look, and wonder marvellously; for I am working a work in your days, which ye will not believe though it be told you. For, lo, I raise up the Chaldeans, that

185

bitter and hasty nation, that march through the breadth of the earth, to possess dwelling-places that are not theirs" (Hab. 1:5, 6).

If this answer of God solves one problem for Habakkuk, it raises another problem which is even greater. How can God do this? "Thou that art of purer eyes than to behold evil, and that canst not look on perverseness, wherefore lookest thou upon them that deal treacherously, and holdest thy peace when the wicked swalloweth up the man that is more righteous than he?" (Hab. 1:13) How can God use the wicked Chaldeans to punish the people of God, who by comparison are more righteous? This the prophet cannot understand.

Again God answers, and this answer has echoed and re-echoed down through the centuries. "Behold, his soul is puffed up, it is not upright in him; but the righteous shall live by his faith" (Hab. 2:4). In these words we find a contrast. The wicked are proud and puffed up. The result of this pride will be destruction. But the true people of God live by faith. And their faith will be rewarded with life—even eternal life. This is the answer to the prophet's problem. The wicked, proud Chaldean nation cannot last; it too will be punished for its sin. Only those who are righteous by faith shall live before God. What a comfort to those true people of God in Judah! Those who trust in Jehovah shall never be moved.

The fate of the Chaldeans is expressed in a series of woes. The various sins of the Chaldeans are called to mind, and woe is pronounced upon those who commit those sins. The multiplication of Judah's sins led God to use Babylon as His instrument to punish Judah. But the sins of Babylon will not be overlooked by God. Upon Babylon will be visited the punishment which is her due.

Habakkuk's Psalm

The last chapter of Habakkuk's prophecy is a beautiful psalm, which is even furnished with musical instructions for singing. It is the only such psalm found in the prophets. The theme is confidence in God. In answer to the prophet's prayer that God will revive His work, he sees a vision of God coming and fighting against His enemies.

The prophet is aware of what lies ahead. Yet he has learned to trust in God through all circumstances.

> *. . . I must wait quietly for the day of trouble,*
> *For the coming up of the people that invadeth us.*
> *For though the fig-tree shall not flourish,*
> *Neither shall fruit be in the vines;*
> *The labor of the olive shall fail,*
> *And the fields shall yield no food;*
> *The flock shall be cut off from the fold,*

And there shall be no herd in the stalls:
Yet I will rejoice in Jehovah,
I will joy in the God of my salvation.

— Hab. 3:16-18

EXERCISES

Factual questions

1. When do we think Habakkuk prophesied?
2. What is the purpose of the book of Habakkuk?
3. Write out four verses from Habakkuk 1 and 2 which summarize Habakkuk's two questions and God's two answers.
4. Describe the Chaldeans who will punish Judah. Hab. 1:5ff.
5. For what sins will the Chaldeans be punished? Hab. 2:4ff.

Thought questions

1. What effect has Habakkuk 2:4 had on the history of God's church?
2. What application may Habakkuk have to the world scene today?

Memory

1. Outline of Habakkuk.
2. Habakkuk 2:4.
3. Habakkuk 2:20.
4. Habakkuk 3:17, 18.

Chapter 39

God's Punishment of Sinful Judah

Jeremiah

INTRODUCTION

Author

This prophecy is the work of the prophet Jeremiah whose name it bears. Jeremiah was a priest, whose home was in the village of Anathoth in Benjamin, about five miles north of Jerusalem. We read nothing of his service as a priest. He was called to be a prophet at an early age, and served Jehovah in this capacity for some fifty years. The prophecies which make up the book were probably written at various times during his ministry.

The Times of Jeremiah

Jeremiah began his prophetic ministry during the thirteenth year of the reign of Josiah, and continued to prophesy until Jerusalem had fallen. Even after this he prophesied to the miserable group which remained in Judah and later fled to Egypt.

Jeremiah's ministry covered the period in which Judah declined and went into captivity. Judah had already been ravaged by the Assyrians in the days of Ahaz and Hezekiah. In Hezekiah's time God had destroyed the Assyrian army of Sennacherib, and Judah had had a time of peace. But the sins of Manasseh again brought punishment at the hand of the Assyrians. Manasseh was taken captive into Assyria, but was returned to his throne. The reign of Manasseh was a turning point for Judah. He led the people into open idolatry, and the people willingly followed. Manasseh's reign was both long and disastrous. God swore that he would punish Judah because of the sin of Manasseh.

When Josiah came to the throne he inaugurated a reform. But this godly young king, though he gave himself diligently to his reforms, was unable to change the hearts of his people. He did curb open idolatry. He did restore the worship of Jehovah in the temple. But he did not change the people. They were hardened in their sins.

It was during the reforms of Josiah that Jeremiah began his labors. He aided the young king by his vigorous preaching and his bold exposure of the sins of all classes of people. But it had little effect. The untimely death of Josiah saw the work of reformation unfinished. Judah's heart was wicked and rebellious, and the punishment of God was sure to come.

The death of Josiah signaled the beginning of Judah's time of troubles. From that time on the nation was under the control of either Egypt or Babylon. Judah's troubles were compounded by her constant plotting and rebelling against her masters. This rebellion finally brought the destruction of Jerusalem in 586 B.C.

From the days of Josiah, Jeremiah had proclaimed that Judah would be taken captive by a nation from the north. Later he made it clear that Babylon was the nation. When the Babylonians were at the gates of Jerusalem, Jeremiah continually counseled surrender. When Jerusalem was finally taken, Nebuchadnezzar carried into captivity all but the poorest and lowliest inhabitants of the land. They were ruled by Gedaliah, a governor who was appointed by the king of Babylon. But he was assassinated and many of those who were left decided to flee to Egypt. Jeremiah prophesied against such action, but the people would not listen. They even carried Jeremiah with them. Jeremiah probably died in exile in Egypt.

The Character of the Prophet

Jeremiah has often been called the weeping prophet. Certainly no other prophet had more cause for weeping. Not only did Jeremiah experience a great deal of suffering; he was obliged to contend for half a century with a people who named the name of Jehovah but would not hearken to His word. At times be became discouraged. He says, "Oh that I had in the wilderness a lodging-place of wayfaring men; that I might leave my people, and go from them! for they are all adulterers, an assembly of treacherous men " (Jer. 9:2).

But Jeremiah never turned aside from his task. Knowing from the beginning of his ministry that punishment must surely come upon his nation, he refused to bring any message that would please his listeners. Nor would he allow others to preach peace to this people who would receive the wrath of God. He was "an iron pillar, and brazen walls, against the whole land" (Jer. 1:18). Yet despite the fact that his message was rejected and he was despised, Jeremiah never ceased sympathizing with the people. He stood before them as the servant of God who was both stern and sympathetic. Like the God in whose name he spoke, Jeremiah embodied both love and justice.

PURPOSE

The prophecies of Jeremiah were given to the people of Judah and to us to show clearly that the terrible calamities that befell Judah and

ended her existence as a nation were God's punishment against her sin.
While Jeremiah also looks forward to a future time of blessing and to
the coming of the Messiah, the theme of punishment for sin is
central in his prophecies.

OUTLINE

ANALYSIS

The Prophet's Call

Jeremiah received his call to be a prophet when he was a young man.
Like Moses, he felt himself to be inadequate for the task. But God
supplied that which he lacked. "Then Jehovah put forth his hand, and
touched my mouth; and Jehovah said unto me, Behold, I have put my
words in thy mouth: see, I have this day set thee over the nations and
over the kingdoms, to pluck up and to break down and to destroy and to
overthrow, to build and to plant" (Jer. 1:9, 10). At the time of his
call God gave Jeremiah two visions. The one taught him that God is
faithful, and would do for Jeremiah all that He had promised. The
other taught him that Judah would be punished by a nation from the
north.

Jeremiah was given no easy task. He was to stand before the nation
and to proclaim the righteous judgment of God. But he did not stand
alone. "And they shall fight against thee; but they shall not prevail
against thee: for I am with thee, saith Jehovah, to deliver thee" (Jer.
1:19).

Jeremiah's Early Ministry

The prophecies of Jeremiah were uttered during the reigns of four
kings. These prophecies are not arranged in chronological order. But
we have many of the prophecies which Jeremiah uttered during the
reign of Josiah collected in Jeremiah 2-20. These prophecies were
spoken long before the destruction of Jerusalem. They tell us what
kind of message Jeremiah preached in the early days of his ministry.

Jeremiah did not spare the feelings of the people. He attacked
sin wherever it was found. His indictment of all Judah is graphic.
"For my people have committed two evils: they have forsaken me, the
fountain of living waters, and hewed them out cisterns, broken cisterns,
that can hold no water" (Jer. 2:13). He was especially strong in his

condemnation of the priests and prophets, who should have led the people toward God but actually led them into sin. "A wonderful and horrible thing is come to pass in the land: the prophets prophesy falsely, and the priests bear rule by their means; and my people love to have it so: and what will ye do in the end thereof?" (Jer. 5:30, 31)

One of the striking features of the ministry of Jeremiah is the small place given in his preaching to a call for repentance. At times he does call upon the people to repent, but his call is less frequent than that of the earlier prophets. To be sure, his messages of judgment implied that repentance was needed. But seldom did Jeremiah issue a summons to repentance. Instead, Jeremiah points time and again to the punishment which will certainly come upon Judah because of her sin. Jeremiah 4 contains a description of the punishment to come. Jeremiah also speaks in these words, "Thus saith Jehovah, Behold, a people cometh from the north country; and a great nation shall be stirred up from the uttermost parts of the earth. . . . O daughter of my people, gird thee with sackcloth, and wallow thyself in ashes: make thee mourning, as for an only son, most bitter lamentation; for the destroyer shall suddenly come upon us" (Jer. 6:22, 26).

While Jeremiah concentrates upon the punishment which Judah will receive, he also strikes a note of promise. In the distant future there is hope of restoration. "And it shall come to pass, after that I have plucked them up, I will return and have compassion on them; and I will bring them again, every man to his heritage, and every man to his land" (Jer. 12:15).

At times God instructed Jeremiah to present some of his messages in symbolic form. Actions like the burial of the loincloth along the Euphrates in Jeremiah 13 and the destruction of the clay bottle in Jeremiah 19 served to drive home to his hearers the message which the prophet had to deliver.

Judgment by the Chaldeans (Babylonians)

The third section, beginning with Jeremiah 21, contains a series of prophecies in which the prophet announces that the Chaldeans are God's weapon of judgment. These prophecies were originally delivered at various times in the reigns of Jehoiakim and Zedekiah, and are gathered in this section because of the similarity of content. In various ways God tells the kings and the people that they will be taken into captivity by the Chaldeans. King Zedekiah and his servants will be captured and killed, the city taken and destroyed by fire. In the light of these predictions, Jeremiah uttered the words that were so distasteful to many of the rulers of Jerusalem: "Thus saith Jehovah: Behold, I set before you the way of life and the way of death. He that abideth in this city shall die by the sword, and by the famine, and by the pestilence; but he that goeth out, and passeth over to the Chaldeans that besiege you, he shall live, and his life shall be unto him for a prey" (Jer. 21:8, 9).

Yet Jeremiah's words were not without a note of hope for the future. Judah's punishment was sure. But her exile would not be permanent. He also brought this word from Jehovah, "These nations shall serve the king of Babylon seventy years. And it shall come to pass, when seventy years are accomplished, that I will punish the king of Babylon, and that nation, saith Jehovah, for their iniquity, and the land of the Chaldeans; and I will make it desolate for ever" (Jer. 25:11, 12).

On another occasion, when the city of Jerusalem was still standing, and many of those who had been exiled during Jehoiachin's reign expected to return shortly to Jerusalem, Jeremiah wrote them a letter. Don't expect to return, he said. Build houses and plant vineyards. "For thus saith Jehovah, After seventy years are accomplished for Babylon, I will visit you, and perform my good word toward you, in causing you to return to this place" (Jer. 29:10).

The Coming Messiah

Jeremiah also looked beyond the return from exile. He saw in the future a time when God would bless His people abundantly. Although the blessing is pictured in terms of material prosperity there are many indications that this is a picture of spiritual prosperity.

The great blessing of God is this: "Behold, the days come, saith Jehovah, that I will make a new covenant with the house of Israel, and with the house of Judah: . . . I will put my law in their inward parts, and in their heart will I write it; and I will be their God, and they shall be my people" (Jer. 31:31, 33).

Jeremiah, like the other prophets, saw that the future blessing of God should come through one whom God would send. "In those days, and at that time, will I cause a Branch of righteousness to grow up unto David; and he shall execute justice and righteousness in the land" (Jer. 33:15). By this prophecy Jeremiah takes the promise which God gave to David and clearly connects it with the Messiah who is to come. Though Jeremiah is rightly called the weeping prophet, he received some wonderful prophecies about the future of God's people which must have caused his heart to rejoice. He had to proclaim the destruction of the nation which had been the Kingdom of God. But he also looked forward to a new and better manifestation of the theocracy. He saw the blessings of the coming Kingdom of Christ.

Historical Narratives

The story of the fall of Jerusalem before the armies of Nebuchadnezzar (586 B.C.) is told in the books of Kings and Chronicles. But

Jeremiah gives us information about the last days of Jerusalem which is not contained in those historical books. Much of the material in Jeremiah deals with the troubles which came to Jeremiah because of his faithfulness to the word which he had received from God. He tells us how King Jehoiakim burned the prophecies which he had written and sought to kill him. He records how he was imprisoned several times because the message he proclaimed did not suit the princes of Jerusalem. He tells of the advice from God which he gave to King Zedekiah. But Zedekiah would not listen, and therefore the king suffered greatly when the city was taken and he was captured by the Chaldeans.

Jeremiah also gives us a more detailed account of the events which occurred after the destruction of Jerusalem. He tells how Gedaliah was made governor, how he was slain by some of the remaining Jews, and how fearful the Jews were of Nebuchadnezzar's wrath. They asked Jeremiah what they should do. He told them to remain in Judah. But they had determined that they would go to Egypt, and they forced the prophet to accompany them there. Jeremiah's experiences in Egypt were no happier than his ministry in Judah. He announced that Nebuchadnezzar would capture Egypt and slay the Jews there. And when he sought to call the Jews away from their idolatry and back to Jehovah, they scorned his words and declared openly their intention to continue worshiping idols.

Prophecies Against the Nations

It was Jeremiah's sad duty to preach to the people of Judah and warn them of the destruction that was to overtake them. They had to be told again and again that this was God's method of punishing them for their constant sinfulness. God had purposed to use the heathen nations to destroy the covenant nation which had rebelled against its God. But Jeremiah's prophecies were not limited to Judah. He also spoke to the nations around Judah, and predicted judgment upon them. The same Babylonians who were to punish Judah would also punish these nations. And at the end of this section of prophecies against the nations Jeremiah unleashes a prediction of punishment against Babylon that is far sterner than any of the other predictions. Although the Chaldeans have been used of God to punish other nations, that does not mean that they will not be punished. God's wrath will also be poured out upon them. As Babylon destroyed other nations, so Babylon will also be destroyed.

A Historical Review

Jeremiah closes his book with a survey of the events surrounding the fall of Jerusalem. This survey in Jeremiah 52, in almost identical language, is also found in Kings. Many scholars do not believe that

Jeremiah is the author of this passage. Then why is it found at the end of his book? That is a difficult question. Perhaps it is appended as a kind of historical proof, from the pen of another writer, of the truth of the prophecies which Jeremiah brought to the children of Judah.

EXERCISES

Factual questions

1. Identify the author of Jeremiah.
2. Describe the times in which Jeremiah prophesied.
3. What type of man was Jeremiah?
4. What is the purpose of the book of Jeremiah?
5. What visions did Jeremiah have at the time of his call? Explain what each meant. Jer. 1:11ff.
6. List three sins that are described in Jeremiah 7.
7. What is the meaning of the burial in the linen girdle? Jer. 13.
8. What lesson did Jeremiah learn in the potter's house? Jer. 18.
9. What is the meaning of the broken clay bottle? Jer. 19.
10. What did Pashhur do to Jeremiah? Jer. 20.
11. What is the meaning of the two baskets of figs? Jer. 24.
12. How did the example of Micah save Jeremiah's life? Jer. 26:10ff.
13. Why was Jeremiah cast into prison? Jer. 37:11ff.
14. How was he released from prison? Jer. 38:7ff.
15. By what sign did Jeremiah indicate that the Chaldeans would conquer Egypt? Jer. 43:8ff.

Thought questions

1. Do you think our times are similar to the times in which Jeremiah lived?
2. What traits of character make Jeremiah a great man?
3. Why did Jeremiah stay in Judah rather than go to Babylon?
4. Has Jeremiah 31:31-34 been fulfilled? Use Hebrews 8:8-12 to determine your answer.

Memory

1. Outline of Jeremiah.
2. Jeremiah 31:33.
3. Jeremiah 33:15, 16.

Chapter 40

The Covenant Nation Mourns Its Destruction

Lamentations

INTRODUCTION

Author

The common tradition of the Jews and of the Christian Church has maintained that Jeremiah is the author of Lamentations. The arguments used to uphold this tradition have not always been sound. But the arguments of those who try to deny this position have been even less sound. While we do not have definite proof, it is best to say that Jeremiah probably wrote Lamentations. The work was composed shortly after the fall of Jerusalem in 586 B.C.

Its Place in the Canon

In the English Bible, Lamentations is placed after Jeremiah. The Hebrews, however, include Lamentations in the Writings. This would seem to contradict the idea that the prophet Jeremiah is the author. But there may be a reason for this. Lamentations is one of the Five Rolls (Megilloth) read at the Jewish holy days. Lamentations is read at the fast commemorating the fall of Jerusalem. This use of Lamentations may explain how a book written by a prophet is found in the Writings.

The Form of The Book

Lamentations is written as an acrostic poem. Chapters 1, 2, and 4 have 22 verses each. The verses begin with the letters of the Hebrew alphabet in order. Chapter 3 has 66 verses. It is composed of groups of 3 verses, each group containing verses that begin with the same letter. The last chapter also has 22 verses, but there is no alphabetic order. This acrostic form is a mark of Hebrew poetry, which served a good purpose. It helped the Hebrew reader to memorize the book more easily. By this form the meaning of the book was more fully grasped.

PURPOSE

Jeremiah wrote Lamentations to express the deep sorrow of the people of God when the covenant nation was destroyed, and to show the reason for this suffering.

195

ANALYSIS

This book consists of five separate lamentations. In each there is the same sorrow and mourning. But in each we find a different emphasis. In each lament the author points up a different aspect of the sorrow surrounding the fall of Jerusalem.

Lamentations 1 expresses with pathetic beauty the sorrow of captive Zion.

How doth the city sit solitary, that was full of people!
She is become as a widow, that was great among the nations!
She that was a princess among the provinces is become a tributary!
                                                          —Lam. 1:1.

Is it nothing to you, all ye that pass by?
Behold, and see if there be any sorrow like unto my
  sorrow, which is brought upon me,
Wherewith Jehovah hath afflicted me in the day of his
  fierce anger.   —Lam. 1:12.

Lamentations 2 points to the fact that this great suffering is from God.

How hath the Lord covered the daughter of Zion with a
  cloud in his anger!
He hath cast down from the heaven unto the earth the
  beauty of Israel,
And hath not remembered his footstool in the day of
  his anger.   —Lam. 2:1.

In Lamentations 3 the author, speaking for Zion, bemoans his condition and expresses hope in the mercy of God.

I am the man that hath seen affliction by the rod of his
  wrath.
For the Lord will not cast off for ever.
For though he cause grief, yet will he have compassion
  according to the multitude of his lovingkindnesses.
Let us search and try our ways, and turn again to Jehovah.
Let us lift up our heart with our hands unto God in the
  heavens.   —Lam. 3:1, 31, 32, 40, 41.

Lamentations 4 is a graphic description of the horrors of the siege of Jerusalem.

The tongue of the sucking child cleaveth to the roof of his
  mouth for thirst:
The young children ask bread, and no man breaketh it unto
  them.   —Lam. 4:4.

> They that are slain with the sword are better than they that
>   are slain with hunger;
> For these pine away, stricken through, for want of the
>   fruits of the field.
> The hands of the pitiful women have boiled their own
>   children;
> They were their food in the destruction of the daughter of
>   my people.
>> —Lam. 4:9, 10.

Lamentations 5 is a plea to God for mercy.

> Remember, O Jehovah, what is come upon us:
> Behold, and see our reproach.
>> —Lam. 5:1.

> Thou, O Jehovah, abidest for ever;
> Thy throne is from generation to generation.
> Wherefore dost thou forget us forever,
> And forsake us so long time?
> Turn thou us unto thee, O Jehovah, and we shall be turned;
> Renew our days as of old.
> But thou hast utterly rejected us;
> Thou art very wroth against us.
>> —Lam. 5:19-22.

EXERCISES

Factual questions
1. Who is the author of Lamentations?
2. Why is Lamentations in the Writings?
3. What is unusual about the form of Lamentations?
4. What is the purpose of Lamentations?

Memory
1. Lamentations 3:21-24.
2. Lamentations 3:41.

Chapter 41

God's Assurance of Blessing after Punishment

Ezekiel

INTRODUCTION

Author

This book is the work of the prophet Ezekiel, a priest who was the son of Buzi. Ezekiel was taken into exile in 597 B.C. during the reign of Jehoiachin. Ezekiel was taken into Babylon along with the nobles and the better classes of the people. There he lived along the river Chebar, in a town called Tel-abib. After he had lived there for five years, he was called of God to be a prophet. At this time he was thirty years old. He continued his prophetic labors for a period of at least twenty-two years.

We see then that Ezekiel was a contemporary of Jeremiah and Daniel. Daniel was taken to Babylon in the first captivity (606 B.C.) and served in the palace of the heathen monarchs. Jeremiah remained in Jerusalem until after its destruction and prophesied to the Jews there. Ezekiel was the prophet whom God sent to the Jews who had gone into captivity.

Ezekiel's Style

Although all the prophets brought the word of the living God, each brought that word in a unique manner. The style of Ezekiel is particularly distinctive. In the first place, Ezekiel uses symbolism more than any other prophet. He does not simply bring the word of God; he acts it out. The siege of Jerusalem is not simply proclaimed; it is portrayed by a miniature city built on a tile (Ezek. 4). The exile of the inhabitants is acted out by Ezekiel himself (Ezek. 12). In addition to these symbolic actions, the prophecy of Ezekiel contains many visions. The vision of the valley of dry bones is probably the best known of these. Even a casual survey of the book will impress the reader with the great amount of symbolism it contains.

In the second place, Ezekiel places a great deal of emphasis on the giving of the message by God. Time and again he begins a prophecy with the words, "The word of Jehovah came unto me, saying, Son of

198

man. . . ." Not only does Ezekiel emphasize that God speaks, but the title which God gives him indicates that he is simply the human servant of the divine master. This repeated introduction adds authority to the words which Ezekiel brings.

PURPOSE

The prophet Ezekiel had two tasks. Before the fall of Jerusalem the exiles were filled with a false optimism. They were sure that they would soon return to Jerusalem. Ezekiel is sent to destroy this idea by insistently preaching that Jerusalem is going to be destroyed because of her sin. After these words were fulfilled and the city had been razed, the optimism of the exiles gave way to an equally strong pessimism. As their temper changed, Ezekiel's message changed. Now God gave him a promise of hope for the future. The purpose of this book is to show that God is righteous, and will punish the sins of His people; and also that God is faithful to His covenant, and will fulfill all His promises.

OUTLINE

I. Messages of judgment   Ezekiel 1-32
II. Messages of hope   Ezekiel 33-46

ANALYSIS

Ezekiel's Call

God called Ezekiel to the prophetic office after he had been in captivity for five years. The call of Ezekiel, like that of Isaiah, involved a vision of God. But Ezekiel's vision is pictured much more fully than is Isaiah's. Ezekiel saw a great cloud and out of it came four living creatures. These are later identified as cherubim, that is, a special class of angelic beings. They are strange and wonderful in appearance, and with them go wheels which are equally strange and wonderful. But these creatures merely prepare the way for the appearance of Jehovah, whose glory is so great that merely seeing it causes Ezekiel to fall upon his face. Then he is called to the prophetic office. Like his contemporary Jeremiah, Ezekiel is given to understand that his work will not be easy. "And he said unto me, Son of man, I send thee to the children of Israel, to nations that are rebellious, which have rebelled against me: they and their fathers have transgressed against me even unto this very day" (Ezek. 2:3).

After seven days God again spoke to the new prophet and explained the solemn duty which was his. "Son of man, I have made thee a watchman unto the house of Israel: therefore hear the word at my mouth, and give them warning from me. When I say unto the wicked, Thou shalt surely die; and thou givest him not warning, nor speakest to warn the wicked from his wicked way, to save his life; the same wicked man shall die in his iniquity; but his blood will I require at thy hand. Yet if thou warn the wicked, and he turn not from his wickedness, nor from his wicked way, he shall die in his iniquity; but thou hast delivered thy soul" (Ezek. 3:17-19).

The Fall of Jerusalem

God gave Ezekiel many different ways to portray the destruction that must befall Jerusalem. If his book is an accurate presentation of his ministry (and it surely is), then Ezekiel seldom preached without using visual aids or casting his message in some graphic form. God told him to take a tile and to build on it the city of Jerusalem. Around the city he was to depict the various instruments of war, thereby showing that Jerusalem would be besieged (Ezek. 4). He was told to cut his hair, then to divide the cut hair into three parts. One part was to be burned, the second cut by the sword, and the third scattered to the winds (Ezek. 5). Thus Ezekiel showed what would happen to the inhabitants of Jerusalem.

The prophet also presented the reason for this destruction of the holy city. In Ezekiel 8-11 he was lifted up and carried to Jerusalem. (This may have been a vision, or God may actually have transported him.) There God showed him the awful idolatries and abominations practiced by the citizens of Jerusalem. Even in the very temple of God such iniquity was practiced. For this reason God would punish the city.

Ezekiel was also shown the punishment. God sent a man with an ink-horn through the city to mark those who were the true worshipers of God. Then six men went through the city to destroy all who were not marked. These men were undoubtedly angels, and they symbolized the destruction that occurred historically when the Babylonians captured Jerusalem.

Once again the prophet was told to puncture the optimistic dreams of his fellow captives. Whereas they looked for a speedy return to Jerusalem, Ezekiel portrayed to them a man beginning a long sad journey. This was a picture of what would happen to the dwellers of Jerusalem (Ezek. 12). Although Jerusalem had not yet fallen, the time of her repentance was past. Jerusalem was doomed to destruction. Nothing could save the city. She was worse than was Sodom in the time of Abraham. Indeed, "though these three men, Noah, Daniel, and Job, were in it, they should deliver but their own souls by their righteousness, saith the Lord Jehovah" (Ezek. 14:14). The punishment which the prophets had foretold is now certain. In a vision Ezekiel sees God departing from His holy city.

The Reasons for Jerusalem's Fall

Ezekiel not only announced to the exiles that Jerusalem would be destroyed. He told them repeatedly the reason for this destruction. The figure of an adulterous woman is frequently used in the Bible to portray the sin of idolatry and departing from God. Ezekiel uses this figure several times. By this comparison Israel is placed in the worst possible light. She has been redeemed by God when utterly helpless in Egypt. She has been given blessing upon blessing. But she has gone aside to other gods. Instead of trusting in Jehovah she has put her trust in alliances with foreign nations. Even the punishment of her adulterous sister, Samaria, did not turn her from her wicked way. Having departed from God, she must now be punished.

The Jews in Ezekiel's time tried to evade responsibility by placing the blame for their sad situation on the sins of their fathers. They used a parable, "The fathers have eaten sour grapes, and the children's teeth are set on edge" (Ezek. 18:2). Thus they tried to blame their evil situation on the sins of their fathers. But such evasion of responsibility God would not permit. He declares, "As I live, saith the Lord Jehovah, ye shall not have occasion any more to use this proverb in Israel. Behold, all souls are mine; as the soul of the father, so also the soul of the son is mine: the soul that sinneth, it shall die" (Ezek. 18:3, 4). These people were sinners. They had not departed from the sins of their fathers. Because of this God's wrath was upon them.

The Final Prophecy of Destruction

Ezekiel began his ministry four years before the final siege of Jerusalem by Nebuchadnezzar. On the day that the siege began God announced it to him, and Ezekiel announced it to the people. It was portrayed by another sign. "Also the word of Jehovah came unto me, saying, Son of man, behold, I take away from thee the desire of thine eyes with a stroke: yet thou shalt neither mourn nor weep, neither shall thy tears run down. Sigh, but not aloud, make no mourning for the dead; bind thy headtire upon thee, and put thy shoes upon thy feet, and cover not thy lips, and eat not the bread of men. So I spake unto the people in the morning; and at even my wife died; and I did in the morning as I was commanded" (Ezek. 24:15-18). This was to teach the exiles how they would act when the news of Jerusalem's fall reached them. "Thus shall Ezekiel be unto you a sign; according to all that he hath done shall ye do: when this cometh, then shall ye know that I am the Lord Jehovah" (Ezek. 24:24).

Prophecies Against the Nations

Ezekiel also included in his book prophecies which he spoke against the nations around Judah. Because of their hatred of God's people they too shall be destroyed. Tyre and Egypt were especially singled out by the prophet. The words which Ezekiel uttered against Tyre are very much like those which describe the fall of Babylon in Revelation 17-18.

Messages of Hope

Ezekiel's ministry changed when Jerusalem fell. That change was marked by a second announcement that God had set him as a watchman over Zion. Now Ezekiel was to bring messages of hope to the depressed and disheartened exiles.

A New Shepherd

One of the causes of Israel's plight lay in the failure of her kings and priests to lead the people in the paths laid out by God. Therefore Ezekiel is told to prophesy against them. "Son of man, prophesy against the shepherds [leaders] of Israel, prophesy, and say unto them, even to the shepherds, Thus saith the Lord Jehovah: Woe unto the shepherds of Israel that do feed themselves! should not the shepherds feed the sheep?" (Ezek. 34:2, 3) These shepherds have led Israel astray, but now Israel shall be led aright for God Himself promises to be the shepherd of Israel. "For thus saith the Lord Jehovah: Behold, I myself, even I, will search for my sheep, and will seek them out. . . . And they shall know that I, Jehovah their God, am with them, and that they, the house of Israel, are my people, saith the Lord Jehovah. And ye my sheep, the sheep of my pasture, are men, and I am your God, saith the Lord Jehovah" (Ezek. 34:11, 30, 31).

New Life for Israel

The vision of the valley of dry bones is well known. It was given to encourage those who had given up hope. By it God promised to breathe new life into His people. "Therefore prophesy, and say unto them, Thus saith the Lord Jehovah: Behold, I will open your graves, and cause you to come up out of your graves, O my people; and I will bring you into the land of Israel. And ye shall know that I am Jehovah, when I have opened your graves, and caused you to come up out of your graves, O my people. And I will put my Spirit in you, and ye shall live, and I will place you in your own land: and ye shall know that I, Jehovah, have spoken it and performed it, saith Jehovah" (Ezek. 37:12-14).

.In connection with this vision God gave another sign. Two sticks, representing Israel and Judah, are miraculously joined together in Ezekiel's hand. This is a sign that God will join the two kingdoms so that they will be one again. We might think that these promises referred to the return from exile. But there is another promise added. "And my servant David shall be king over them; and they all shall have one shepherd: they shall also walk in mine ordinances, and observe my statutes, and do them" (Ezek. 37:24). This promise refers to Christ, the king who reigns on the throne of David. Thus we know that God is speaking of a spiritual restoration of His people—a restoration which began at Pentecost.

The promise of new life for the Church of God is followed by a prophecy about Gog and Magog. These represent nations that will come against the renewed Israel, but will be destroyed by God. This prophecy has been interpreted by some as a prediction of an alliance of modern nations that will fight against the Jews. But it is closely connected to the previous vision. The people of God have been renewed. And immediately there are enemies who seek to destroy them. Satan is always attacking the Church of God. But God will destroy the enemies. By means of the symbolism of these nations warring against the renewed Israel, Ezekiel presents the truth that the gates of Hell shall not prevail against the Church of God.

These prophecies draw our attention again to the Kingdom of God. We are reminded again that destruction of the covenant nation is not the end of God's kingdom. Only outwardly shall the theocracy fall. It will still continue in the small group of pious Israelites who really love Jehovah. It will lie dormant for some time, so that many will think that God's kingdom has been destroyed. But in the fullness of time God will make it clear to all men that His kingdom yet lives. For He will send His king, Jesus Christ, to establish the spiritual theocracy that will continue until the end of time. The Kingdom which once was limited to the nation of Israel will spring to renewed life in the universal Church of Jesus Christ.

The New Temple

The final vision of Ezekiel is very long. It is an elaborate description of a temple, its services, its location in the land, and the arrangement of the twelve tribes around it. This temple cannot be the temple of Solomon, nor the temple that was built after the return from captivity. The temple of Ezekiel's vision is much larger than either of those temples. And there are important differences. There is no most holy place. There is no ark of the covenant. The priests are limited to the family of Zadok instead of the house of Aaron. And there is no mention of a high priest. In fact, to take Ezekiel's description of the temple literally leads to many difficulties. What then does this vision mean?

We must remember that it is a vision. It was never intended to be taken literally. It is a symbol, designed to teach a lesson. And that lesson is contained in the last words of the prophecy, "Jehovah is there" (Ezek. 48:35). This vision pictures, in the language of the Old Testament, the great truth that God dwells in the midst of His people. It presents in Old Testament form the great glory of New Testament Christianity — that God dwells in the hearts of His people. This is certainly a message of hope. Although Jerusalem was destroyed, those who truly loved God could look forward to a day when Jehovah would dwell in the midst of His people. In that hope they could wait and watch.

EXERCISES

Factual questions

1. When and where did Ezekiel prophesy?
2. What is distinctive about Ezekiel's style?
3. What is the purpose of the book of Ezekiel?
4. How was Ezekiel's call symbolized? Ezekiel 2:8ff.
5. In Ezekiel 4 and 5 there are three symbolic actions performed by Ezekiel, and an explanation of each. Describe each action and its meaning.
6. How was Ezekiel to picture the coming exile? Ezek. 12.
7. How was the king of Babylon to decide whether or not he would go against Jerusalem? Ezek. 21:18ff.
8. By what two signs was the destruction of Jerusalem announced to the exiles? Ezek. 24:6ff.
9. What did the exiles think of Ezekiel? Ezek. 33:30ff.
10. Explain what happened in the valley of dry bones. Ezek. 37.
11. What is the meaning of the vision of the valley of dry bones?
12. When God destroys Gog and Magog, how long will it take to clean up the results of the battle? Ezek. 39:11ff.
13. The "long cubit" used in measuring the temple was about two feet long. Ezek. 40:5. How large was the court of the temple in feet? Ezek. 42:15ff.
14. What is the meaning of the vision of the temple?

Thought questions

1. Why did God tell Ezekiel to use so many visions and symbolic actions to bring His word to the people?
2. Some people think that the description of the king of Tyre in Ezekiel 28:11-19 cannot refer to any human being but refers to Satan and his fall. Do you think this is a good interpretation of this passage?

Memory

1. Outline of Ezekiel.
2. Ezekiel 18:4.
3. Ezekiel 33:8, 9.

Chapter 42

The Covenant People under Gentile Dominion

Daniel

INTRODUCTION

The Period of Theocratic Transition

The beginning of the Exile brings us to a new period in the history of the Old Testament, which we call the period of theocratic transition. In our study, we have traced the history of Israel as the covenant nation. We have seen her redeemed from Egypt by the hand of God. We have seen her established as the covenant nation at Sinai, and given the land of Canaan. We have seen the fulfillment of ancient promises when David became the theocratic king. But we have also seen Israel's sinfulness and apostasy. We have seen how this sin led to the division of the kingdom, and finally to the downfall and captivity of both the northern and southern kingdoms.

God had warned Israel that sin would bring punishment, even the punishment of exile. But God had also promised, as we have seen in the Prophets, that He would restore His people to their land, renew them by His Spirit, and erect His kingdom under the Messiah.

So we see that the Exile is not the end of the theocracy. This is not the period of theocratic termination, but of theocratic transition. The Exile had a purpose. It was designed to remove from Israel the sin of idolatry and prepare a people who should receive the fullness of God's covenant promises in Christ.

The Purpose of This Period

"The exile forms a great turning point in the development of the Kingdom of God which He had founded in Israel. With this event the form of the theocracy established at Mt. Sinai comes to an end, and then begins the period of the transition to a new form, which was to be established by Christ, and has been actually established by Him" (Keil). No longer was Israel to be an earthly kingdom. This stage in the development of the theocracy was past. It had served its purpose, and was never to be restored. When the exiles returned to Jerusalem and established again a Jewish state, this was not a restoration of the theocratic nation. Only a small remnant returned. This group was still under the control of heathen powers. And although the temple was rebuilt and the walls of Jerusalem restored, things were never the same. Sacrifices were offered as of old, but now there was no ark of the covenant in the most holy place, and no real presence of God in the sanctuary. The Day of Atonement could no longer be celebrated. Though for a time God gave His word through prophets, after the work of Nehemiah was completed prophecy ceased. There was a period of waiting until God would begin the next step in His program. And this period of waiting prepared Israel for that which was to come. Not a restoration of the national theocracy, but the arrival of the spiritual theocracy in Christ—this was God's plan for His people.

This period performed two great tasks. The time of captivity winnowed the chaff of idolatry out of Israel. Never since the Babylonian captivity have the Jews been known to commit idolatry. And the period of waiting aroused in them a sense of expectancy. They began to long for the coming of the Messiah. The prophets had often spoken of the Messiah, but the people had paid little attention. But now the temple, which lacked the real presence of God, reminded them constantly that their religion lacked something. Now they began to look forward earnestly to the coming of the Messiah.

Historical Background

In order to place properly the events recorded in the books we are about to study, we need to review some important dates and to learn some new ones.

722 B.C. — Samaria fell to Assyria; end of the kingdom of Israel
625 B.C. — The Assyrian empire fell to Babylon
606 B.C. — First Babylonian captivity in the reign of Jehoiakim
597 B.C. — Second Babylonian captivity in the reign of Jehoiachin
586 B.C. — Third Babylonian captivity and destruction of Jerusalem in the reign of Zedekiah
538 B.C. — Babylonian empire fell to Medo-Persia
536 B.C. — First return of Jews under Zerubbabel by decree of Cyrus
458 B.C. — Second return of the Jews under Ezra
445 B.C. — Third return of the Jews under Nehemiah

INTRODUCTION TO DANIEL

Place in the Canon

In the Hebrew Bible, Daniel is included in the Writings, that group of books which was written by men who were not prophets. It may seem strange that Daniel is not considered as one of the prophetical books. It is true that there is a great deal of prophecy in Daniel.

But, technically speaking, Daniel himself was not a prophet; that is, he was not called of God to receive God's word and communicate it to the people. Daniel was a statesman, serving heathen kings. He never occupied the office of prophet, and therefore his book is part of the Writings.

Language

The Old Testament is composed of books that were originally written in Hebrew. But in Daniel about sixty per cent of the book (Daniel 2:4-7:28) is written in Aramaic, the language of the Babylonians. It is difficult to explain this use of two languages. Probably the best explanation is this: Aramaic, being the language of the Babylonian empire, is used in those sections which deal primarily with the world empires. Hebrew, the language of God's people, is used in those sections which deal primarily with the Kingdom of God. This explanation is not without difficulties, but it is accepted by many excellent scholars.

Author

This book was written by the man whose name it bears. We find evidence for this in the book itself. In Daniel 8-12 the author refers to himself as "I, Daniel." In Daniel 12:4 he is told to preserve the book in which these words are written. Jesus has reference to Daniel 9:27 and 11:31 when He speaks of the "abomination of desolation which was spoken of through Daniel the prophet" (Matt. 24:15). All the biblical evidence points to Daniel as the author.

We have seen in our previous study of the Old Testament that men do not always accept what the Bible teaches about the authorship of Old Testament books. So it is with Daniel. Many scholars try to place the book of Daniel at a later date. They say that it was written in the Maccabean period. (This period runs from about 165-63 B.C. The name Maccabean refers to a family of high priests who became the leaders of a rebellion which won independence for the Jews.) This late date would mean that Daniel could not have been the author.

Why do men deny that Daniel wrote this book? Their denial is based upon the idea that predictive prophecy is impossible. These men believe that God cannot reveal what will happen in the future. Some may admit that God can present broad outlines of the future, but deny that He can give the details. In either form, this is a denial of God's sovereignty. God's revelation of future events is based upon His control of future events. Men deny that God reveals the future because they do not believe that He controls the future.

When one studies the book of Daniel he is brought face to face with some remarkable prophecies. Several visions trace broadly the future history of the Gentile empires. The last vision is most specific. The history of Antiochus Epiphanes, a king who ruled in Syria from 175-164 B.C., is presented in great detail. While this king is not mentioned by name, the description is so clear that all scholars agree that the prophecy speaks about him. This leaves only two alternatives. Either one believes that Daniel was given this revelation about Antiochus in advance, or else one must insist that this account was written after Antiochus lived. The Critics take the latter view. But those who believe that God controls the future will gladly confess that He can also predict the future.

Daniel

The author of this book is also its chief character. Daniel is an outstanding figure. Even in his lifetime he was so highly regarded that Ezekiel pointed to him as an example for the other Israelites. Daniel was taken into captivity in 606 B.C. He was a child of noble birth, perhaps of royal parentage. He was educated to serve in the court of Nebuchadnezzar. He became the most learned man in Babylon, and rose to a position of honor. After Nebuchadnezzar's death he seems to have lost favor, but was restored to a position of honor just before the death of Belshazzar. He continued in this high position under Darius and Cyrus, the Medo-Persian rulers.

Daniel was a youth of perhaps fifteen to eighteen years of age when carried to Babylon. He was still active when the seventy years of captivity ended. He did not return with the exiles, but remained at the court. His last vision came two years after the first group of exiles returned to Jerusalem. At this time he was an old man approaching the age of ninety. His life spanned a dark period in the history of Israel. Throughout his life he was a faithful servant of God.

PURPOSE

The Exile had ended the national existence of God's people. The Jews were captives, controlled by heathen rulers. This time of exile must have caused the pious Jews to wonder if God's plan had failed. Were the promises to Abraham and David to be forgotten? The book of Daniel provides convincing proof that they were not forgotten. God's plan does not fail. God is still sovereign. He rules over the heathen rulers. And He guides the course of history so that His purposes will be fulfilled.

OUTLINE

I. God's control of Gentile empires   Daniel 1- 7

II. The future of the Kingdom of God   Daniel 8-12

ANALYSIS

Miracles

Anyone who has read the book of Daniel must admit that miracles play an important part in the book. There are miracles that show God's omnipotence (almighty power) and those that show His omniscience (knowledge of all things). When we study the Bible carefully, we discover that there are four periods when miracles abound — the time of the Exodus, the days of Elijah and Elisha, the time of Daniel, and the Apostolic Age. These clusters of miracles come at important points in the history of the theocracy. The first and fourth periods come when a new form of the Kingdom is being established: the national theocracy in Israel and the spiritual theocracy in the Church. The second and third come when the Kingdom is endangered by the forces of Satan: the false worship of Baal and the heathen power of Babylon. By means of miracles the theocracy is established, and by means of miracles the Kingdom is protected.

This point is important in our study of the book of Daniel. We must not think of the miracles and visions in this book as mere curiosities. They played an important part in the divine plan of redemption. Even as God used mighty signs and wonders to deliver Israel from the bondage of Egypt, so now He used miracles and visions to show clearly that He alone is God. The miracles of the book of Daniel help to achieve the purpose of the book — to display God's sovereignty to Israel and the Gentile nations.

God's Care of His People

The contents of the book of Daniel may be classified into three groups. There are stories which show God's care of His people in their captivity, accounts of God's control of the heathen rulers, and visions about the future.

The stories which display God's protection of His people are very familiar. They are found in Daniel 1, 3, and 6. By means of these incidents the captive Israelites were reminded that God had not changed. He still protected and blessed those who were faithful to His covenant.

God's Control of Heathen Rulers

In caring for His people, God overruled some of the plans of the heathen rulers. But there are two striking accounts which show directly how God controls even the greatest rulers of world empires. One of those stories is an account of God's mercy as well as His justice. Nebuchadnezzar, warned in a dream of the humiliation that awaited him, nevertheless continued in his pride. As God had declared, he became like a beast. He was affected with a disease known as lycanthropy, in which the sufferer thinks that he is an animal and acts like that animal. Nebuchadnezzar continued in this existence for a considerable length of time, until he prayed, and confessed that God is truly sovereign. His confession is most beautiful. "I blessed the Most High, and I praised and honored him that liveth for ever; for his dominion is an everlasting dominion, and his kingdom from generation to generation; and all the inhabitants of the earth are reputed as nothing; and he doeth according to his will in the army of heaven and among the inhabitants of earth; and none can stay his hand, or say unto him, What doest thou?" (Dan. 4:34, 35) After this Nebuchadnezzar was restored to his throne.

The other incident concerns Belshazzar, who ruled as coregent with his father Nabonidus during the last days of the Babylonian empire. In the midst of a drunken reveling, a hand appeared and wrote on the wall. As Daniel interpreted it, the writing spoke of judgment. And even that night the judgment fell, for Babylon was captured and Belshazzar was slain.

Visions about the Future

The visions in this book are all rather closely connected. They all deal with the period from the time of Daniel to the time of Christ. Two of them are especially close. The dream of Nebuchadnezzar (Dan. 2) and the vision of Daniel (Dan. 7) both deal with the great Gentile world powers that will arise. Babylon, Medo-Persia, Greece, and Rome are presented in symbols. Nebuchadnezzar's dream about a great statue of various metals presents the outward glory of these empires. Daniel's vision about the beasts which arise from the sea shows their internal characteristics. Each vision ends with a picture of the Kingdom of God triumphing over the kingdoms of men.

These two visions teach a common lesson. They show that no world power is lasting. Each has its day of glory, then sinks before the onslaught of another. And each in its turn becomes less glorious and more vicious. In striking contrast to these is the Kingdom of God. It is eternal and universal. It judges the wickedness of the heathen, and establishes righteousness in the earth.

Antiochus Epiphanes

The outline indicates that in Daniel 8-12 the emphasis shifts from God's control of the heathen empires to the future of the Kingdom of God. This shift in emphasis needs to be explained. It is in this section that the most detailed prophecies are to be found. In Daniel 8 and 10 - 12 we have two visions which are quite similar. Both deal with Persia and Greece. Both focus our attention on a figure in history who was a great persecutor of the Jews, Antiochus Epiphanes. The first of these visions is general; the second is very specific.

Why is our attention called to this man? It is for two reasons. Antiochus tried to wipe out the worship of Jehovah and establish a Grecian worship in Judea. His terrible persecutions and blasphemous actions provoked a revolt which won independence for the Jews. It also brought about a reaction which turned the people back to God in great numbers. In this way Antiochus prepared for the coming of Christ.

Antiochus is also important because he is a type. In his hatred of the true God and fury against those who worship Jehovah, Antiochus pictured the Antichrist, whom Paul describes as "he that opposeth and exalteth himself against all that is called God or that is worshipped; so that he sitteth in the temple of God, setting himself forth as God" (II Thess. 2:4). The prophecy about Antiochus in Daniel 10 - 12 leads into a prophecy about the Antichrist. In this prophecy we learn of the final destruction of the Antichrist and the complete triumph of the Kingdom of God.

The Coming of Christ

Daniel 9 is the keystone of the second section of Daniel. In this chapter we have a clear promise of the coming of the Messiah. Daniel's study of Jeremiah teaches him that the time of captivity is nearly over. This leads to a penitential prayer in which he confesses the sins of Israel. Then he receives a vision. He is told of seventy weeks which have been decreed. In that time Jerusalem will be rebuilt. In that time the Messiah will come and carry out His work of redemption. And after that the city will be destroyed. This vision points directly to the coming of Christ.

VALUE

The book of Daniel supplied a need for Daniel and his people. In a very dark hour, it was a ray of light. It assured them that God was still sovereign. The heathen empires, which seemed so strong, were really under His control. And He was bringing to pass His own will. The Kingdom of God was still coming. The Messiah would appear.

This book is also helpful to us. Sometimes the future of the Church seems dark. All the world seems to be against her. Yet, as we read Daniel, we are reminded that God is still on the throne. He has sent the Messiah, as He promised. And He is still guiding His covenant people toward the final victory, when Christ shall return to judge the living and the dead. All the hosts of Hell cannot prevent that victory. And until that day, even the gates of Hell cannot prevail against God's church.

EXERCISES

Factual questions

1. What was the purpose of the Exile?
2. What two tasks were accomplished by the period of theocratic transition?
3. Why is the book of Daniel in the Writings?
4. Why do some men reject the belief that Daniel wrote this book?
5. What was Daniel's work?
6. What is unusual about the language of the book of Daniel?
7. When was Daniel taken captive?
8. Under what rulers did he serve?
9. What is the purpose of the book of Daniel?
10. Why are miracles so important in the book of Daniel?
11. Into what three groups may the book of Daniel be classified?
12. What three stories tell of God's protection of His faithful servants? Dan. 1, 3, 6.
13. What judgment came upon Nebuchadnezzar? Dan. 4:28ff.
14. What brought this judgment upon him? Dan. 4:28ff.
15. Why was Belshazzar punished? Dan. 5.
16. How was Belshazzar punished? Dan. 5:29ff.
17. What empires are represented by the various parts of the statue in Nebuchadnezzar's dream? Dan. 2:36ff.
18. Name the four beasts of Daniel's vision and tell which empire each represents. Dan. 7.
19. Whom do the ram and goat in Daniel 8 represent?
20. Why is Antiochus Epiphanes important?
21. For what purpose were the seventy weeks decreed? Dan. 9:24ff.

Thought questions

1. Why did Daniel refuse the king's food? Lev. 11.
2. What does the stone in Nebuchadnezzar's dream represent? Dan. 2.
3. How can we apply the example of the three Hebrews to our own lives? Dan. 3.
4. Who was in the fire with the three Hebrews? Dan. 3.
5. Was Nebuchadnezzar saved? Read Dan. 2:46, 47; 3:14, 15; 3:28, 29; 4:29, 30, 34, 35.
6. Do all nations have special angels? Dan. 10:13, 20, 21.

Memory

1. Outline of Daniel.
2. Daniel 4:35.
3. Daniel 7:13, 14.
4. Daniel 12:2, 3.

Chapter 43

The Covenant People under Divine Protection

Esther

INTRODUCTION

Canonicity of Esther

The right of the book of Esther to a place in the Old Testament has often been disputed. Martin Luther disliked it heartily, and once said that he wished that it had never been written. The Higher Critics have attacked the book, and even some Christian scholars have questioned it.

As we read the book of Esther we may understand why this is so. Not once in the book is God mentioned. There is no record of any worship, except one mention of prayer and fasting. It seems quite different from the other books of the Old Testament. But in spite of all contrary opinions we may safely regard this book as part of the Word of God. Both the content of the book and the judgment of history lead us to that conclusion.

Even though the book of Esther does not mention the name of God, the hand of God is clearly visible in the book. There is a satisfactory explanation for the lack of the divine name and of all the usual practices of public worship. And just as we would not admit that every book that uses the name of God is inspired, so we cannot flatly declare that a book which does not use His name is not inspired. In Esther we see the providence of God displayed in a striking way. In this way it is a revelation of God.

We must not ignore the fact that the Jews have never questioned the right of Esther to a place in the canon. They have always accepted it. It is true that the Jews can be charged with many sins. But never have they been accused of corrupting the Word of God. Christ accepted the Jewish Bible as the Sacred Scriptures. And Esther was in the Jewish Bible.

Place in the Canon

The book of Esther is placed in the Writings, which indicates that the Jews believed that it was written by someone who was not a prophet. Since the story of Esther occurs near the end of the Old Testament period, the Jews who made the final collection of the Old Testament books were in a good position to know who the author was. So we may be reasonably certain that Esther is properly considered as part of the Writings.

Within the Writings, Esther is included in that division known as the Megilloth, or the Five Rolls. This includes those books which were read at the five feasts of the Jewish year. Esther was read at the feast of Purim. This is most natural, since the story of Esther tells how the Purim festival came to be instituted.

Author

The author of Esther was not a prophet. Apparently, the only prophets after the return from exile were Haggai, Zechariah, and Malachi. They all prophesied to the returned exiles. But it is most probable that the author of Esther was one of the Jews who had not returned to Judea. Living in Persia, where the events of Esther took place, he would be better able to record the narrative found in this book.

Date

The Persian ruler who took Esther as his queen is known to us as Xerxes, who ruled over the Persian empire from 485-465 B.C. This places the events of this book in the same time as those recorded in Ezra. The first return to Jerusalem had occurred, but Ezra had not yet led his group back to Judea. The book itself was written after the death of Xerxes, probably sometime during the last half of the fifth century B.C.

PURPOSE

To understand the purpose of the book of Esther we must consider the times in which these events took place. We should also try to understand why the author does not use the name of God.

Cyrus had issued his edict allowing the Jews to return to their land. But only a small minority had chosen to go. Among this remnant the flame of zeal for the theocracy still burned brightly. But most of the Jews had settled themselves in the heathen lands. Their zeal for the Kingdom of God was only a dying ember, if it had not altogether been extinguished. They had no desire to leave their homes and businesses. Their religion occupied a secondary place in their lives. The punishment of exile had removed the sin of outward idolatry from among the Israelites. But, for this majority, the punishment had not truly turned their hearts back to Jehovah.

This people had forsaken Jehovah. They had been faithless to His covenant. This probably explains why the book of Esther makes no mention of the name of God, nor does it picture any public worship. But God is faithful, even when His people are faithless. He who visits the sins of the fathers upon the children, upon the third and fourth generation also shows lovingkindness unto thousands of generations of those who love Him and keep His commandments. So in the book of Esther we see how God providentially protected His covenant people from destruction, even though they had departed from Him.

But the book of Esther also has a definite connection with the further development of God's kingdom. The characters in the book are those who had not returned to Jerusalem. But the events which took place had great significance for those who had returned. That little band led by Zerubbabel, now residing in Judah, was not outside of the Persian empire. The decree of Cyrus did not free the Jews. It only permitted them to remove themselves to that part of his empire from which they had been deported. So the danger which the Jews faced affected also the remnant in Judah, from which the Messiah was to come. The work of Esther influenced the whole future of the Kingdom of God.

OUTLINE

    I. The deliverer of the Jews is crowned   Esther 1, 2
   II. The extermination of the Jews is planned   Esther 3, 4
  III. The enemy of the Jews is killed   Esther 5- 8
  IV. The victory of the Jews is celebrated   Esther 9, 10

ANALYSIS

The Workings of Providence

In much of the Old Testament we see God working in a supernatural way. But in Esther we see how He works in and through the natural events of daily life. We call this the providence of God.

In this book we may trace how many events—large and small, good and evil—work together to carry out the purposes of God. The king makes an unusual request of his queen. She refuses to do as he commands. The king's counselors advise a divorce and the choice of a new queen. The king is pleased to choose Esther. What a strange combination of circumstances brings this Jewish girl to the Persian throne!

And when the wicked Haman plots the destruction of the Jews, it is again a strange set of circumstances that foils his plot: the opportunity that Mordecai gets to be of service to the king by informing him of a plot against his life, the failure to do anything to honor Mordecai at the time, a sleepless night for the king, a call for a reading of the history of the kingdom, and the honor heaped upon Mordecai at a time when it was most necessary. God uses strange events to bring His purposes to pass.

Mordecai appears to be a man like Nehemiah. He was a godly man, but was prevented from returning to Judah because of his position at the palace. He believed in Jehovah, and he believed that Jehovah would save His people. The thought of God's providence is clearly seen in his challenge to Esther. "For if thou altogether holdest thy peace at this time, then will relief and deliverance arise to the Jews from another place, but thou and thy father's house will perish: and who knoweth whether thou art not come to the kingdom for such a time as this?" (Esther 4: 14)

The Defeat of Evil

The entire Bible shows how Satan and his evil forces will be defeated. The story of Esther is one historical example of the defeat of evil. Haman, the villain of the story, is surely an evil character. He is altogether self-centered, and he will stop at nothing to accomplish his goals. He is contrasted to Mordecai, the godly Jew, who will not give worship to any man, although everyone else bows to Haman. Haman will not rest until he is avenged of this insult to his pride. Not only Mordecai, but all the Jews, must die. And Haman's influence with the king makes it possible for him to further his evil purposes.

Yet Haman is defeated. By the workings of God's providence, the tables are turned. Haman is hanged on the gallows he had prepared for Mordecai. The Jews are enabled to defend themselves and to defeat their enemies. And Mordecai ascends to the place of honor which Haman had held.

EXERCISES

Factual questions

1. Why is the canonicity of the book of Esther questioned?
2. Why should we accept Esther as part of God's word?
3. Where do the Jews place Esther in the Old Testament canon?
4. When and where was Esther probably written?
5. What is the purpose of the book of Esther?
6. How do the events of Esther fit into the development of the theocracy?
7. Why did Ahasuerus divorce Queen Vashti? Esther 1:9ff.
8. How did Mordecai save the king's life? Esther 2:19ff.
9. Why was Haman determined to wipe out the Jews? Esther 3.
10. How did Esther risk her life to save her people? Esther 4:9-5:4.
11. How was the honor to be given Mordecai decided upon? Esther 6.
12. What is the feast of Purim? Esther 9:26ff.

Thought questions
1. Was Vashti right or wrong in refusing the king's demand?
2. Why did Esther make two banquets before telling the king what she wanted?
3. What examples of "poetic justice" can you find in this book?

Memory
1. Outline of Esther.

Chapter 44

The Covenant People Returns to Its Land

Ezra-Nehemiah

The Jews, when they arranged the books of the Old Testament, united the two books of Ezra and Nehemiah into one. They did not think that these books were both written by the same author. It is difficult to explain the reason for so uniting them. Perhaps it was due to the fact that they deal with the same story, have the same purpose, and combine to present a finished narrative. At any rate, we will find it profitable to deal with them together.

INTRODUCTION

Authors

Some Higher Critics have maintained that Chronicles, Ezra, and Nehemiah were all written by one author. We have seen that Chronicles and Ezra were probably written by one man. From the book of Ezra we may gather that they were written by Ezra, the priest who was also a scribe of the law of God. In the last few chapters of Ezra the author speaks of himself in the first person singular. There is no reason to question the authorship of Ezra.

But Ezra did not write Nehemiah. In this book we find the author of Nehemiah speaking of himself in the first person singular. Each of these books was written by the man whose name it bears. In each the author is the main character.

Since Ezra and Nehemiah wrote the books which bear their names, two matters are clear. First, these books were written about the middle of the fifth century B.C. They are some of the last books to be included in the canon of the Old Testament. Second, these books properly belong in the Writings. Ezra was a priest. Nehemiah was an official in the Persian court. Neither of them was a prophet. Their works are therefore included in the historical books of the Writings.

PURPOSE

The Exile had ended the theocratic nation. But God had not cast off His people whom He had loved. He gathered a remnant from among the heathen and brought them back to the land which He had given them. Through this group He prepared the way for the next step in the development of His kingdom—the coming of Christ. Ezra and Nehemiah show us how God re-established His people in their land, and guided their life by His holy law.

EZRA

OUTLINE

I.	Return under Zerubbabel	Ezra 1, 2
II.	Restoration of temple and worship	Ezra 3 - 6
III.	Return under Ezra	Ezra 7, 8
IV.	Reforms led by Ezra	Ezra 9, 10

ANALYSIS

The Decree of Cyrus

The words of the prophets had been fulfilled. Israel and Judah had continued in sin, and the prophetic predictions of punishment had been fulfilled. But the words of the prophets had not ended there. Jeremiah had said, "These nations shall serve the king of Babylon seventy years. And it shall come to pass, when seventy years are accomplished, that I will punish the king of Babylon, and that nation, saith Jehovah, for their iniquity" (Jer. 25:11, 12). And long ago through Isaiah God had spoken of Cyrus, saying, "He is my shepherd, and shall perform all my pleasure, even saying of Jerusalem, She shall be built; and of the temple, Thy foundation shall be laid" (Isa. 44:28). And this word of God was also fulfilled. Seventy years after the captivity of Judah, Babylon was taken by Cyrus, the Medo-Persian king. And this Cyrus issued a decree permitting the Jews to return to the land of Judah.

The Return

The response to the decree was not overwhelming. Many of the exiled Jews were content to remain in the land of captivity. They had no wish to leave their homes and businesses and the land of their birth. But there was a godly minority who longed to return to Jerusalem and re-establish the worship of Jehovah according to His law. And so, in the year 536 B.C., Zerubbabel led about fifty thousand men and women back to Judah and Jerusalem.

Rebuilding the Temple

Back in Judah, the returned exiles began the work of rebuilding the temple. All did not go well. At first the half-breed Samaritans wished to join them. But when the Jews rejected the help of those who did not truly worship Jehovah, the Samaritans became their enemies. They harried the Jews in every way possible. They were so successful in their efforts that work on the temple ceased. But the prophets of God,

Haggai and Zechariah, stirred up the people. In the reign of Darius the work was again begun and in the year 515 B.C. the temple was completed and dedicated.

The rebuilding of the temple and the re-establishment of the ancient sacrifices were important events in the lives of these people. But these events did not signify the rebirth of the covenant nation. The old order of things was not to be restored. There was no theocratic king ruling in Jerusalem. The Jews were still very much under the control of the heathen rulers. And when the temple was dedicated, the glory of God did not fill the most holy place as it had done in the past. God's purposes do not move backward. These people were not to restore the theocratic nation but to prepare for the coming of the theocratic King.

The Return of Ezra

Almost eighty years after the first group of exiles returned, Ezra led a second group back to Jerusalem. This group brought an offering from the Jews who did not return and from the Medo-Persian ruler for the temple in Jerusalem. Ezra carried a letter from the king Artaxerxes ordering all the treasurers in that part of his kingdom to give to Ezra whatever he needed for the worship of God. God's blessing was resting on His covenant people.

The Reforms of Ezra

The Exile had been God's punishment upon Israel for her sin. By the Exile Israel was purified from her tendency to commit idolatry. But the people were not free from sin. In fact, the returned exiles fell into one of the grievous sins which had afflicted their forefathers. They married heathen women of the surrounding nations. When Ezra learned of this he was horrified. He fasted and prayed for the people. And then he began a reformation movement which resulted in the complete separation of the people from their foreign wives. It was not easy to divorce wives and separate families. But the covenant people of God were still called to be separate from the world.

NEHEMIAH

OUTLINE

    I. The rebuilding of the walls   Nehemiah 1- 7
   II. The reforms of Ezra and Nehemiah   Nehemiah 8-13

ANALYSIS

Nehemiah Rebuilds the Walls

The opening scenes of the book of Nehemiah give us insight into the character of its author. Although he had remained in Persia, probably because of his important position in the court, Nehemiah had the welfare of Jerusalem and the returned exiles at heart. When news came to him that "the remnant that are left of the captivity there in the province are in great affliction and reproach: the wall of Jerusalem also is broken down, and the gates thereof are burned with fire" (Neh. 1:3), he was extremely sad. He gave himself to fasting and prayer. He could not hide his sadness from the king. When he had explained the cause, the king sent him to Jerusalem to remedy the situation.

After first surveying the situation, Nehemiah revealed to the elders his plan for rebuilding the walls. The people, led by the priests, willingly joined in the work. But again the work of reconstruction aroused enmity. Tobiah and Sanballat, heathen leaders of nearby peoples, conspired to stop the work. They threatened an armed attack, but Nehemiah provided defenses and armed the builders, and the work continued. They tried to trick Nehemiah, but their plans failed. In fifty-two days the walls were rebuilt. Jerusalem was again secure from its adversaries.

The Reforms of Ezra and Nehemiah

Unfortunately, the rebuilding of the walls was not the only work that needed to be done. There were sins among the people that must be dealt with. Nehemiah even had to pause in the building of the walls to deal with those who were unjustly treating the poor.

The work of Ezra and Nehemiah continued after the walls were rebuilt. There was an important work yet to be done. The people needed to be reminded again of the importance of God's law for them. This was done at a great service, where all the people gathered to hear Ezra read the law of Moses and explain it to them.

As a result of this reading of the law, two significant events took place. The people learned about the Feast of Tabernacles. This feast had been neglected for generations. But now it was celebrated again. And this service led to a full-scale confession of sin, after which they formally renewed their covenant with Jehovah. The people promised not to mingle with the heathen, to observe the Sabbath faithfully, and to provide offerings for Jehovah according to the law.

Nehemiah returned to Persia, to the court of the king. How long he remained there is not known. But he did return to Jerusalem again, and there discovered that the people had gone back on their covenant promises. Precisely the things they had promised to do were not being done. Tobiah, the heathen leader, had been given a place of honor in the city, the Sabbath was being broken, and the offerings were not being brought to the house of God. Nehemiah had to exert his authority to put an end to these sins.

CONCLUSION

The story of Ezra and Nehemiah brings us to the conclusion of the inspired history of the ancient Jews. Therefore it would be well at this juncture if we surveyed once more the development of the theocracy.

The story of the Bible is the record of the rebuilding of the theocracy which replaces the first theocracy that was destroyed by sin. Since sin not only destroyed that original theocracy, but also plunged mankind into a state of sin and misery which results in eternal death, the second theocracy must necessarily be a redemptive theocracy. It must restore man to his proper relationship to God by destroying both sin and the effects of sin. This redemptive theocracy came into being by a process of development. Let us review the steps by which such development occurred.

The giving of the first promise of redemption in the Garden of Eden lit the flame of the theocracy in a world suddenly darkened by sin. For some centuries the flame was small, carried by the line of Seth, and limited at one time to the family of Noah. But the flame received new fuel in the patriarchal period. The promise to Abraham that the theocracy would be established with him and his children both protected the flame from the blasts of unbelief and limited its glow to Abraham's family.

Again there was a time when the theocratic flame burned low. The centuries of bondage in Egypt threatened to extinguish it. But instead the powerful work of God, redeeming His chosen people from bondage and forming them into a nation, fanned the dying spark into a lively flame. And the continued work of God throughout the days of Moses and Joshua added fuel to that flame, so that a truly theocratic nation was firmly established in the promised land at the time of Joshua's death.

But it seems to be necessary, in the wise providence of God, that every forward step in the development of the theocracy must be prefaced by a time of darkness. In the days of the judges the flame burned low indeed. The revival under Samuel was threatened by the selfish rule of Saul. But suddenly the flame of the theocracy burned again, more brightly than ever before, in the theocratic kingdom of David and Solomon.

If only the glories of such a time could remain! But the all-pervasive influence of sin ever tends to reduce that theocratic flame. The sins of Solomon and his successors brought the theocratic nation slowly but surely down to destruction. Finally it came—the Babylonian captivity.

Was the flame of the theocracy extinguished? Was the work of God destroyed? No! Even in the darkness of the Exile the flame burned on—tiny but unextinguished. The nation, which had been for so many centuries the home of the theocracy, had perished. But the theocracy did not die with it. "Except Jehovah of hosts had left unto us a very small remnant, we should have been as Sodom, we should have been like unto Gomorrah" (Isa. 1:9). But God did leave that remnant. Out of the ruins of the captive nation, He restored to Judah and Jerusalem a godly minority, who again established a temple and again lived by His law. The flame grew in size once more.

But again the flame flickered. Ezra, Nehemiah, and the prophets after the Exile labored with the sinful descendants of the godly remnant. And when after this time the voice of God ceased, when four hundred silent years followed each other with never a word from Jehovah, the flame seemed sure to go out. But it never did. A godly remnant ever continued, looking forward to the day when the promises of God would be fulfilled and the Messiah of God would come.

That day dawned—the great and glorious day when God sent His own Son into the world to establish His kingdom in a new and wonderful form. That, of course, is the story of the New Testament. But it is also the day of glory to which the entire Old Testament points.

EXERCISES

Factual questions

1. Who was the author of the the book of Ezra? Of Nehemiah?
2. When were these books written?
3. What is the purpose of these books?
4. What did Cyrus give to those who were willing to return to Judah? Ezra 1:5ff.
5. What was the first thing that the returned exiles did to restore the worship of Jehovah? Ezra 3.
6. What was the reaction of the people when the foundation of the temple was laid? Ezra 3:10ff.
7. How did the enemies of the Jews stop the work on the temple? Ezra 4:7ff.
8. What did Darius do when he found the edict of Cyrus? Ezra 6.
9. What did Ezra do when he learned of the mixed marriages of the Israelites? Ezra 9:3ff.
10. What did the men do who had married foreign wives? Ezra 10:9ff.
11. How did Nehemiah protect the builders of the wall from their enemies? Neh. 4:9ff.
12. What two types of strategy did Tobiah and Sanballat use to try to get rid of Nehemiah? Neh. 6.

13. Tell exactly how the Jews broke the promises to God which they had made in Nehemiah 10. Neh. 13.

Thought questions

1. Why did the Jews refuse to allow their neighbors to join with them in building the temple?
2. What was lacking when this temple was dedicated? See I Kings 8:1-11. What significance does this have?
3. Why are mixed marriages so dangerous for God's people?
4. Why did the people, when they were confessing their sin (Neh. 9), make so much mention of sins which had been committed a thousand years before?
5. Describe the character of these people who had returned from exile and now dwelt in Jerusalem.

Memory

1. Outline of Ezra.
2. Outline of Nehemiah.

Chapter 45

God's Philosophy for the Covenant People

Ecclesiastes

INTRODUCTION

Author

For many years it was thought that the introductory words of this book indicated that the author was King Solomon. This was the view of the Jews. For centuries it was the view of the Christian Church, and no one thought to question it. Luther was apparently the first man to raise doubts about the Solomonic authorship. And modern scholars are almost unanimous in agreeing that it was not written by Solomon, but was written after the Exile.

What caused this change of opinion? Some of the reasons are technical, but a few simple reasons may be easily understood.

1. This book does not claim to be written by Solomon. It is the work of "the Preacher." Every other work written by Solomon bears his name. His name stands before the psalms he wrote, at the beginning of his proverbs, and as a title to the Songs of Songs. If Solomon wrote this book, why did he not use his name? It is true that many have taken the title "Preacher" as a title belonging to Solomon. But the book does not clearly state that it is written by him.

2. The book says, "I the Preacher was king over Israel in Jerusalem" (Eccles. 1:12). If this is interpreted strictly, it teaches that the writer was king and is king no longer. This was never true of Solomon who reigned until his death.

3. The language of the book is the language of the period after the Exile. Languages change. Shakespeare could not have written in twentieth-century English. Nor could Solomon have written in post-exilic Hebrew.

4. The conditions of Israel are not those of Solomon's time. (a) The people say, "What is the cause that the former days were better?" (Eccl. 7:10). The people would not say that in Solomon's day, when Israel was at the height of its glory. (b) The writer sees wickedness in the place of justice (Eccles. 3:16). This does not fit Solomon's day for he received wisdom from God to rule the people well. (c) In the writer's

time it was dangerous to criticize the king (Eccles. 10:20). Certainly King Solomon would not have written that.

Since the book does not actually claim to be the work of Solomon, and since the language and the circumstances do not fit Solomon's time, scholars have concluded that he did not write the book. And since the language and the circumstances do fit the time of Nehemiah when the Israelites were under the Persian rule and were oppressed and heavily burdened, it is almost certain that Ecclesiastes was written in this period. The writer surely refers to Solomon. He uses Solomon as the personification of wisdom. But he writes to the people among whom he lived, and he seeks to help them.

PURPOSE

This book was written to explain the ways of God to His oppressed people, in order to comfort them in sorrow, encourage them in their labors, and direct them to godliness. This is accomplished by showing the vanity of earthly things apart from God and by leading them to a recognition of the great duty of man—to fear God and keep His commandments.

ANALYSIS

The Theme

The author of this book begins with a statement of the theme he is going to develop. "Vanity of vanities, saith the Preacher; vanity of vanities, all is vanity. What profit hath man of all his labor wherein he laboreth under the sun?" (Eccles. 1:2, 3) This world with all that fills it is just so much emptiness, and all that man can get of this world's goods and pleasures is but a puff of smoke. This is the author's estimate of the world he lives in—and it is a true estimate of the world which is in bondage to sin and subjected to vanity (Rom. 8:20). Having stated his theme, he goes on to demonstrate how true it is. He points out from his experiences the truth of his theme.

The Vanity of Wisdom

First he shows the vanity of wisdom. Wisdom is the highest of this world's possessions, sought after by the noblest of men. "And I applied my heart to seek and to search out by wisdom concerning all that is done under heaven: it is a sore travail that God hath given to the sons of men to be exercised therewith. . . . For in much wisdom is much grief; and he that increaseth knowledge increaseth sorrow" (Eccles. 1:13, 18). Even wisdom, that is, the wisdom of the world, is empty and vain.

The Vanity of Pleasure

From wisdom the Preacher turns to pleasure. Pleasures of all sorts are his, yet he retains wisdom so that he may evaluate pleasure. And his conclusion is this: "And whatsoever mine eyes desired I kept not from them; I withheld not my heart from any joy; for my heart rejoiced because of all my labor. . . and, behold, all was vanity and a striving after wind, and there was no profit under the sun" (Eccles. 2:10, 11).

The pleasure of the Preacher was not limited to feasting and drinking and other such pleasures of the flesh. He also took great delight in architecture, gardening, and other useful pleasures. What made these pleasures so empty? Behind all his labors, and all the pleasurable activities which the Preacher filled his time, there was a thought which filled him with bitterness. "And I hated all my labor wherein I labored under the sun, seeing that I must leave it unto the man that shall be after me. And who knoweth whether he will be a wise man or a fool?" (Eccles. 2:18, 19) All man's labor is also emptiness. So what shall a man do? He may as well enjoy what he has, and not covet. "There is nothing better for a man, than that he should eat and drink, and make his soul enjoy good in his labor. This also I saw, that it is from the hand of God" (Eccles. 2:24).

The Providence of God

The Preacher pauses to think about these things, and he sees in it all the working of God's providence. There is a time for everything; it is all in God's hands. God has made all things. He has given man a unique position. And yet man cannot understand the world in which he lives. "He hath made everything beautiful in its time: also he hath set eternity in their heart, yet so that man cannot find out the work that God hath done from the beginning even to the end" (Eccles. 3:11). Man can only wait for that which God brings to him, and do good while he waits. Even when there is wickedness in the seat of justice, we must remember that there is a time for everything, and God will judge in the proper time.

All Is Vanity

Oppression, envy, a man piling up riches and having no one to share them—all these the Preacher surveys and again sees vanity on every side. In contrast to such vanity of the things of earth is set the worship of God. The Preacher is aware how prone we are to bring the world's standards into the house of God. He warns against it. "Be not rash with thy mouth, and let not thy heart be hasty to utter anything before God; for God is in heaven, and thou upon earth: therefore let thy words be few. . . . When thou vowest a vow to God, defer not to pay it; for he hath no pleasure in fools: pay that which thou vowest" (Eccles. 5:2, 4).

Why does the Preacher emphasize the vanity of all worldly things? When we remember the times in which he wrote, we can find a good reason. The Jews were heavily oppressed by their Persian rulers. They were unhappy, especially when they compared their miserable state to the glory of Solomon's time. They were despondent. So the author seeks to comfort them in their misery by reminding them that all things are vanity. Riches or poverty, sickness or health, freedom or oppression—all is emptiness. So why be depressed about that which you do not have? Rejoice in what God has given you.

This comfort is applicable to all God's people who are in miserable conditions. It teaches us to take our eyes off the things we lack and to count the blessings we have. And learning that lesson is one of the important steps to happiness.

Words of Wisdom

Now the Preacher presents to his people words of wisdom to guide them in their affliction. He reminds them that the end of a thing is better than the beginning. Therefore they should not murmur about their present condition. "In the day of prosperity be joyful, and in the day of adversity consider; yea, God hath made the one side by side with the other, to the end that man should not find out anything that shall be after him" (Eccles. 7:14).

What lies at the root of all this vanity? Why is it that our world is so full of emptiness? The Preacher sees the answer. "Behold, this only have I found: that God made man upright; but they have sought out many inventions" (Eccles. 7:29). Here is the root of the problem— the sinfulness of man. Despite the fact that man was made in the image of God, mankind has sought after all manner of sinful things. And this is the reason why everything is vanity. Sin has divorced the world from God and it is God who gives meaning to all things.

From this point on there is a slight shift in the Preacher's thought. He still points out the vanity in the world, and gives instructions for living in this vain world. But more frequently now he emphasizes that God is behind all things and is governing all things. For instance, he says in Ecclesiastes 8:12, 13: "Though a sinner do evil a hundred times, and prolong his days, yet surely I know that it shall be well with them that fear God, that fear before him: but it shall not be well with the wicked, neither shall he prolong his days, which are as a shadow, because he feareth not before God."

Since all things are in God's hands, and the same end awaits all men, the Preacher commends the enjoyment of those blessings which God gives. "Go thy way, eat thy bread with joy, and drink thy wine with a merry heart; for God hath already accepted thy works" (Eccles. 9:7). Though the sinfulness of man may bring many foolish things to pass, yet the people of God are not to be dismayed. Rather they are to continue in good works, for this has God's blessing. "Cast thy bread upon the waters; for thou shall find it after many days" (Eccles. 11:1).

Advice to Young People

The Preacher ends his words of wisdom by exhorting the young people. "Rejoice, O young man, in thy youth, and let thy heart cheer thee in the days of thy youth, and walk in the ways of thy heart, and in the sight of thine eyes; but know thou, that for all these things God will bring thee into judgment. Therefore remove sorrow from thy heart, and put away evil from thy flesh; for youth and the dawn of life are vanity. Remember also thy Creator in the days of thy youth, before the evil days come, and the years draw nigh, when thou shalt say, I have no pleasure in them" (Eccles. 11:9-12:1).

The End of the Matter

God has given His people the one source of wisdom—His Word. It is to this that the Preacher points Israel. "The words of the wise are as goads; and as nails well fastened are the words of the masters of assemblies, which are given from one shepherd. And furthermore, my son, be admonished: of making many books there is no end; and much study is a weariness of the flesh" (Eccles. 12:11, 12). Much of the despondency among the people was caused by a neglect of God's Word. How true it is that there are innumerable books to guide us in this life. But this life is vanity, and much study simply wearies us. But that is true only of study which is not based on God's Word. The Preacher calls us to a study of the Scriptures. For only the Scriptures can give meaning to life. To study the world apart from God's Word is to find vanity. But a study based on the Scriptures finds real meaning in life and the world.

Thus the Preacher draws to his conclusion. Perhaps we can trace the steps by which he has arrived at that conclusion. He has shown us the vanity of all that this world contains. He has provided words of wisdom to guide us through life. He has pointed to the Holy Scriptures as the guidebook which we should study. Now he says: "This is the end of the matter; all hath been heard: Fear God, and keep his commandments; for this is the whole duty of man" (Eccles. 12:13). His conclusion is the only correct one for any people in any age. No matter what our circumstances, no matter when or where we live, this is our duty—to fear God and keep His commandments.

Factual questions   Exercises

1. When was Ecclesiastes written?
2. What is the purpose of Ecclesiastes?

3. What pleasures did the Preacher sample? Eccles. 2.
4. Why is it good for man to enjoy what he has? Eccles 3:12-15.
5. Summarize the advice given about worship. Eccles. 5.
6. What five things does the Preacher say are "better"? Eccles. 7.
7. What happens to all men? Eccles. 9:1-6.
8. What is the Preacher describing in Ecclesiastes 12:2-7?
9. Rewrite Ecclesiastes 12:2-7 without using figures of speech.

Thought questions

1. What value does the book of Ecclesiastes have for young people today?
2. How does Ecclesiastes 12:13 agree with or differ from Matthew 22:37-40?

Memory

1. Ecclesiastes 3:11.
2. Ecclesiastes 12:13.

Chapter 46

God's Call to Faithful Service

Haggai

AUTHOR

This short book contains a summary of the prophecies uttered by Haggai. We know little about this prophet. He was probably born in Babylon and returned to Palestine with the first band of exiles. His ministry is dated very clearly. He prophesied in the second year of Darius the king (Hag. 1:1; 2:1; 2:10). This is considered by competent scholars to be 520 B.C. His words are directed primarily to the rulers of the people, Zerubbabel the governor and Joshua the high priest.

PURPOSE

The message of Haggai centers around the rebuilding of the temple. By his rebukes for failure to finish the temple and his promises of God's blessing which would attend the resumption of the work, Haggai inspired the exiles to labor faithfully for God. That such inspiration was necessary is clear from the history found in the books of Ezra and Nehemiah.

OUTLINE

    I. Rebuke for failure to rebuild the temple   Haggai 1
   II. Blessings connected with rebuilding the temple   Haggai 2

ANALYSIS

Haggai's book is composed of four prophecies, all delivered in the same year (520 B.C.). These cover two main subjects, as indicated in the outline.

The Call to Build

When the exiles had returned to their native land, they had immediately begun to rebuild the temple. The altar had been built and the foundation had been laid. But the opposition of their hostile neighbors dimmed the enthusiasm of the people, and they said, "It is not the time for us to come, the time for Jehovah's house to be built" (Hag. 1:2). To this came God's answer through Haggai, "Is it a time for you yourselves to dwell in your ceiled [paneled] houses, while this house lieth waste?" (Hag. 1:4) Because of their failure to finish the work of rebuilding, God's blessing had been withheld from them. "Now therefore thus saith Jehovah of hosts: Consider your ways. Ye have sown much, and bring in little; ye eat, but ye have not enough; ye drink, but ye are not filled with drink; ye clothe you, but there is none warm; and he that earneth wages earneth wages to put it into a bag with holes" (Hag. 1:5, 6).

This divine call did not fall on deaf ears. God put it in the hearts of the people to obey. "And Jehovah stirred up the spirit of Zerubbabel the son of Shealtiel, governor of Judah, and the spirit of Joshua the son of Jehozadak, the high priest, and the spirit of all the remnant of the people; and they came and did work on the house of Jehovah of hosts, their God, in the four and twentieth day of the month, in the sixth month, in the second year of Darius the king" (Hag. 1:14, 15). Within a month after Haggai brought his message the work on the temple was resumed.

The Glory of the Rebuilt Temple

When the foundations of the second temple were laid, it was so much smaller than the first that "the old men that had seen the first house, when the foundation of the second house was laid before their eyes, wept with a loud voice" (Ezra 3:12). This dimmed the enthusiasm for building. It seemed obvious that the second temple would never be as glorious as the first. Therefore God asks: "Who is left among you that saw this house in its former glory? and how do ye see it now? is it not in your eyes as nothing?" (Hag. 2:3) But what seems obvious is not true. "The latter glory of this house shall be greater than the former, saith Jehovah of hosts; and in this place will I give peace, saith Jehovah of hosts" (Hag. 2:9).

This promise of God is a spiritual promise. The glory will not be an earthly glory. God is not speaking of great splendor and beauty. The second temple was made glorious because Christ appeared in it. In the first temple God came in the cloud of glory that dwelt between the cherubim. But in the second temple God came in the person of Jesus Christ. This was the greatest glory that the temple could possibly have.

The Promise of Prosperity

God spoke again through Haggai. The prophet used a question about the levitical law of uncleanness to explain why Israel had not been blessed. Her sin in failing to rebuild the temple had polluted all her life. But now since the temple was being built, God promised to send them abundant harvests. Here we see a spiritual law in operation. Obedience to God's commands brings blessing; disobedience brings punishment.

The Line of David

The final prophecy is short. God tells Zerubbabel, the governor of the people, of His plan to shake the kingdoms of the world and overthrow the might of the wicked. And He promises, "In that day, saith Jehovah of hosts, will I take thee, O Zerubbabel, my servant, the son of Shealtiel, saith Jehovah, and will make thee as a signet; for I have chosen thee, saith Jehovah of hosts" (Hag. 2:23). This is another promise that the line of David (of which Zerubbabel was the representative) would continue forever. This prophecy was finally fulfilled in Christ. The theocracy which came to its highest Old Testament expression in David, the theocratic king, will come to still higher expression in the great Son of David, Jesus Christ.

EXERCISES

Factual questions

1. When and where did Haggai prophesy?
2. What subject is the center of his messages?
3. What is the purpose of the book of Haggai?
4. What was the result of the failure to rebuild the temple? Hag. 1:7ff.
5. Express in your own words the question Haggai put to the priests. Hag. 2:11ff.
6. How did this question apply to the people? Hag. 2:14ff.

Thought question

1. Why was it so important that the temple be rebuilt?

Memory

1. Outline of Haggai.
2. Haggai 2:9.

Chapter 47

God's Promise of Future Glory

Zechariah

AUTHOR

This book contains the prophecies of Zechariah, the son of Berechiah. Ezra calls him the son of Iddo, but he was probably Iddo's grandson. Zechariah was possibly a priest. He was a contemporary of Haggai, beginning his prophetic labors just two months after that prophet. Ezra gives both prophets credit for stirring up the people to rebuild the temple.

OUTLINE

I.	Visions of judgment and blessing	Zechariah 1- 6
II.	The necessity of obedience	Zechariah 7- 8
III.	The future glory of Zion	Zechariah 9-14

ANALYSIS

The Call to Return

The first words of Zechariah's prophecy may well be considered the theme of the book. "Therefore say thou unto them, Thus saith Jehovah of hosts: Return unto me, saith Jehovah of hosts, and I will return unto you, saith Jehovah of hosts. Be ye not as your fathers, unto whom the former prophets cried, saying, Thus saith Jehovah of hosts, Return ye now from your evil ways, and from your evil doings: but they did not hear, nor hearken unto me, saith Jehovah" (Zech. 1:3, 4).

Visions in the Night

Three months after the above prophecy was given, Zechariah had a series of visions. One vision introduced the others. He saw riders on horses. They were led by a rider on a red horse, who is identified as the angel of Jehovah, that is, the Lord Jesus Christ appearing before His incarnation. These riders report that the earth is at peace. But Jerusalem is still troubled. How long will this continue? God answers that the nations will be destroyed and "Jehovah shall yet comfort Zion, and shall yet choose Jerusalem" (Zech. 1:17). Then Zechariah sees seven visions which portray what will happen:

235

1. A vision of four horns which are broken by four smiths. This pictures the future overthrow of the four world empires of which Daniel spoke.

2. A man with a measuring line measuring Jerusalem. This teaches that Jerusalem will be so enlarged that walls will not contain it.

3. Joshua the high priest clothed in filthy garments which represent sin. He is clothed with rich apparel by God. This teaches that the priesthood is to be cleansed so that it will typify the Messiah.

4. A golden lampstand fed by pipes from two olive trees. The lampstand is the Church, and the trees are the Spirit of God. From this comes the promise: "Not by might, nor by power, but by my Spirit, saith Jehovah of hosts" (Zech. 4:6).

5. A flying roll which symbolizes that God will punish sinners.

6. An Ephah containing a woman named Wickedness being borne away to Shinar. This symbolizes that God will remove iniquity from His people.

7. The four chariots, which are the winds of Heaven. These symbolize the judgments of God.

These visions combine to show clearly that God is going to destroy the nations which oppress Israel, that He will purify Israel by removing her sin and punishing her sinners, and that He will bring about a new and glorious state for His people. To these visions is connected a prophecy. Joshua the high priest is crowned. The meaning of this action is explained as a prophecy of the Messiah, who "shall build the temple of Jehovah; and he shall bear the glory, and shall sit and rule upon his throne; and he shall be a priest upon his throne; and the counsel of peace shall be between them both" (Zech. 6:13).

Obedience Is Better

The visions and prophecies of Zechariah are interrupted by the record of men of Bethel who came to the priests with a question. They have faithfully held a fast annually commemorating the destruction of Jerusalem. Shall they continue? This brings a word from Jehovah. "When ye fasted and mourned in the fifth and in the seventh month, even these seventy years, did ye at all fast unto me, even to me?" (Zech. 7:5)

The fasts of these people were not acceptable before God because they fasted only outwardly and did not humble their hearts before Him. These people were guilty of formalism. In this we see the seeds of the sins of formalism and hypocrisy which Jesus rebuked in the Pharisees. So now God rebukes these people by His prophet, and tells them that He wants obedience and godliness, not formal fasting.

The Deliverance of Zion

The heathen powers had always been a source of trouble for Israel. Even now Israel was under the control of the Persian rulers. But God promises that He will overthrow the heathen. He will send His king. "Rejoice greatly, O daughter of Zion; shout, O daughter of Jerusalem: behold, thy king cometh unto thee; he is just, and having salvation; lowly, and riding upon an ass, even upon a colt the foal of an ass. And I will cut off the chariot from Ephraim, and the horse from Jerusalem; and the battle bow shall be cut off; and he shall speak peace unto the nations: and his dominion shall be from sea to sea, and from the River to the ends of the earth" (Zech. 9:9, 10). It is evident that this is a promise of Christ, and therefore that this whole promise is spiritual. Christ's kingdom is not of this world. The enemies of His church are spiritual powers of wickedness. These, the most dangerous of all enemies, He has overcome and now He gives peace to Zion. The prophets speak in Old Testament language, but they frequently give us beautiful pictures of New Testament truths.

The fact that the prophets at times use Old Testament language to express New Testament truths has significance. The Kingdom of God is repeatedly spoken of as Israel, Zion, or Jerusalem. But this does not mean that we should equate the theocracy with the nation of Israel. For many centuries, from the Exodus to the Exile, the nation of Israel was the earthly expression of the Kingdom of God. But it was not always so. The theocracy existed before Israel was born. The theocracy continued after the covenant nation was destroyed. And in New Testament times it has come to expression as the Church of Christ. The Jews of Jesus' time failed to realize that the prophets, while speaking in Old Testament language, could refer to a higher form of God's kingdom. They expected the Messiah to come and re-establish the nation of Israel as the ruler of the world. When Jesus spoke of a spiritual kingdom they rejected Him and crucified Him. But it was of Christ and His spiritual kingdom that the prophets spoke.

In contrast to this blessing that will come upon Zion is the story of the shepherds. God, the good Shepherd, relates what He has done for Israel. He has destroyed her enemies, even three world powers that ruled over her. But Israel repaid Him with ingratitude. The final blow came when He asked the people to show whether they appreciated His work by paying Him. "So they weighed for my hire thirty pieces of silver" (Zech. 11:12). This was the price of a slave — a sign of contempt. Therefore God rejected them and gave them a false shepherd who would not take care of them. Matthew tells us that this prophecy was fulfilled when Judas was paid thirty pieces of silver for betraying Christ. So we see that future blessings on Zion are not thereby blessings

on the nation Israel. Israel has been rejected for her continual
ingratitude which came to a climax when she rejected Christ. Israel
has been rejected, and given over to false shepherds who led her away
from the truth of God. The pictures of God's blessing upon Zion are
fulfilled in the Church of Jesus Christ.

God's Victories for His People

The entire book of Zechariah is difficult to interpret. Some reliable
commentators have confessed their inability to explain the book. This
is due to the symbolism and to the rapidity with which the symbols
shift. The last prophecy, which is entitled "The burden of the word of
Jehovah concerning Israel," is very difficult. Perhaps it is best to
consider it as three separate visions with a common theme. These
visions deal with things which will happen at the end of time. Because
of the way in which the prophets group together everything after Christ,
they may have some partial fulfillment in the Church. But they are also
intended to picture the final judgment. In Zechariah 12 we see Jerusalem
besieged by her enemies but saved by God. In Zechariah 13 we see that
Israel is purified and refined by suffering and a remnant is saved. In
Zechariah 14 there is a picture of the nations fighting against and taking
the city, and then going up to Jerusalem to keep the Feast of Tabernacles. All these visions have the same basic thought. The people of
God will always have enemies. God uses these enemies to purify His
church. But the enemies can never be finally victorious. God Himself
will fight for His people, and they shall be saved.

PURPOSE

Zechariah, like Haggai, sought to encourage the people in their tasks.
He shows them the punishments coming to sinners and calls upon them
to repent of their sins. But especially he holds before their eyes the
glories of the messianic future, so that they may see what God has in
store for His people. So the book served to encourage the people of
Zechariah's time, and shows us how God's blessing is given to His people
in all ages.

EXERCISES

Factual questions

1. What is the theme of Zechariah? Zech. 1.
2. What can you learn about the Messiah from Zechariah 1:7-17;
   3:6-10; 9:9-10; 11:4-14; 14:1-8?
3. How was the prophecy of Zechariah 9:9, 10 fulfilled? Matt. 21.
4. What is the meaning of the parable in Zechariah 11:4-14?
5. What do the visions in Zechariah 12-14 teach?
6. What is the purpose of the book of Zechariah?

Memory
1. Outline of Zechariah.
2. Zechariah 9:9.

Chapter 48

God's Demand for Full Repentance

Malachi

AUTHOR

This book declares that it is "the burden of the word of Jehovah to Israel by Malachi" (Mal. 1:1). Concerning this statement there have been two schools of thought. Since Malachi means "my messenger" some have thought that this was simply a title or a name taken by the writer when he wrote this book. Others have insisted that Malachi is the prophet's proper name. Since nothing else is known about the prophet we cannot be certain. But since none of the other Latter Prophets are anonymous, it seems likely that Malachi is the name of the prophet.

DATE

Malachi was the last of the Old Testament prophets. He does not date his prophecies. But the similarity between the conditions apparent in Malachi and those set forth in Nehemiah make it clear that Malachi prophesied in the days of Nehemiah. Many scholars think that this prophecy was given during the interval when Nehemiah was absent from Jerusalem (Neh. 13:6).

OUTLINE

    I. The sin of Israel   Malachi 1, 2
   II. The call to repentance   Malachi 3, 4

ANALYSIS

The Sin of Israel

The prophet begins his message by showing that God loves Israel. "Was not Esau Jacob's brother? saith Jehovah: yet I loved Jacob; but Esau I hated" (Mal. 1:2, 3). God's love for Jacob is shown by the fact that Judah has been restored from her captivity, but Edom has been utterly destroyed.

In contrast to this love of God for Jacob, the prophet points out the sins of the priests and the people. He does this in a unique style. He makes a point, then presents an objection, and then answers the objection. This procedure is used seven times. Here is an example:

> *Will a man rob God? Yet ye rob me.*
> *But ye say, Wherein have we robbed thee?*
> *In tithes and offerings. Ye are cursed with the curse;*
> *for ye rob me, even this whole nation.*
>
> —Mal. 3:8, 9.

Malachi particularly attacks the priests, because they lead the people astray. The priests bring for sacrifices animals that are not fit. Their worship is formal. God even condemns them for carrying on the sacrifices. And their sin is the greater because they have broken the covenant which God made with Levi, and are not faithful to their office. "For the priest's lips should keep knowledge, and they should seek the law at his mouth; for he is the messenger of Jehovah of hosts. But ye are turned aside out of the way; ye have caused many to stumble in the law; ye have corrupted the covenant of Levi, saith Jehovah of hosts" (Mal. 2:7, 8).

The people likewise have sinned against God. One of their chief sins was divorce. The people put away their wives in order to marry foreign women. Because of this God will not receive their offerings nor hear their prayers. "Therefore take heed to your spirit, and let none deal treacherously against the wife of his youth" (Mal. 2:15).

The Call to Repentance

This state of affairs could not last. God declared that it would not. He Himself would change it. "Behold, I send my messenger, and he shall prepare the way before me: and the Lord, whom ye seek, will suddenly come to his temple; and the messenger of the covenant, whom ye desire, behold, he cometh, saith Jehovah of hosts. But who can abide the day of his coming? and who shall stand when he appeareth? for he is like a refiner's fire, and like fullers' soap: and he will sit as a refiner and purifier of silver, and he will purify the sons of Levi, and refine them as gold and silver; and they shall offer unto Jehovah offerings in righteousness" (Mal. 3:1-3). This occurred when God appeared in the form of Jesus Christ, and took away the sins of His people.

The call to repentance includes a call to deal faithfully with God. They have robbed God by failing to bring their tithes to Him. He pleads with them to repent, to turn unto Him, and to bring in their tithes. Then He will pour out a blessing "that there shall not be room enough to receive it" (Mal. 3:10).

These words of God through Malachi did not affect every one. But there were some whose hearts were touched. "Then they that feared Jehovah spake one with another; and Jehovah hearkened, and heard, a book of remembrance was written before him, for them that feared Jehovah and that thought upon his name" (Mal. 3:16). These are the

true people of God. In the day of judgment He promises to bless them.
"But unto you that fear my name shall the sun of righteousness arise
with healing in its wings; and ye shall go forth, and gambol as calves
of the stall" (Mal. 4:2).

The closing words of the Old Testament look both backward and
forward. They point back to the law of Moses, which is God's Word by
which His people must guide their lives. These words also point forward to the coming of Christ who will restore the covenant relations between fathers and sons. This last promise of the Old Testament is the
first promise of the New Testament (Luke 1:17). Since it prepares the
way for Christ, it is like a bridge between the two Testaments. It directs
our eyes to the coming of the Christ of God.

PURPOSE

Malachi obviously preached to a sinful people. By unveiling their
sins, by calling them to repentance, by prophesying of the blessings found
in Christ, he sought to turn them again to God. In a real sense he was
seeking to prepare the way for the coming of Christ by preparing the
hearts of men to receive Him.

CONCLUSION

Malachi is the last of the prophets. With Malachi we come to the
end of our study of the Old Testament. But the Old Testament ends
with a comma, not with a period. There is more to be added. The Old
Testament requires the New Testament to complete it. What is the
connection between the end of the Old Testament and the beginning of
the New?

The end of the Old Testament shows why Christ had to come. In the
Old Testament we have seen the Kingdom of God develop. It has
developed within the borders of Israel. But we have seen how the
children of Israel failed to keep God's covenant. Their sin was so great
and so persistent that the nation was finally destroyed. The future hope
of the Kingdom of God no longer rests in Israel. The Kingdom must
take a new and better form. And Christ is the answer to that need. In
Him the Kingdom of God comes to its perfect expression.

The end of the Old Testament helps us to understand the circumstances at the beginning of the New Testament. Throughout the Old
Testament we have seen how susceptible Israel was to the sin of idolatry.
It was that sin that led to her captivity. The Exile proved to be a
furnace of affliction which purged that particular sin from Israel. After
the Exile we find no more traces of idolatry. However, the Exile did
not turn Israel's heart back to Jehovah. It simply turned her sin into
other channels. In the Exile the Jewish tendency to limit salvation to
the Jews became stronger. With this growing nationalism there

sprang up a spirit of formalism. Worship lost its vigor. It was outward, not from the heart. Hypocrisy began to flourish. Religion was often divorced from ethics. The Jews combined a formal worship of Jehovah with lives that were utterly void of godliness. This is the picture of the Jewish character that we find in Malachi and in Nehemiah. And this character persisted during the four hundred silent years. When Christ arrived it had developed into Pharisaism. The Pharisees were Christ's worst enemies. They were responsible, at least in part, for His execution.

Yet even in this we see the hand of God. For the death of Christ at the hands of wicked men was the means whereby the Kingdom of God was eternally established. Through His death and resurrection Christ now reigns in Heaven from whence He shall come to initiate the perfect, eternal Kingdom of God in that new Heaven and new earth, where only righteousness dwells.

EXERCISES

Factual questions

1. When was Malachi written?
2. What unusual style do we find in Malachi?
3. Against what sins does Malachi speak? Mal. 1:6ff.; 2:14ff.; 3:7ff.
4. What work of Christ is pictured in Malachi 3:1-3?
5. Who is the Elijah of Malachi 4:5? Luke 1:17.
6. What is the purpose of the book of Malachi?
7. How does the end of the Old Testament prepare for the beginning of the New Testament?

Thought questions

1. Find in Malachi evidence that the seeds of Pharisaism were already sown.
2. Does God still feel the same way about tithes? Mal. 3:7-14.

Memory

1. Outline of Malachi.
2. Malachi 3:1.

REFERENCES

This list of references is restricted to volumes which were consulted in the preparation of this guide and which will be of value to teachers whose time for further study is limited.

Alexander, J. A. *The Prophecies of Isaiah.* Grand Rapids: Zondervan Publishing House, reprint ed.

Edersheim, A. *The Bible History, Old Testament.* 2 vols. Grand Rapids: Wm. B. Eerdmans Publishing Co., reprint ed.

Fairbairn, P. *The Typology of Scripture.* Grand Rapids: Zondervan Publishing House, reprint ed.

Halley, H. H. *Bible Handbook.* Chicago: Henry H. Halley, 1955.

Keil, C. F. and Delitzsch, F. *Commentaries on the Old Testament.* Grand Rapids: Wm. B. Eerdmans Publishing Co., reprint ed.

Robinson, G. *The Minor Prophets.* Grand Rapids: Baker Book House, reprint ed.

Vos, G. *Biblical Theology.* Grand Rapids: Wm. B. Eerdmans Publishing Co., 1948.

Young, E. J. *An Introduction to the Old Testament.* Grand Rapids: Wm. B. Eerdmans Publishing Co., 1952.

Isaiah 53. Grand Rapids: Wm. B. Eerdmans Publishing Co., 1952.

My Servants the Prophets. Grand Rapids: Wm. B. Eerdmans Publishing Co., 1953.

The Prophecy of Daniel. Grand Rapids: Wm. B. Eerdmans Publishing Co., 1949.